LOUIS KAHN

ON THE THOUGHTFUL MAKING OF SPACES

Michael Merrill

# LOUIS KAHN ON THE THOUGHTFUL MAKING OF SPACES

## THE DOMINICAN MOTHERHOUSE AND A MODERN CULTURE OF SPACE

Lars Müller Publishers

CONTENTS

"Architecture deals with spaces,
the thoughtful and meaningful making
of spaces." Louis Kahn, 1973

## INTRODUCTION
## ON THE VALUE OF UNCOMPLETED THINGS

***Form is something mobile, something becoming, something passing. The doctrine of formation is the doctrine of transformation.***

Johann Wolfgang von Goethe, Diary, 1796

***The value of uncompleted things is very strong.... If the spirit is there and can be recorded, what is lost? The drawing is important, the incomplete scheme is important, if it has a central gravitational force which makes the arrangement not just an arrangement but something which gives a richness to the associations which are lost. Recording of that which has not been done must be made much of.*** Louis Kahn, 1965

***That which has not been built is not really lost. Once its value is established, its demand for presence is undeniable. It is merely waiting for the right circumstances.*** Louis Kahn

### Prologue: Philadelphia, 1965–1969: An Iconic Plan, Enigmatic Drawings

It had taken Louis Kahn a long time to master his craft, but considering the forces at play this probably could not have been accomplished any sooner. Now, with both the century and the architect in their mid-sixties, his long-nurtured skill had reached full bloom. The recently completed Richards Medical Research Laboratories (1957–64) and First Unitarian Church (1959–63*) had gained the attention of an international audience; the Salk Institute for Biological Studies (1959–65)—his first fully mature work—was nearing completion; and career-crowning projects for the Indian Institute of Management (1962–74) and the Capitol of East Pakistan at Dhaka (1962–84) were steadily unfolding on his drawing boards, as accolades, assignments, and invitations poured into his office from around the globe. In the midst of those prolific and expansive years, Kahn was presented—separately and within the space of a few months—the

1 Louis Kahn in his office, 1960

opportunity to design two monasteries: the Dominican Motherhouse near Media, Pennsylvania (1965–69), and St. Andrew's Benedictine Priory in Valyermo, California (1965–67). Figs. 2–3 For a man who had sown so much and reaped so little for much of his career, this must have seemed like some kind of late restitution. How could he have not have been thrilled at the chance? Accordingly, and in spite of all uncertainties, he and his associates poured hours of thought onto reams of paper in what would turn out to be months and years of designing.[1]

In spite of all efforts by the architects, both designs were destined to join those other "unbuilt offerings" which make up such a large and important part of Kahn's oeuvre.[2] Among the unrealized projects of that later period, which include such seminal designs as those for the U.S. Consulate in Angola (1959–61), the Mikveh Israel and Hurva Synagogues (1961–72 and 1967–74), or the Salk Institute's Meeting House (1959–65), the monasteries occupy a privileged yet enigmatic position in Kahn literature. While both projects have been regularly published, it is particularly the protagonist of this study, the Dominican Motherhouse, with its eccentric, shifting, and bricolage floor plan, which rarely fails to appear in any comprehensive look at Kahn's work, representing—depending on the author's point of view—either the apotheosis of his thinking about

1 The project dates are given in the Louis I. Kahn Collection, Architectural Archives of the University of Pennsylvania (hereafter referred to as "Kahn Collection") as follows: St. Andrew's Priory (cat. no. 715): earliest date: November 16, 1965 (Kahn had been contacted by St. Andrew's Priory as early as 1961, and according to a letter from his office to the convent, seems to have worked on it before March 1965. Letter, David Wisdom to Mother Mary Emmanuel, April 2, 1965, Box LIK 10, Kahn Collection.); date of contract: May 19, 1965; last dated drawing: November 29, 1966; termination of project: February 6, 1967. Dominican Motherhouse (cat. no. 700): earliest date: March 26, 1965; date of contract: August 7, 1967; last dated drawing: December 15, 1968; termination of project: March 18, 1969.

2 This is Robert McCarter's term; see McCarter, *Louis I. Kahn,* p. 443.

**spatial organization or an odd episode, the exception to the rule of the otherwise geometrically-so-disciplined plans.**[3]

**It is not only the conflicting views of its interpreters that have made the Dominican Motherhouse such an enigmatic case; in spite of its repeated publication, our knowledge of Kahn's design has remained sketchy at best. Usually a single ground-floor plan, occasionally an elevation study or two (more often than not of an incomplete intermediate scheme) will have sufficed to illustrate the project—no upper or basement floor plans, no perspectives, rarely sections or models; little to explain the means of construction, the intricacies of interior space, or the interaction of the building with its site.**[4] **Curiously, though, this limited information has not hindered the project from attaining something approaching iconic status within Kahn's oeuvre and within the history of late-twentieth-century architecture.**[5] **The capacity of the unrealized design to engage the imaginations of architects and historians—as it surely has—must lie, then, more in the power of its evocative diagram than in our detailed knowledge of its internal workings, its constructive and spatial nuances, or its material intentions. More promise than evidence, it is perhaps the very incompleteness and openness of its images which, together with the compelling "gravitational force" of its plan, have inspired other architects to explore with their own designs the potentials suggested by the unrealized scheme.**[6]

3 For representatives of the former view, see, for example, Gregotti, "Louis Kahn: Modern Connection," p. 4; Sabini, "Between Order and Form: Fragments and the Idea of Architecture," p. 14; Norberg-Schulz, *Roots of Modern Architecture,* p. 169; McCarter, *Louis I. Kahn,* pp. 288–95. For representatives of the latter view, see Moneo, "End of the Century Paradigms," pp. 198–203; and Lewis, "The Dominican Motherhouse," pp. 384–89.

4 The "iconic" and until now by far most published drawing is the ground-level floor plan (and occasionally, the North and South elevations) of the scheme from April 22, 1968. (See, for example, in the Bibliography: Giurgola, Norberg-Schultz, Gast, Saito, McCarter, and A&V, special issue, February 2001.) The most comprehensive overview of the project to date in a widely available publication remains Heinz Ronner and Sharad Jhaveri's *Louis I. Kahn: Complete Work, 1935–1974,* in which nine pages (pp. 302–11) are dedicated to the various design stages using both Kahn's sketches and his associates' plans. This is one of the few publications that include information on the site and the building's section. The fourth volume of Garland Publishing's *The Louis I. Kahn Archive* (p. 316) contains eighty-five drawings and sketches for the Motherhouse project that have been accredited to Kahn himself. The most informative description of the project's development and the client-architect relationship to date is Michael J. Lewis's essay in Brownlee and De Long's *Louis I. Kahn: In the Realm of Architecture* (pp. 382–89), while David Brownlee's essay "The Houses of the Inspirations" (pp. 94–111) in the same publication remains an authoritative source for the positioning of the Motherhouse project among Kahn's related works of the sixties. Robert McCarter makes a strong case in his book on Kahn for ranking the Dominican Motherhouse among Kahn's important works. The plan and elevation drawings that had been prepared for that text are more "hybrids," consolidated from different plans and aimed at giving a general understanding of the project, than accurate reconstructions of the actual final schemes. To the enigma of the Motherhouse project belongs both the final reason for its termination and the terminating party: with Lewis and McCarter stating that Kahn elected to withdraw from the project (Lewis, p. 388; McCarter, p. 293), while in fact it was the congregation that terminated the contract (see pp. 101–14).

5 "Iconic," an overused but, in this case, fitting adjective.

6 See the epilogue, note 248 (p. 206), for some possible influences of and from the Dominican Motherhouse.

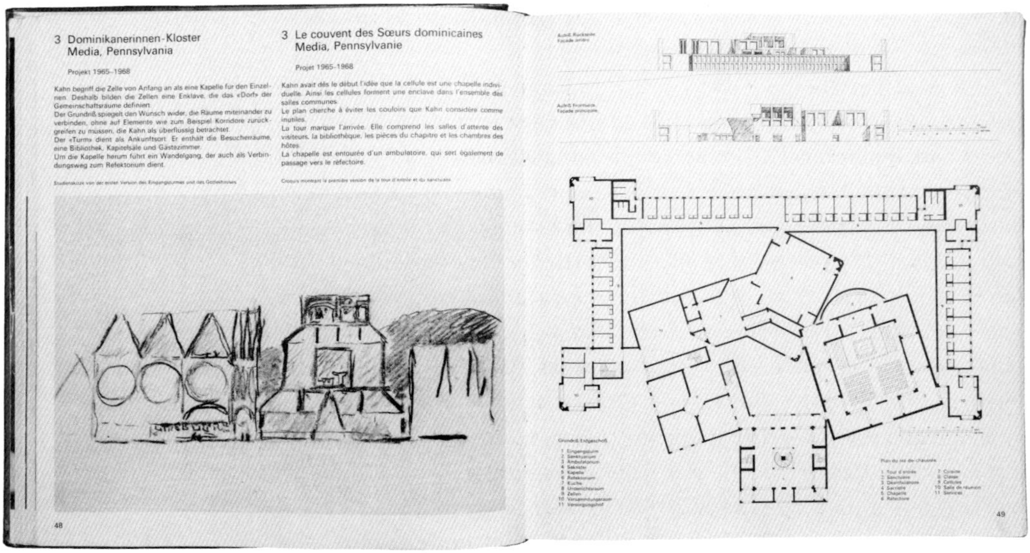


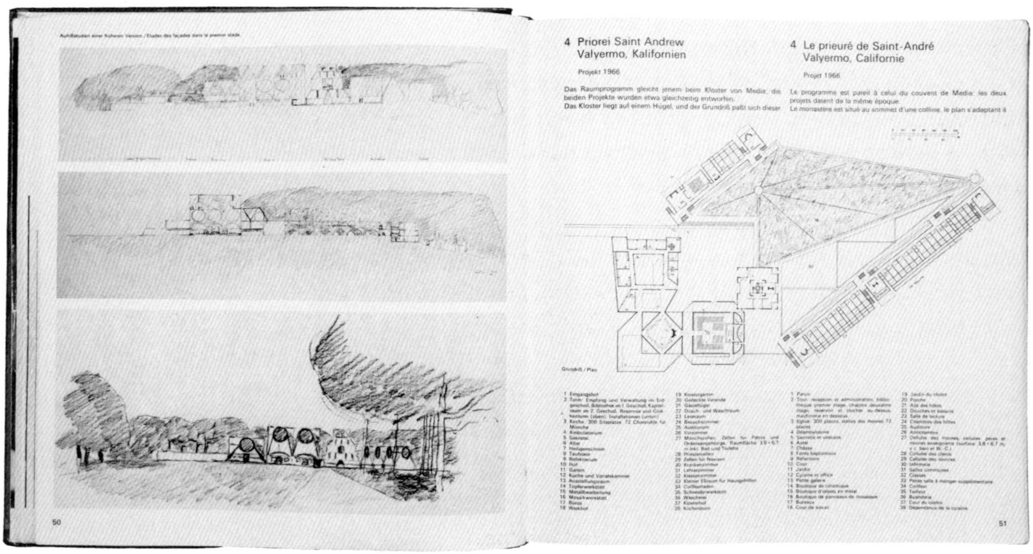


**2** Dominican Motherhouse, 1965–69, in Giurgola and Mehta's *Louis I. Kahn,* Zurich, 1975
**3** St. Andrew's Priory, 1966–67, in Giurgola and Mehta's *Louis I. Kahn,* Zurich, 1975

## Revisiting the Motherhouse: Drawings as Objects to Think With

What a revelation for the architect seeking instruction to find neatly garnered in the Architectural Archives of the University of Pennsylvania sixteen portfolios holding the hundreds of unpublished sheets that make up this project. Kahn's charcoal probings, his associates' meticulously drafted plans, messages in margins from master to assistant, area calculations, untold themes and variations, etc. More than merely filling in the missing details of the final design, these drawings, together with an equally large file of notes and correspondence, transport the patient viewer into the thicket of its three-year genesis.[7] If architecture is poorer for the fact that this willful masterpiece was never built, this loss may in one respect be seen as a gain. By allowing us to immerse ourselves in a rich and extensive set of drawings which stop abruptly on the threshold of the mature project's realization, the evidence directs our attention to those generally less-studied conditions of architecture's existence, conditions which remain "untainted" by the realities of building, inhabitation, and reception. On the one hand, the close-to-construction design—thought through to its masonry courses and window details—gives us precise information on the building's intended reality. On the other hand, through these drawings, by their very nature incomplete, we can—indeed must—make this building "our own" by investing it with our own images.

One aspect of our fascination with good architectural drawings is that through a combination of precision and incompleteness, they make of us collaborators in the process of making. Martin Steinmann has observed:

> "A building and a drawing of that building are different expressions, or more correctly, different existence-forms of the same thing. One difference is in the way in which we perceive them. With a building, the form stands before us at the beginning; from it we reach, through the means of abstraction, that which Adolf Loos called the 'basis of the form.' On the other hand, with the drawing our perception begins at this basis. We must construct the resultant form in our head according to the instructions the drawing provides us.... While reading these drawings we can't conjure up just any picture though. When 'fir' is notated, we can't imagine anything else. Only, how does 'fir' look? How does this wood look when it is new? How does it age, and how does it look then? In order to read these drawings, which are so exact, we must create a world of things in our head on the basis of our experience: boards, planed; wire, rods,

7 Regarding patience: the visitor to the Archive should bring a good working week of free time in order to view all of the (chronologically unsorted) drawings.

galvanized; shingles.... This seeing, which leads from things to images, describes then exactly the opposite way than that which the designer goes: the one that leads from images to things."[8]

In the case of the Dominican Motherhouse, of perhaps even greater interest than our "participation" in fleshing out the final design is our "collaboration" in the development of that design. To follow the thoughts of Kahn and his associates over the three-year course of the project is to re-enact an engrossing journey, one complete with all the false starts, contradictions, slow accumulations, leaps of faith, and hard-won insights which belong to making architecture. A hypothesis is wagered and a next coherent step is sought; the plot thickens as the sheets are successively, carefully, taken from the portfolios. Why was one configuration found better than another? Why was an entire scheme redrawn in order to change a few lines? Why was a convincing detail abandoned in favor of a less compelling one? From sheet to sheet the forms shift, turn, evolve. Our privileged knowledge of the outcome does nothing to reduce the fascination of the story, for while leafing through the schemes and their accompanying notes it becomes apparent just how precarious was the existence of that well-known final design, how often it skirted failure, and how ready it was to embark on alternative paths. For those of us who attempt to make architecture, a heartening surprise may be coupled with a mild shock of recognition: Kahn—made remote through time, canonization, layers of interpretation (and yes, by that sometimes simply-too-sagelike persona)—feels suddenly quite near. Not everything we find in the portfolios can be called "masterly," and indeed, some of it looks quite rough or even naive, with frustration and uncertainty at times almost tangible: "A building is a struggle, not a miracle."[9] We who have similarly struggled *know* something of what our more accomplished colleague and his associates are going through here. Kahn's favorite medium, charcoal on thin yellow sketching paper—at once delicate and apparently impervious to time—seems expressly made to preserve the immediacy of thoughts. With his drawings spread out on the big archive table, the viewer may, over forty years after the fact, be overcome with the uncanny feeling that the master and his assistants have just stepped out for a break.

In a concrete architectural project, ideas and ideals which are general, abstract, and long-term meet specific, circumstantial realities and attempt to become manifest through them. A decisive portion of this takes place through the daily handcraft of the architect—through acts of conjecture

8 Steinmann, "Techne: zur Arbeit von Peter Zumthor," pp. 6–8.

9 Kahn, "The Architect Speaks," 1953.

and refutation made visible in acts of enclosing, juxtaposing, shifting, comparing, rejecting, etc. Astonishingly little has been written in the past decades regarding this part of our métier, even though it forms such a large part of our efforts as architects. While much recent theory has been written leading either *toward* or *away* from architecture, comparatively little has been reported from the locus of its making: the drawing board (or monitor). This may be due to lack of evidence for study—projects as comprehensively archived as the Dominican Motherhouse are truly rare treasures—or because the monumental failed attempts of the sixties to codify a systematic and rational methodology of design have lastingly discouraged inquiry into this area of architecture's reality. Until now, at least, most attempts at constructing even an operational theory of design have remained mute in regard to those small daily acts of ordering, forming, juxtaposing, testing, rejecting, etc., which become so apparent in the scores of drawings for the Dominican Motherhouse.

## Between a Culture of Drawing and a Culture of Architectural Space

"Theory" is not the prime goal of this book; rather, an extended visit to Kahn's conceptual space through his drawings as an opportunity to ruminate on the goals, procedures, tools, and craft/culture of thinking architecture: to meditate on that which gives rise to coherence and depth in a work, to reflect on that which changes in this process of making and that which remains the same. A companion volume has provided the chance to foreground the rough-and-delicate, loose-and-disciplined beauty of the drawings and to reflect at greater length upon what they might have to say in our contemporary digital culture.[10] Recognizing that there are both concrete architectural lessons to be learned from watching Kahn at work, as well as glimpses from between the lines into the tacit realms of *ethos,* skill, and embodied knowledge, the book before you attempts to combine the virtues of both narrative and primer (with the primer breaking into parts what the narrative attempts to gain sight of as a whole). In the narrative of the first half of this study, a selection of the Dominican Motherhouse's drawings are accompanied by a commentary and excerpts from Kahn's texts to tell the story of the design's development, illuminating the intended realities of the project and the path of its making. This narrative then forms a point of departure for a second section, an analytic excursion into Kahn's culture of architectural space. Thus, the Dominican Motherhouse is treated as both an end in itself and as a window onto selected aspects of architectural space.

10 Michael Merrill, *Louis Kahn: Drawing to Find Out,* Baden, 2010.

One good reason to dwell on (in) the Dominican Motherhouse as a means of getting closer to Kahn lies in the elementary nature of its space-defining means. In Kahn's monastery—from the start conceived as a simple masonry structure—technical and constructive aspects play only secondary roles. There is no need for virtuosic long spans such as at his Yale University Art Gallery or Kimbell Art Museum, no major form-shaping technical parameters like at his Richards Medical Laboratories or the Salk Institute. The constructive challenges and handcraft opportunities which played such major roles in the Indian Institute of Management and the National Assembly at Dhaka are not present at Media, nor is the budget which allowed the material richness and density of the Yale Center for British Art or the Exeter Library. The size and nature of the project make serialism and prefabrication such as that found at the Tribune Review Building or the Olivetti Factory uninteresting. With the Dominican Motherhouse, Kahn's main source of architectural expression—and our interest—shifts to those most fundamental elements of architecture: the simple acts of enclosing and configuring spaces—represented here by the shifting and ordering of rectangles against each other on paper.[11] The resulting design is extremely rich and complex; its richness and complexity, though, lie not in its advanced use of technology nor in its illustration of a particular theory, but in those basic acts of delimiting, placing, measuring, juxtaposing, of finding distance; in other words, of finding depth and magic in doing what is both necessary and familiar: "The making of a room."

Kahn's mature work—which spans from the end of the fifties until his death in 1974—represents a continuous research-through-designing on a very few fundamental architectural themes. While Kahn is rightly regarded as an heir to the modernist program and as one of its last great protagonists, it is at least equally valid to see in him one of modernism's boldest revisionists. This is nowhere more evident than in Kahn's culture of space. In place of modernism's abstract and neutral paradigm of space—a paradigm which continues to erode our environment—Kahn patiently sought the origins of architectural meaning in that spatial raw material which forms the human psyche. As much excavations into that which makes up our inner archaeologies as solutions to everyday problems, Kahn's best spaces are as much *revealed* as *made,* evoking responses which are both deeper and broader than those generated by the narrow abstractions of the last century. Following Kahn and his associates on their search for the Dominican Motherhouse is a compelling and rewarding way for us to begin to plumb those spaces.

11 Again, if you are an architect, chances are that you have spent many, many hours doing something that looks quite similar.

## SECTION I
## LOUIS KAHN AND THE DOMINICAN MOTHERHOUSE, 1965–1969

### PRELUDE TO A PROJECT
### CONGREGATION, PROGRAM, AND ARCHITECT

*Constantly the question, What is a Monastery? What inspired the first Monastery? You needn't know the truth of the circumstantial fact because that is not a guide at all. Anything in history which happens circumstantially is of little worth. What in history is a sign of the inevitable is of tremendous worth.* Louis Kahn, "The Institutions of Man," lecture at Princeton University, 1968

*A building is a world within a world.* Louis Kahn, "White Light, Black Shadow," lecture at Rice University, 1969

**The congregation**

The drawings that tell their story over the following pages are to be found in Kahn's archive under the rather formidable title of "The Mary, Queen of All Saints Motherhouse, Dominican Congregation of St. Catherine de Ricci."[12] The commissioning congregation was founded in 1880 by Lucy Eaton Smith near Albany, New York, as a convent and laywomen's retreat house, the first of its kind in America. Under the guidance of Lucy and her younger sister Lilly, the congregation flourished in its first decades, establishing new foundations in Philadelphia and Cuba by 1900.[13] In 1964, after over eighty years in upstate New York, the Albany sisters were forced to leave their aging wooden home after it failed to meet the fire department's new regulations. A plan to move in with the second foundation in the Philadelphia suburb of Elkins Park was short-lived; there the sisters had operated the William L. Elkins estate[14] as a convent and retreat

12 Unless otherwise noted, the source of the original drawings of the Dominican Motherhouse used in this text is Kahn Collection: Project File 700, Folders LIK 030.I.A.700.1–LIK 030.I.A.700.4 and Folders LIK 030.I.C.700.001–LIK 030.I.C.700.012, as well as correspondence and project files in Box LIK 10. A second source was the archive of the Dominican Motherhouse in Elkin's Park, PA.

13 Sources of information on the congregation: website of the Dominican Motherhouse of St. Catherine de Ricci, http://www.elkinsparkop.org (accessed January 2005); interview, author with Sister Mary Irene Lolli, O.P., and Sister Eileen Patricia Primrose, O.P., Dominican Motherhouse, Elkins Park, PA, April 15, 2006; correspondence, author with Sister Mary Irene Lolli, O.P., October, 2007.

14 The opulent Elkin's Estate, "Elstowe," was built in 1898 by the prominent Philadelphia architect Horace Trumbauer, best known for the Philadelphia Museum of Art and villas for the turn-of-the-century high society; see http://landconservancyofelkinspark.org/elkins.html (accessed April 15, 2010). In 2007, the congregation, now smaller, older, and burdened by the upkeep of the large property, sold the estate and relocated to Upper Darby, PA.

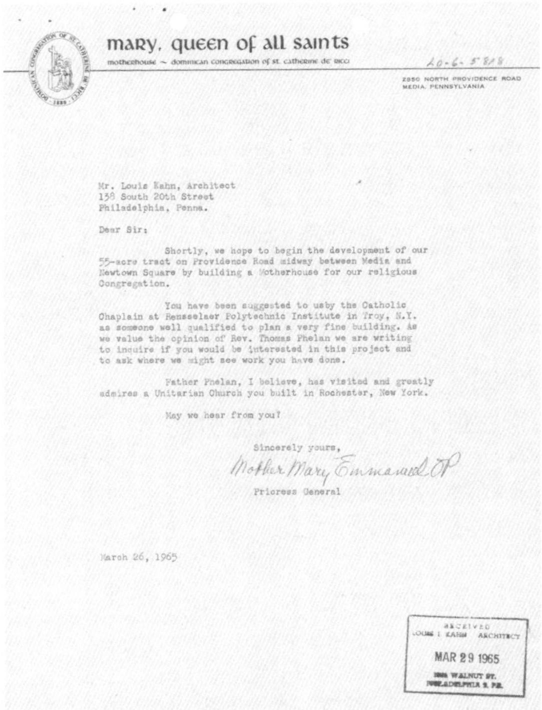

mary, queen of all saints

motherhouse ~ dominican congregation of st. catherine de ricci

2850 NORTH PROVIDENCE ROAD
MEDIA, PENNSYLVANIA

Mr. Louis Kahn, Architect
138 South 20th Street
Philadelphia, Penna.

Dear Sir:

Shortly, we hope to begin the development of our 55-acre tract on Providence Road midway between Media and Newtown Square by building a Motherhouse for our religious Congregation.

You have been suggested to usby the Catholic Chaplain at Rensselaer Polytechnic Institute in Troy, N.Y. as someone well qualified to plan a very fine building. As we value the opinion of Rev. Thomas Phelan we are writing to inquire if you would be interested in this project and to ask where we might see work you have done.

Father Phelan, I believe, has visited and greatly admires a Unitarian Church you built in Rochester, New York.

May we hear from you?

Sincerely yours,

Mother Mary Emmanuel OP

Prioress General

March 26, 1965

RECEIVED
ARCHITECT
MAR 29 1965
WALNUT ST.

**4** Letter from Mother Mary Emmanuel to Louis Kahn, March 26, 1965

house since 1932, but postwar materialist culture had sparked such renewed interest in spiritual life that the estate—at times brimming with over three hundred guests—was simply too full for the Albany sisters. Opportunity soon presented itself thirty miles to the south, though, near Media, Pennsylvania, in a country estate named Windy Hill. **Figs. 5–7** Not long after the sisters had bought and settled into their new home, the ongoing spiritual groundswell reached Media, bringing with it a growing number of new postulants and the need for more space.[15]

Deciding to build a new motherhouse on their property, the congregation, under the leadership of its Prioress General, Mother Mary Emmanuel, began its search for an appropriate architect. Mother Emmanuel's good friend, the Reverend Thomas Phelan, was quick to suggest Kahn. Chaplain at Rensselaer Polytechnic Institute, specialist on liturgical art, and consultant for church architecture in the Albany diocese, Father Phelan was familiar with Kahn's work and recommended his recently completed First Unitarian Church in Rochester (1959–63*) as a model of modern religious architecture.[16]

15 Interview with Sisters Mary Irene Lolli, O.P., and Eileen Patricia Primrose, O.P. Property sales information in the Archive of the Dominican Motherhouse, Elkins Park, PA.

16 Lewis, "The Dominican Motherhouse," pp. 383–89. On Kahn's particular brand of religiousness, see Benedikt, "God, Creativity and Evolution: The Argument from Designers."

Kahn, although Jewish, was not an unlikely candidate for the Dominicans, his freewheeling religiousness seemingly at home in all faiths and in none: "I can't speak about religious sects. I just know about the Catholics, the Jews, and the Moslems—I have a vague idea of the various sects. But I don't have a vague idea about religion itself. I feel conversed with religion as a very sacred part of the intimate. But as far as people practicing their philosophies of religion, I can frankly say I don't know anything about them. None of them seem to be of the quality of religion itself."[17] While building the First Unitarian Church, Kahn had served as a member of the art and architecture panel of the Catholic Liturgical Conference in Philadelphia in 1963 and later lectured at the Twentieth Liturgical Conference in Chicago in 1965.[18] Fittingly, by the end of his career he would build for the Jewish, Christian, and Islamic faiths.

**First contact**

At the end of March 1965, Kahn's office received Mother Emmanuel's inquiry in the form of a letter.[19] **Fig. 4** Kahn was away in Pakistan at the time involved in planning twin capitals at Dhaka and Islamabad, but his senior associate David Wisdom responded promptly in a letter dated April 2, 1965.[20] Affirming Kahn's interest in their project, listing several buildings he thought relevant to the congregation, and mentioning that the office was beginning work on another monastery, St. Andrew's Priory in California, Wisdom invited Mother Emmanuel to visit the office to view works in progress. After this brief exchange it would take a full year, though, before Kahn and the sisters would meet: by no means a small undertaking for the congregation; before embarking the sisters needed to reassess their needs and to arrange the project's funding. After much deliberation, they agreed on a schematic program and calculated a budget of $1,500,000 before again taking up contact with the architects.[21]

On April 26, 1966, Kahn and his assistant Galen Schlosser finally met with the congregation's building committee in Media.[22] In this and the following meetings Kahn was accompanied by an assistant who took notes as Kahn led the discussion. The first encounters between the architects and the sisters quickly broke the ice, with Kahn questioning on the traditions and rules of the order while sifting through their schematic program. This was the beginning of a project-long

17 Louis Kahn, in conversation with Richard Saul Wurman, October 1973, in Wurman, *What Will Be Has Always Been*, p. 231.

18 Lewis, "The Dominican Motherhouse," p. 384.

19 Letter, Mother Mary Emmanuel to Kahn, March 26, 1965, Box LIK 10, Kahn Collection.

20 Letter, David Wisdom to Mother Emmanuel, April 2, 1965, Box LIK 10, Kahn Collection.

21 The budget of $1,500,000 appears several times in the correspondence for the Dominican Motherhouse. Box LIK 10, Kahn Collection.

22 Meeting Minutes, Galen Schlosser and Louis Kahn, April 26, 1966. Box LIK 10, Kahn Collection.

**5–6** Auction poster, Windy Hill, 1964
**7** Surveyor's plan, April 16, 1966

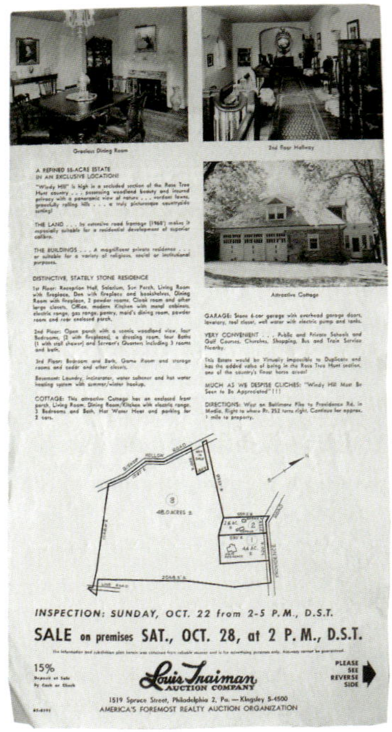

process of self-education through questioning in which Kahn would gradually refine his—more than mildly romantic—understanding of monastic life in general and of the sisters' needs in particular.[23]

**David Polk, project architect**

Soon after the first meeting Kahn awarded his assistant David Polk the position of project architect. Polk, a graduate of the University of Pennsylvania, had been a member of the office for over four years. A talented designer and draftsman, he belonged to those associates who were equal to the considerable challenge of serving as Kahn's sparring partner in the early rounds of designing. In what must have seemed a divine coincidence of timing, the project for another monastery, the Benedictine St. Andrew's Priory, had been on Polk's drawing board for less than a month; Kahn now had the unique chance to develop the twin projects in dialogue with a single trusted partner.[24]

### The Site

The congregation could scarcely have wished for a more fitting setting for their new monastery. Their property consisted of fifty-five acres (22 hectares) of wooded land with a handsome manor house and outbuildings embedded in a rural landscape near the small town of Media, Pennsylvania, thirty miles south of Philadelphia. **Figs. 5–7** Located at the highest point in Delaware County, the site was skirted by the historic Providence Great Road, the first route to be cleared into Pennsylvania's backcountry by early settlers in 1683.[25] Given that the existing house was to be used for guests and older sisters, the topography, which ranged from a gentle slope on the north of the property to a steep ravine in the south, and considering the extent of the woods, the natural site for the new monastery presented itself immediately: a lightly sloping hillock on the edge of a meadow. Secluded deep within the property and surrounded by deciduous forest on its south, east, and west sides, the hill could be accessed either from the northeast over North Providence Road or from the northwest over Bishop Hollow Drive. The site—dubbed "Daffodil Hill" by the sisters for the lush blanket of flowers that covered it each spring—had the virtues of good drainage, solar exposure, and being relatively free of trees. The forest edge, meadow, and mild terrain joined in an idyllic setting, with the reciprocal qualities of openness and closure, the twin promises of prospect and refuge.

23 Interview, author with David Polk, Chestnut Hill, PA, October 20, 2004. Confirmed in interview with Sisters Mary Irene Lolli, O.P., and Eileen Patricia Primrose, O.P.

24 Polk would bring the shorter-lived St. Andrew's project to completion and accompany the Dominican Motherhouse until leaving the office in late 1968, at which time Anant Raje, a young architect who had joined the office in 1964, assumed the role of project architect. Interview with David Polk.

25 Property sales information in Archive of the Dominican Motherhouse, Elkins Park, PA. Information about Providence Road: Historical Landmark, Media Borough Council, 1977.

### The Sisters and Their Program

The leaders of the congregation were women of intellect and experience. With biographies in foreign missionary activity, scholasticism, education, and administration, their interests were anything but purely "monastic." Although not profoundly steeped in modern architecture, in seeking out Kahn the sisters were intently seeking a modern interpretation of their institution. While Dominican rule largely dictated their program, there remained a certain freedom in defining its individual components and, perhaps more importantly, in deciding how these were to relate to each other. The program Kahn and the sisters worked out in their first meetings was more qualitative than precisely quantitative in nature: while types of use and approximate numbers of users were specified, exact room sizes, adjacencies, and detailed functional requirements were left for the architects to develop in dialogue with the sisters by means of their designs.[26]

**From programming to "reprogramming"**

This programming as an open-ended dialogue between client and architect was well suited to Kahn's holistic ideal of the design process, one that stands at odds with conventional prescriptive practice in which the architect is presented with a comprehensive written document at the beginning of a project. For Kahn, architecture can never result from the simple translation of predefined "functions" into spatial diagrams and further into buildings. The role of the architect in programming is to be active rather than passive: thanks to his (ideally) enlightened education and experience it is he, rather than the client, who is likely best equipped to plumb the deeper societal and cultural nature of the institution at hand; he who has the insight to see beyond circumstantial "needs" to the deeply seated "desires" from which all institutions spring. "There are few clients who can understand philosophically the institution they are creating.... Few clients have it or even sense the lack of it. Usually a written program is handed to you and you must assume the role of the philosopher for the client."[27] Given a program consisting of functions, areas, and relationships, it is the architect's duty to "reprogram," to reshape that program in light of a transcendent image of man, liberating it from the narrow paths laid out by functionalism or modern behavioral science. "Our profession is shabby only because we do not change the programming. If you change that programming, you release wonderful forces because the individual then never makes the mistake of making something which just pleases himself. You please society in your

26 Interview with Sisters Mary Irene Lolli, O.P., and Eileen Patricia Primrose, O.P.; meeting minutes, Schlosser and Kahn, April 26, 1966; interview with David Polk.

27 Kahn, quoted in Wurman, *What Will Be Has Always Been,* p. 120.

programming, not in the way you do your lousy building. The architect trains himself in expression which is true."[28] A remarkable statement from an architect often judged for his formal and technical skill! In this statement and others like it, Kahn effectively shifts the creative focus of designing away from the aesthetic making of an object ("the way you do your lousy building") toward its social grounding and toward the often-overlooked creative potential inherent in the initial framing of the project.[29]

With his emphasis on the architect's intuition, cultural memory, and sense of appropriateness in arriving at this "expression of what is true," Kahn stood miles apart from those many colleagues in the fifties and sixties who attempted to systematize architectural programming, either by making it a judgment-free, quasi-scientific branch of problem-solving, or a democratic participatory act.[30] Kahn's insights into relationships between program (or "function") and form—modernism's most oft-repeated and perhaps least understood pair of terms—belong to his most profound. We will return to them often in the following chapter.

**From areas to spaces: the threshold**

Not surprisingly, then, that at the first meeting Kahn spontaneously proposed an element not previously considered by the sisters: a gatehouse, tower, or ceremonial place of arrival to mark a threshold between convent and outer world. Within this threshold building could be an entry hall, administrative offices, and guest rooms. Kahn suggested the entry hall be decorated with symbols of all world religions, assembled as reminders of the universality of belief. Their position at the building's threshold, rather than inside the monastery, was to celebrate the Dominicans' particular form of worship and life. "The monastery which I am doing has an entrance place which happens to be a gate. It is decorated in the invitation of all religions, something which is now being started. But they are given a place only at the gate, because the sanctity of the monastery must be kept."[31] The sisters

28 Kahn, *Conversations with Students,* p. 54.

29 "It is normally assumed that the most creative part of design is concerned with the building as object ... but it may be argued that the most important, and most creative part of the process is the formulation of the brief ... The creative brief is about negotiating a new set of social relations, it is about the juxtapositions of actions and activities, it is about the possibility to think outside the norm, in order to project new spatial, and hence social, conditions. The process of evolving a brief may not provide the immediate rush of visual stimulation that is associated with the creative design of an object—a rush which has proved addictive to architects over the ages—but it does have a much longer-term and profound effect." Till, *Architecture Depends,* p. 168.

30 For influential literature on the programming/problem-solving approach to design in the sixties and seventies, see, for example, Alexander, *Notes on the Synthesis of Form;* Broadbent, *Design Methods in Architecture;* or Pena, *Problem Seeking: An Architectural Programming Primer.* The other side of the "programming argument" tended to shun a tight fit between form and function and to advocate flexibility and the accommodation of mass production to individual use. See, for example, the "mat" buildings of Candelis, Shadrach, and Woods, or N. John Habraken and the University of Eindhoven's SAR planning method. The participatory model was strongly advocated by architects such as Lucian Kroll.

31 Kahn, quoted in Ronner and Jhaveri, *Louis I. Kahn: Complete Work,* p. 301.

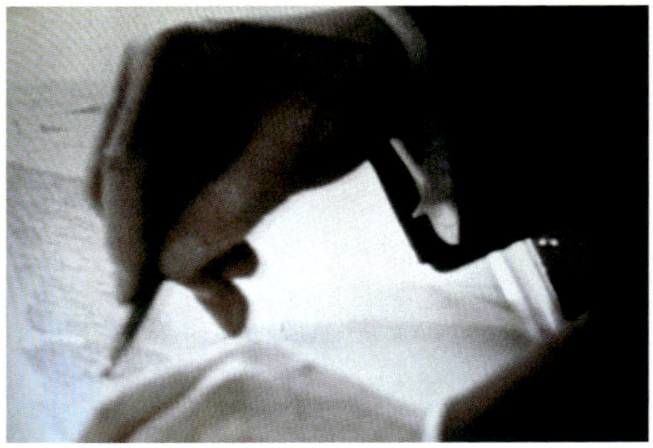

**8–11** Louis Kahn and Mother Mary Emmanuel, Sister Eileen Patricia Primrose, Kahn and David Polk, Kahn at work; from *Signature Against the Sky*, 1967

were immediately enthusiastic about these suggestions. As Kahn later elaborated:

> "I have a gateway building. This gateway is the transition between the inside and the outside—I mean—is the center of the Ecumenical Council. It is not in the program. It comes from the spirit and nature of the problem. This is why I think it is so important that the architect does not follow the program but simply uses it as a point of departure of quantity and not of quality.... The program that you get and the translation you make architecturally must come from the spirit of man, not the program. The program is not architecture—it is merely instruction, it is like a prescription by a druggist. Because in the program there is a lobby which the architect must turn into a place of entrance. Corridors must be changed into galleries. Budgets must be changed to economy and areas must be changed to spaces."[32]

**The double life of the sisters, internal hierarchies**

That Kahn would have great sympathy for a monastery's program is not difficult to imagine. The ideals of secluded contemplation, learning, and ritual community; the interaction between the inner world

32 Ibid., p. 303.

of the nuns and that of visitors from outside; the internal hierarchies of the sisters: all these were the stuff of a finely grained society based on transcendental values which could have only deeply inspired the idealistic Kahn. Kahn and the sisters soon assembled a schematic program as a point of departure. The program divided itself according to the "double life" of the Dominicans into two distinct and equal halves: the nuns' private quarters, which included dormitories for 120 sisters, and the communal spaces, which consisted of a chapel, an auditorium, classrooms, a library, and a refectory. The sisters were ordered according to a four-tiered hierarchy: newly arrived postulants, novices who had taken their first vows, younger professed sisters who had entered the order, and, finally, older professed sisters.[33] Each different rank of sisters was to be housed separately, each group with its own living room. The cells of the professed sisters would be larger and contain private bathrooms; those of the postulants and novices would be smaller and have access to shared bathing and toilet rooms. In addition to ancillary spaces such as a kitchen, housekeeping, storage, and administration, gardens might be included for contemplative work and recreational facilities were to be considered. As to the material of construction, Kahn was certain: stone would be the most sympathetic to the existing buildings on the site.[34]

With budget, site, and schematic program in place, the architects were now ready to bring first thoughts to paper.

33 First typed program (undated); meeting minutes, Schlosser and Kahn, April 26, 1966.

34 Meeting minutes, Schlosser and Kahn, April 26, 1966.

## "ARCHITECTURING"
## THE DESIGNS, APRIL 1966–DECEMBER 1968

*I am no longer speaking of the things that exist in a house, but of the way in which those things have been put together, that is to say, the way things have been "architectured."* Le Corbusier, "In Defense of Architecture," 1929

*Painting has nothing to do with thinking, because in painting thinking is painting. Thinking is language—record-keeping—and has to take place before and after. Einstein did not think when he was calculating: he calculated—producing the next equation in reaction to the one that went before—just as in painting one form is a response to another, and so on.* Gerhard Richter, "Notes," 1962

*A building is a struggle, not a miracle, and the architect should acknowledge this.* Louis Kahn, "The Architect Speaks," 1953

### First Steps, a First Scheme: April–June 1966

**Grasping quantities**

There are no shortcuts to architecture. Kahn's first sketches remind us of this. A sixty-four-year-old architect with over forty years of experience, Kahn, as does any student, needs to grasp the quantities of the program before he can begin to translate its raw square feet into any sort of meaningful spatial arrangement. **Fig. 12** He starts with the sisters' cells—the raison d'être of the program—drawing them freehand and to scale: thirty newly-arrived postulants, forty-five novices, thirty junior professed sisters who have taken their vows and entered the order, and thirty older professed sisters. The cells are tentatively dimensioned: smaller cells (10 × 15 ft. [3 × 4.5 m]) for the younger sisters, larger (10 × 20 ft. [3 × 6 m]) for the elder sisters. Kahn had already proposed, conflating geometry and behavior, that the squarish geometry of the younger sisters' cells would in some way serve to "measure the[ir] servitude."

This linear graphic summary begets linear plan diagrams. The chapel is blocked out on a square-feet-per-person basis in a conventional rectangular plan. Further below, probing toward a first disposition

**12** Elements of the plan, Spring 1966, Louis Kahn
**13–14** Plans, Spring 1966, Louis Kahn
**15** Chapel, Spring 1966, Louis Kahn

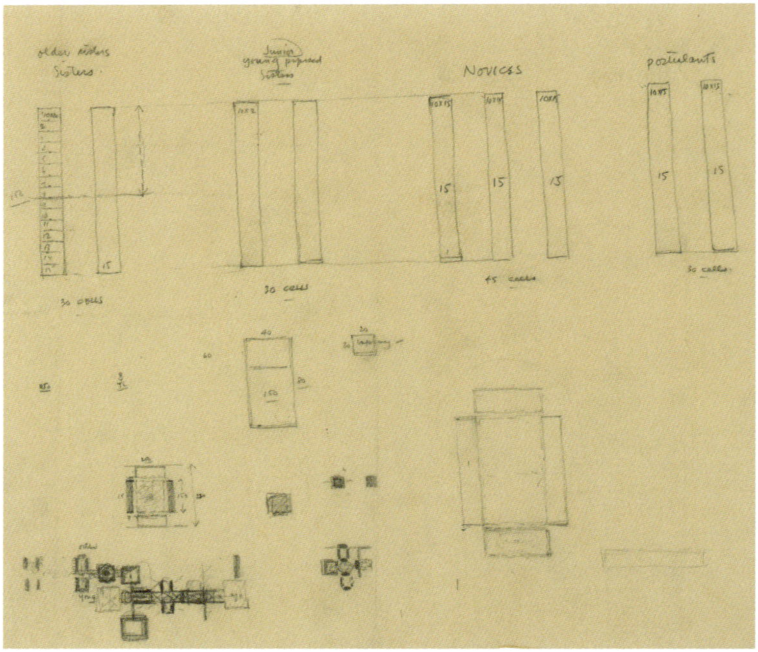

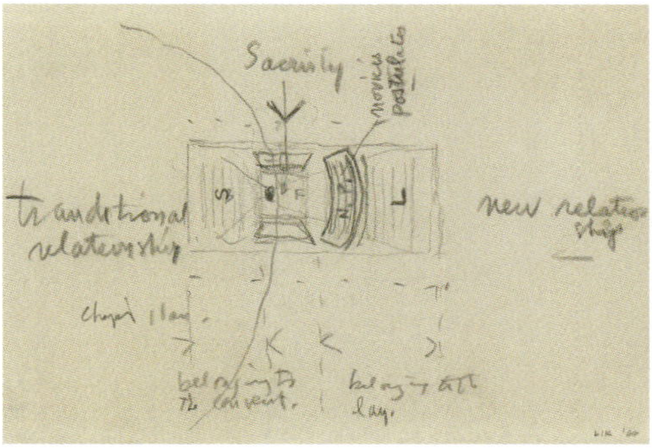


of main spaces, Kahn demonstrates to himself that by stacking the four groups of cells around the chapel, this portion of the program could take a shape similar to that of his First Unitarian Church. Still further below and now thinking in terms of the whole program, he draws a tiny linear scheme with the elements of the program strung along a shifting, street-like axis.

**The cross schemes**

The linear elements are regrouped in second and third, larger-scale sketches. Figs. 13–14 In both drawings an ambulatory describes the thick outer edge of a nave, circumscribing the chapel, the adjacent refectory, and a large court occupying the center of the plan. Minor axes are made of cells and their respective sub-courts, which in turn open to the main court. The schemes resemble rather rudimentary Beaux-Arts plans: symmetrical, processional, and tightly ordered within their tartan grids, with secondary bays dedicated—in somewhat schoolbookish Beaux-Arts manner—to galleries and minor spaces. In spite of their spare hieroglyphics, we can glean much information from these little drawings. All elements of a traditional Western monastic type have been considered—ambulatories, inner and outer cloisters, etc.—though assembled to a typology that has no obvious antecedent. The hierarchic plan unfolds in layers of sanctity: opening near the studio and school, bypassing the novices and then the sisters' cells to the chapel, and terminating in the refectory at its apex. Although it is not exactly clear how this plan relates to its site, tufts of forest in the first sketch seem to indicate that the major axis runs in an east-west direction. The main entry is indicated on the western end of this axis and a second arrow points in the direction of what must be North Providence Road (the "R" in plan). A crescent-shaped pond forms a threshold in this direction.

**The chapel**

In a separate early sketch Fig. 15, Kahn considers the chapel. In a long rectangle, a traditional monastic type is schematically yet conscientiously laid out, with altar and rood screen separating the professed sisters' choir from that of the lay. Kahn's cryptic notes are intriguing:

in contrast to the "traditional relationship" which he has drawn, he apparently seeks a "new relationship," one dependent upon just what area "belongs to the convent" and what "belongs to the lay." If an overlapping of inner convent life and outer world is at the crux of his questioning, the means of achieving this are impossible to determine from the sketch at hand. Though soon abandoned, what makes this sketch interesting is its early proposal of intertwining inner and outer worlds, a theme which will later resurface in the planning.

It is easy to see in Kahn's first drawings more a first means of engaging hand, paper, and program than attempts at fitting a building to this particular site. More architectural stick figures than comprehensive diagrams, the evidence from this earliest phase of the project deals exclusively with the inner world of the program: shifting its linear components against each other in search of resolution while leaving the specifics of context unaddressed. But this was not at all atypical for Kahn's initial approach; by this time in his life he had come to see the act of building first and foremost as a social act, "an offering to an institution of man." When confronted with a design problem, the search for that configuration of parts that spoke most profoundly of the institution in question had become his first priority, transcending the contingencies of material, construction, or site.

**"Form and Design"**

After several attempts in the fifties, Kahn's mature description of how architectural artifacts might come into being emerged in 1960 in what he identified as a process of "Form and Design." Oft quoted but worth repeating here is his description of what he found to be the twofold nature of the architectural act:

"Form encompasses a harmony of systems, a sense of Order and that which characterizes one existence from another. Form has no shape or dimension. For example, in the differentiation of a spoon from Spoon, Spoon characterizes a form having two inseparable parts, the handle and the bowl. A spoon implies a specific design made of silver or wood, big or little, shallow or deep. Form is 'what,' Design is 'how.' Form is impersonal. Design belongs to the designer. Design is a circumstantial act, how much money there is available, the site, the client, the extent of knowledge. Form has nothing to do with circumstantial conditions. In architecture, it characterizes a harmony of spaces good for a certain activity of man.

"Reflect then on what characterizes House, a house and home. House is the abstract characteristic of spaces good to live in. House is the Form, in the mind of wonder it should be there without shape or dimension. A house is a conditional interpretation of these spaces. This is Design. In my opinion the greatness of an architect depends on his powers of realization of that which is House, rather than the design of a house, which is a circumstantial act."[35]

For Kahn, our institutions—of home, learning, government, etc.—were all "on trial," their meanings clouded by layers of cultural detritus and circumstance: "When we think of the simple beginnings which inspired our present institutions, it is evident that some drastic changes must be made which will inspire the re-creation of [their] meaning."[36] The search for "Form" is a metaphorical search for these "simple beginnings." Here lies for Kahn the deeper purpose of architecture: not in the expression of "program," personal whim, or other conditions of circumstance, but in providing access to the root human inspirations behind that program, beyond personal taste, beyond circumstance. The grasp of Form, grounded in man's "sense of appropriateness" or "sense of commonality," belongs to his intuition and embodied knowledge of human history; Design, through its questioning of Order, belongs to his reason. Said Kahn of his own neo-Beaux-Arts training, "The design begins with the sketch (which) depended on our intuitive powers. But the intuitive power is probably our most accurate sense. The sketch depended on our sense of appropriateness. I teach appropriateness. I don't teach anything else."[37]

The Form-Design hierarchy structures the work of the architect. In practice, presented with a project the architect searches the mind for the most suitable among the archetypical forms which it has stored away; this becomes the hypothetical "Form" of the building at hand, be it "House," "School," "Library," etc. These archetypes are not abstract forms existing in some distant realm, but rather represent

35 Kahn, radio lecture for "Voice of America," November 1960, quoted in Latour, *Louis I. Kahn,* p. 113.

36 Kahn, quoted in Jordy, "The Span of Kahn," p. 332.

37 Ibid. The influence of Kahn's Beaux-Arts training on his mature concept of "Form and Design" is evident in his description of that training. In this interest, following is a longer excerpt from Jordy's interview: "First, the sketch or esquisse. For beginning design problems Beaux-Arts training typically presented the student with a written program without comment from the instructor. He would study the program, be given a few hours in a cubicle (en loge) during which he would make a quick sketch of his solution without consultation. This sketch was filed as the basis for the elaboration of the problem which followed. Final drawings could not violate the essence of the original esquisse. The sketch, or esquisse, was the beginning exercise issued by the central office, the Beaux-Arts Institute. This was registered as the first impression as to how the student saw the building. It was something that every student trained himself for. In order not to be at great variance with the nature of a library, or the nature of a legislative chamber, we looked up these places to see what they were in preparation for the esquisse. Once the sketch was made we had to adhere to it during the time of study. This particular aspect of Beaux-Arts training was probably the most controversial because there was no exchange between the advocates of the program and those who interpreted it, the architect. So the sketch depended on our intuitive powers. But intuitive power is probably our most accurate sense. The sketch depended on our intuitive sense of appropriateness. I teach appropriateness. I don't teach anything else. I don't teach how I do things. I'm at my best when I don't tell anything about how I do things. I'm at my best when I talk about the nature of things—the nature of a library. It is not derived so much from knowledge because the examples are very ragged. It is derived because you revere the sense of the beginning.... I don't think that appropriateness comes from examples of what has been done. They are a test of what is done, but not the beginning, the source. The esquisse gave us this sense of a source, because we knew little about how things were done. We couldn't go to the books and really research the problem before the esquisse was made. So I think that the esquisse was valuable in giving a sense of what, out-of-the-blue, a library should be, as though we had never seen a library."

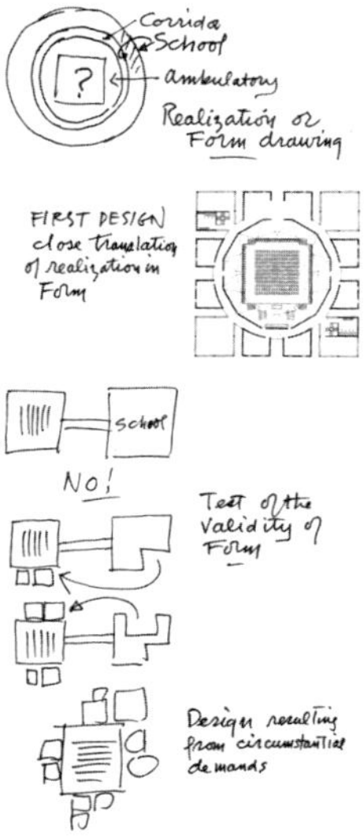


**16** First Unitarian Church, 1959–63*: "Form diagram," Louis Kahn

basic modes of being-in-the-world. For Kahn, the "Form" of a project defined the hierarchical and reciprocal relationships between its activities and was thus the architect's insight into the unchanging essence of the institution in question. This spatial order, whether expressed verbally or laid out in a diagram is, then, an intuition to which all further decisions must be referred. (Kahn's now-famous description of his "Form diagram" accounting for the genesis of the First Unitarian Church gives insight into this priority of decisions.[38] **Fig. 16**) As in Karl Popper's description of conjecture and refutation in a scientific process,[39] once proposed the educated guess of "Form" is to be proven or refuted by confronting it with the many contingencies of reality during the "Design" phase: budget, site, materials, building codes, etc. If the "Form," however deformed by "Design," holds true against these tests, it is the "true" Form; if not, a new "Form" diagram must be conceived and the process begins anew.

Kahn's insight into the architectural process as one uniting intuition and ratio, Platonic idealism and realism, cultural heritage and empiricism, representation and its transcendence—especially provocative against the background of modernism's empiricist tabula rasa methodology—remains one of his most helpful thoughts for fellow architects. For whether or not we share Kahn's depth-giving paradigm of architecture's common "simple beginnings," most of us would agree to some degree upon architecture's dual, ideal-real, nature. Kahn's "space" of designing not only addresses this nature but provides a structure for its unfolding. Bearing this in mind, we return to the drawings.

### The First Scheme and its Variations: June 1966–July 1966

**Between site and program**

After this initial probing, Kahn gave David Polk his tentative sketches to develop into a first, scaled study. Polk, having spent more time on the site than Kahn, suggested that the forest might be used as a natural edge against which the diverse elements of the convent could be positioned. The sisters' cells could engage in an intimate relationship with the woods while defining a place for the communal rooms.[40] To Polk's great satisfaction, Kahn approved of his suggestion for further development during his upcoming absence from the office and continued to consider the idea while away. A series of tiny sketches on the back of an invitation to lecture in Stockholm on April 2, 1966, may have been drawn while en route to that very appointment. **Figs. 17–18** They show four variations in which the basic elements of the program—the four bars of cells (one for each group of sisters) and a more or less solid block of common spaces—are juxtaposed across a large open space. Regardless of where Kahn sketched these diagrams, Polk's reading of the site seems to have helped him focus his thoughts on

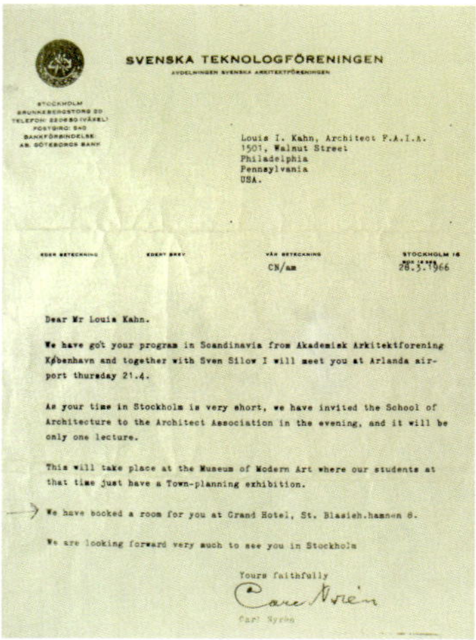

SVENSKA TEKNOLOGFÖRENINGEN

Louis I. Kahn, Architect F.A.I.A.
1501, Walnut Street
Philadelphia
Pennsylvania
USA.

CN/am

STOCKHOLM 16
28.3.1966

Dear Mr Louis Kahn.

We have got your program in Scandinavia from Akademisk Arkitektforening København and together with Sven Silow I will meet you at Arlanda airport thursday 21.4.

As your time in Stockholm is very short, we have invited the School of Architecture to the Architect Association in the evening, and it will be only one lecture.

This will take place at the Museum of Modern Art where our students at that time just have a Town-planning exhibition.

We have booked a room for you at Grand Hotel, St. Blasieh.hamnen 8.

We are looking forward very much to see you in Stockholm

Yours faithfully

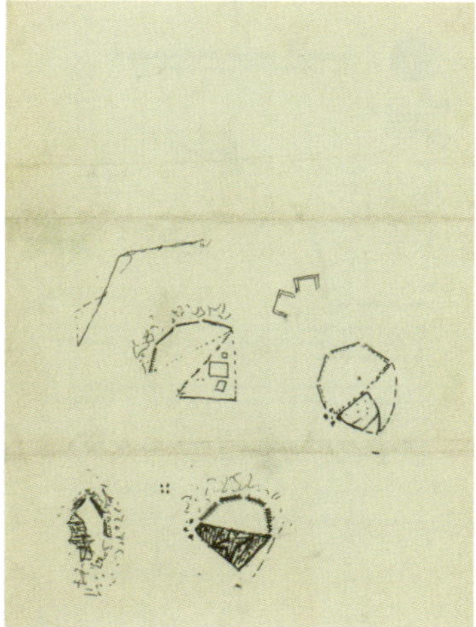

**17–18** Letter with plan sketch (verso), March 28, 1966, Louis Kahn

the program, for in contrast to his earliest sketches, the spatial intention of this simple two-part parti—which holds monastic seclusion in equipoise with communal life—is now abundantly clear.

If the resulting diagram overlays neatly with plans of medieval Carthusian charterhouses, this is less a case of historicist or academic quotation (to which Kahn was loathe) than a result of an "essentialist" method. Expressed in Kahnian terms, both the Carthusians and Kahn, working some seven hundred years apart, had sought and found the appropriate "Form" for "Monastery." A spatial archetype—according to Kahn—does not belong to anyone, any more than "the waltz belongs to any musician or oxygen to the discoverer of that element," it is simply that "one finds a certain nature, and as a professional we must find that certain nature."[41]

38 Kahn often related the genesis of his First Unitarian Church (1959–63*) to illustrate the process of "Form and Design" at work. Presented with the program, Kahn—so he told—quickly realized that the sanctuary ("the center of questioning") and the required classrooms ("which raise the spirit of the question") were in fact inseparable. Kahn represented this realization in a "Form" ideogram, with "questioning" center, ambulatory, and ancillary classroom spaces. The clients, though, had imagined a binuclear scheme, with sanctuary and school separated by a linking foyer. Kahn was then able to demonstrate to the congregation how the individual spaces of the school "wanted" to take part in the presence of the sanctuary; piece by piece, the clients' binuclear scheme morphed back into Kahn's original diagram—the "Form" was thus saved. The pithy final plan, in which the individual sizes of the rooms have been respected (the circumstances of "Design"), shows how the "Form" was strong enough to hold through to realization (see "A Discussion in Louis I. Kahn's Office," pp. 9–18). In contrast to Kahn's description, which tends to suggest that the intuition's way to the correct "Form" is always a quick and certain one, this was not at all the case with several of his projects, as we shall see in the following pages. We might also note at this point that not all programs move with the same vehemence toward "Form"; whereas a church, an auditorium, a school tend to suggest a strong (that is socially charged) Form, a speculative office building or a fast-food restaurant do not. See also Vincent Scully's introduction to *Kahn Libraries.*

39 Popper, *Conjectures and Refutations,* 1963.

40 Interview, author with David Polk, Chestnut Hill, PA, October 20, 2004; see also Polk interviewed by Kazumi Kawasaki in *Architecture and Urbanism,* p. 234: "He wasn't too much aware of the site when working on the original schemes, and when I went to look at the site and I found the woods in relation to a clearing to be a certain way and proposed the idea of the cells sort of related to the woods in a kind of inter-edge to the woods and making a place within which the other things could sit."

41 Kahn, *Conversations with Students,* p. 54.

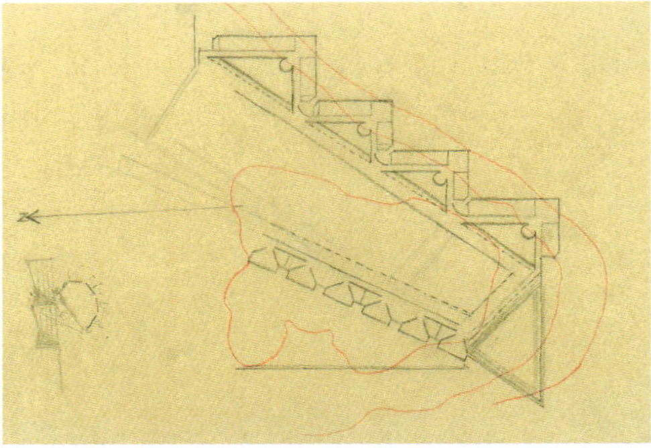

**19–20** Elements of the plan, May/June 1966, David Polk

Fitting sketches to site, we see that the cells are arranged in an arc corresponding roughly to the natural topography and to the course of the sun, leaving the crest of the hill unbuilt. The communal rooms are still portrayed as a single triangular block. Rudimentary as they may be, already laid out in these diagrams are the inherent dichotomies of the problem: on one hand the private world of the sisters, on the other the communal areas and the interface with the public world; on one hand the wish for a comprehensive form, on the other the wish to articulate the program's constituent parts; on one hand the particulars of topography and site, on the other the will of geometry to assert itself. The sum of these frictions and reciprocities would equal Kahn's first serious translation of this monastery's "Form."

Polk completed the first scheme over the next weeks in dialogue with Kahn. Like Kahn, he began by drawing the elements of the program as scaled building blocks. **Figs. 19–20** Attempts to grow Kahn's "Form" using some kind of serialism generated by the cells and the interlocking classrooms (compare these sketches, for example, with the plan of Kahn's Indian Institute of Management) were quickly abandoned and a large, comprehensive plan in 1 in. = 50 ft. (1:600) scale showing the new monastery in relationship to the topography, forest, and existing buildings was submitted to the sisters along with a description from David Wisdom on June 22, 1966, while Kahn was once again away in Asia.[42] **Fig. 21 (See Appendix for room legends to this and the following plans)** Wisdom's letter succinctly walks the sisters through the plan:

*My Dear Reverend Mother:*

*We respectfully submit for consideration the Site Development Plan showing new proposed buildings and surroundings for the Motherhouse, and the general character of the buildings.*

42 Letter, David Wisdom to Mother Mary Emmanuel, June 22, 1966, Box LIK 10, Kahn Collection.

*The approach is obliquely through an orchard replanted where the old orchard grew, arriving at a paved entrance platform, the Gateway and Administration Building lying ahead, and the Chapel, Refectory, School and related courts stretching away to the right.*

*The individual cells are organized in an arc facing South along the brow of the hill in the woods beyond the main platform. They are placed so that each room has its own private relationship with the woods—the serenity of the woods being felt to be in harmony with the nature of the cell.*

*The rooms are arranged in three tiers with access being from the middle level which is also the main ground level of all buildings. Thus one descends one flight of stairs to the first level and ascends one flight to the third level. All the rooms are connected by an interior gallery and open cloister which looks across one of the four sunken gardens to that portion of the woods encircled by the arc of rooms. The sunken gardens are at the first level giving light and outlook to the galleries and cloisters at that level.*

*The Chapel, Refectory and School are organized linearly along the main platform forming, with their courts, a community of buildings, each being accessible from the principle gallery which widens to form a generous hall at the entrances to the major spaces. These buildings begin to become a realm of spaces appropriate to their purpose.*

*As shown the number of cells is 105 [135] consisting of:*
*45 novices*
*30 postulants*
*30 younger professed sisters*
*30 older professed sisters*

*The cells for the novices, postulants and younger sisters are 9 feet 4 inches wide and 12 feet long. Those of the older professed sisters are 11 feet 4 inches wide and 15 feet long.*

*The Chapel will accommodate 164 persons with the possibility of expansion to 200 for special occasions.*

*The Refectory will accommodate 160 persons at the four long tables indicated on the plan.*

*The Auditorium will accommodate 160–200 persons.*

*Please let us know when another meeting may be held to discuss further development of your program.*

*Very truly yours,*
*David Wisdom*

**21** Site plan, June 22, 1966, David Polk (attributed)

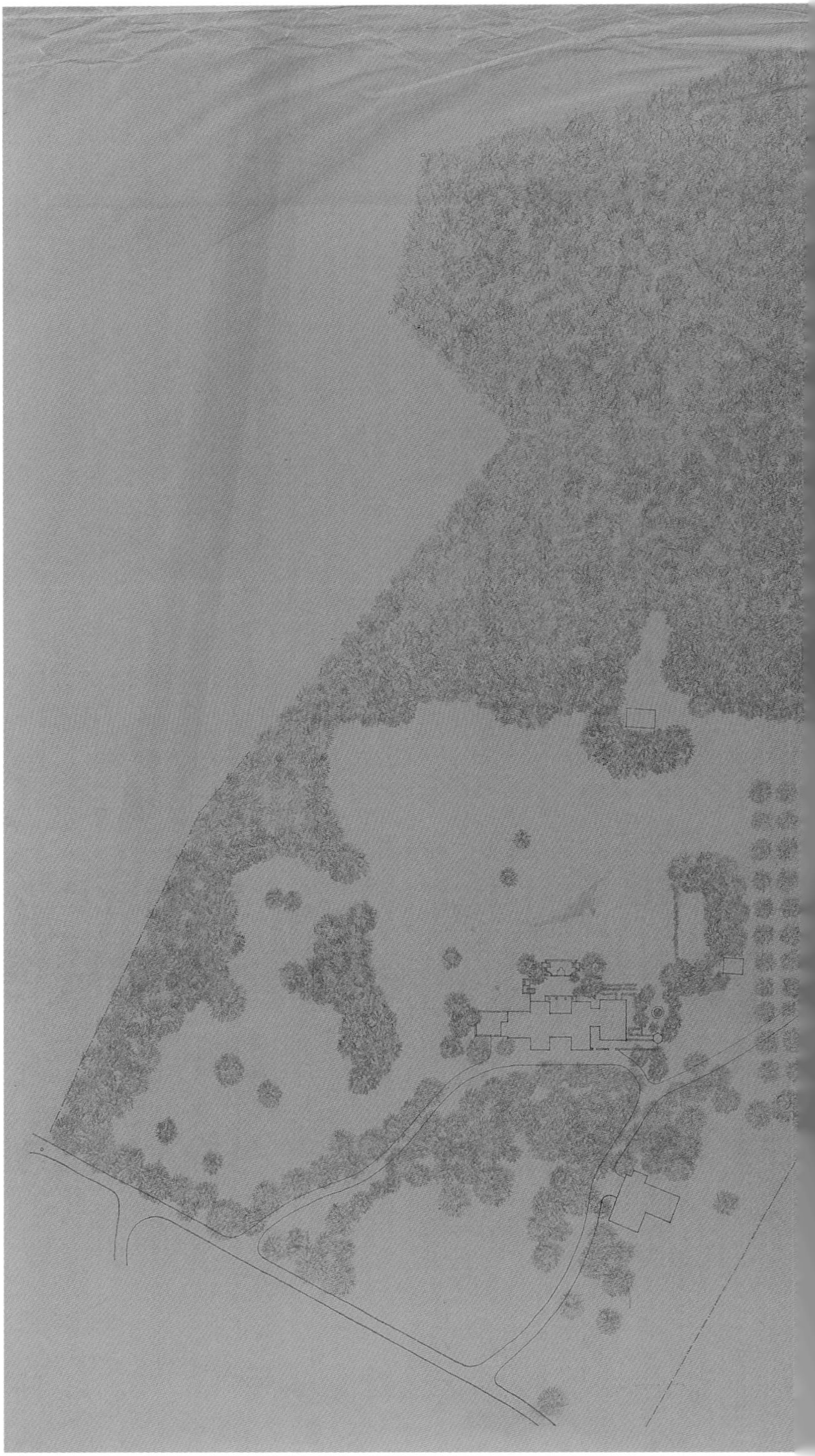

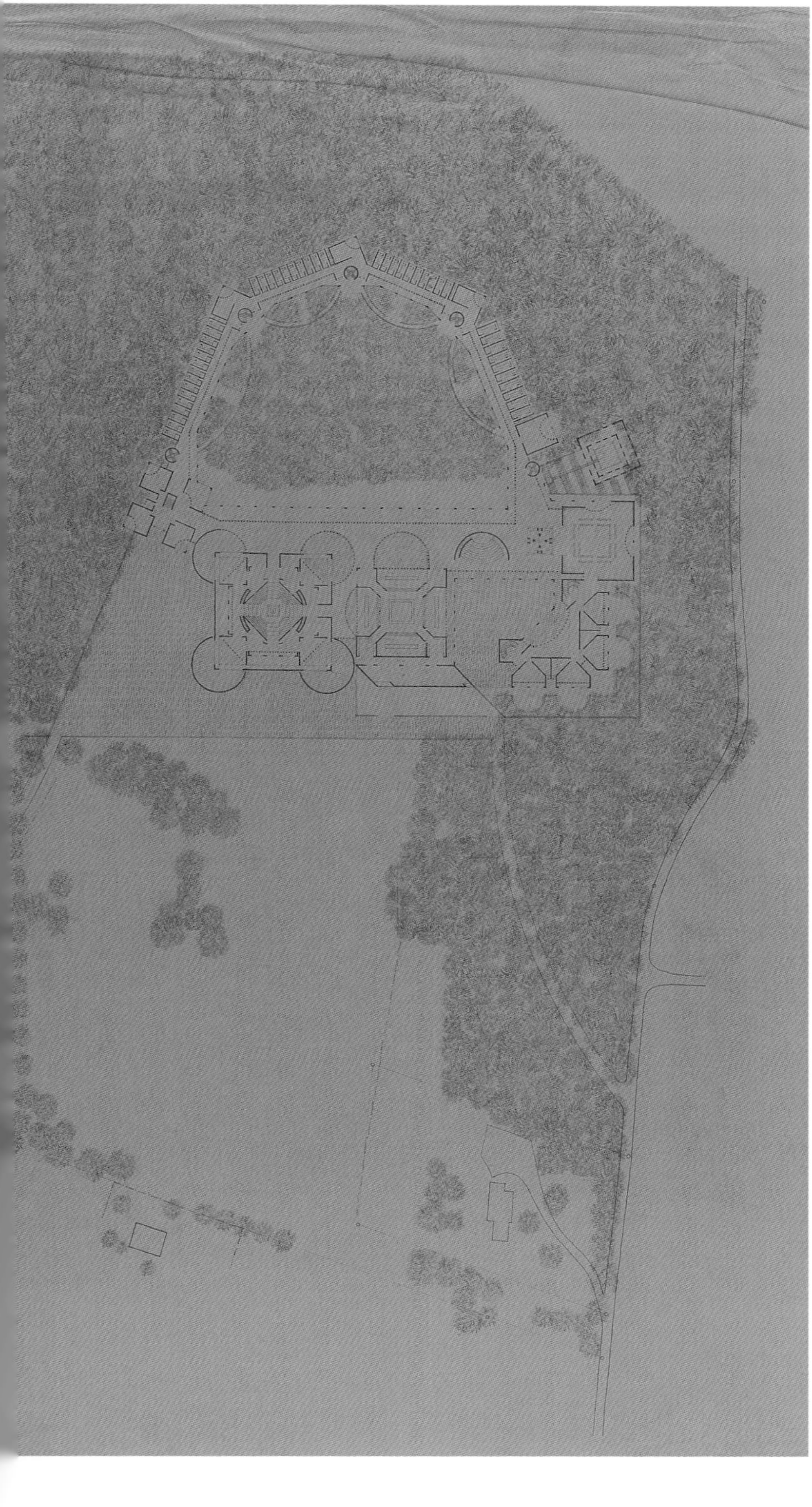

"Form" and landscape, typos and topos

Immediately clear is to what great degree Polk's drafted scheme remained true to the miniature "Form" diagrams on the back of Kahn's letter. But the plan reveals more than just a direct translation of a type; further study reveals that—in contrast to Kahn's first attempts with the cross scheme—program and site are in fact beginning to engage in a relationship based on something more than mutual negation. In the new scheme, the "double life" of the congregation is spatially accentuated by the way in which the program's private and public halves are divided along the edge between forest and meadow. To the north of this edge, the communal buildings, and to the south, the cells, submerging into the forest like so many hermitages. Fitting the four cell tracts to the topography and adding the counter-arcs of retaining walls and sunken gardens strengthens the centrifugal movement of the plan, fortifying the cells' reclusive gesture.

It is not only that the features of the site are now engaged to underscore the program by anchoring it in a concrete situation; rather, the effect of the institution on the site is reciprocal. What had previously been a relatively insignificant event in the landscape—a single hillock among many in a rolling topography—is now crowned by that program, making it a focused place in its context—a "Hill among hills." Heidegger acolytes will recall his famous "revealing and gathering" bridge, through which "the banks emerge as banks only as the bridge crosses the stream."[43]

This said, further consideration of the site plan reveals that things are more complex than at first glance. For in the aforementioned charterhouse—as in most Western monasteries—the courtyard makes a strong figure, centering and anchoring the whole. But here, the figure inscribed within the cloisters is overgrown with the forest, challenging its focal clarity. What in the first reading of the plan is a strong "figure," has in the second become a part of the "ground" of the forest. Our reading of the plan flickers: a traditional cloister type has been both implied by the plan's geometry and "crossed out" by the growth of the forest across that plan.[44]

Communal spaces

Facing the clearing, the communal spaces—entry tower, chapel, refectory, auditorium, library, and school—have been arranged in a thick row. While the cells disappear into the forest, the elevation studies show the communal buildings coalescing into a strong figure against the backdrop of trees. **Figs. 23–25** Free from the formal conventions of

43 "The location is not already there before the bridge is. Before the bridge stands, there are of course many spots along the stream that can be occupied by something. One of them proves to be a location, and does so because of the bridge." Heidegger, "Building Dwelling Thinking," p. 145.

44 "I cross out the words so that people notice them. When something has been obscured, it makes you want to read it." Basquiat, quoted in *Jean-Michel Basquiat,* p. 24.

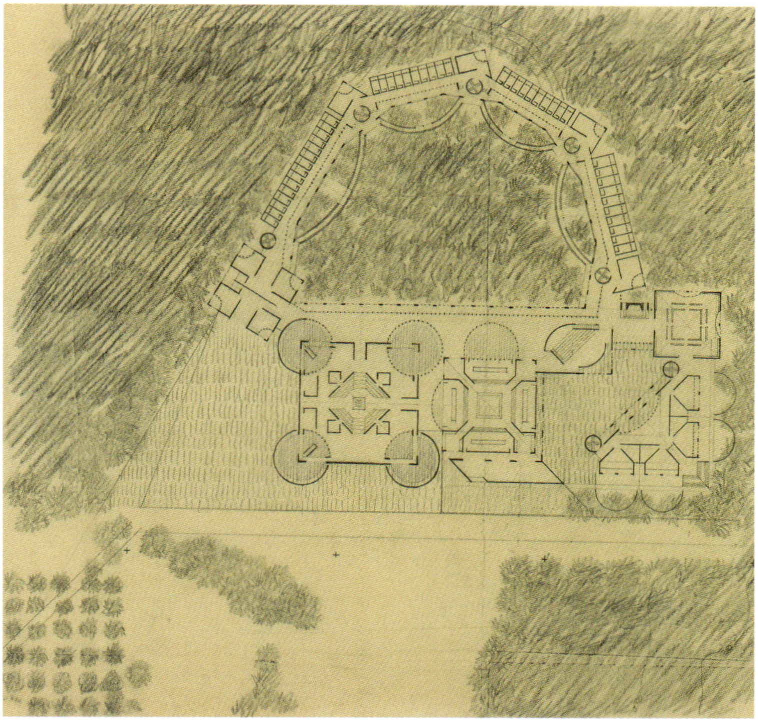

**22** Plan: first floor, June 22, 1966, David Polk (attributed)

Kahn's rejected neo-Beaux-Arts composition and not subject to the same topographical and natural lighting parameters that had determined the positioning of the cells, each of the communal components is theoretically free to take on any shape and to find its most favorable position in respect to the other volumes. In spite of this freedom, common to all of the major spaces is the use of the eroded square as a basis in plan. (Kahn: "I use the square to begin my solutions because the square is a non-choice, really. In the course of development, I search for forces that would disprove the square." [45]) The conch-shaped auditorium is the single exception to this exercise in theme-and-variations.

**"An architecture of connection"**

Kahn and Polk have devised a lavish "architecture of connection": an arcaded cloister that rings the wooded center and a series of galleries, courts, and sub-courts that mediate between the elements of the program. Judging from the generosity of these spaces—they account for nearly half of the scheme's total area—we might assume that the cloisters of a traditional monastery have shrugged their ancillary roles to become the raison d'être for building. We might imagine how Kahn imagined the sisters in these spaces: silently walking the galleries, lost

45 Kahn, quoted in: Ronner and Jhaveri, *Louis I. Kahn: Complete Work*, p. 209.

**23** North elevation, June 1966, Louis Kahn

**24–25** North elevation, June 1966, Louis Kahn

in meditation, or perhaps spontaneously engaged in philosophical discourse. It is an elaborate architecture of that which has no instrumental function: contemplation and chance encounter.

Arrival, movement, and encounter: for Kahn, each deserving of its own architecture, a more or less autonomous space within which to unfold. Indeed, these spaces—in themselves and as spacings between programmed uses—were for Kahn a primary means of interpreting the institution at hand. Tellingly, it is these spaces that most often fail in the client's program: "The architecture of connection is that which the architect has to offer the client ... The architecture of connection, that which connects the usable space: this is the measure of the architect ... The organization of the connecting spaces is that which gives the man walking through the building a feeling for the entire sense of the institution." [46] Or again, later: "The places of entrance, the galleries that radiate from them, the intimate entrances to the spaces of the institution form an independent architecture of connection. This architecture is of equal importance to the major spaces, though these spaces are designed only for movement and must before be bathed in natural light. This Architecture of Connection cannot appear in the program of areas, it is that which the architect offers the client in his search for architectural balance and direction." [47]

Considering the two-part parti as given, a series of variations worked out during the weeks before presentation explore the communal section of the plan. Figs. 26–28 What is at issue here are minor variations of the individual parts (the strict adherence to the square loosening, some sort of centralized chapel remaining a constant), their relationships to each other, and their degree of autonomy or submission to a larger whole. The architects additionally test the consequences of rotating the communal spaces eastward in order to establish frontal rather than oblique access.

Theme and variations

Reading in the meeting minutes that only the first of these variations Figs. 21–22 was presented to the sisters, one may ask why this solution was deemed better than the others. (A question that will soon become familiar in this process.) In this case, Kahn himself might help appease our speculation; speaking to students at Rice University, he explained:

Direct vs. remote association

"Suppose you had a great kind of alley, or gallery, and walked through this gallery, and connected to this gallery are the schools which are associated in the fine arts, be it history, sculpture, architecture, or painting, and you saw people at work, in all these classes. It was designed so that you always felt that you were walking through a place where people were at work. Then I present another way of looking at it, say as a court, and you enter this court. You see buildings in this court, and one is designated as painting, one as sculpture, another as architecture, as history. In one, you rub against the presence of the classes. In the other, you can choose to go in if you want to. Now, without asking you which is better, which is a very unfair question, let me tell you what I think is better. I think the latter is greater by far. In the halls that you go through, you will absorb by some osmosis ... you will see things. If you can choose to go in there, even if you never do, you can get more out of that arrangement than you can of the other. There is something that has to do with the feeling of association which is remote, rather than direct, and more remote association has a longer life and love." [48]

This preference for a combination of free choice and "remote" contact with what Kahn called "the Availabilities" provides a means for deciphering virtually all of Kahn's mature plans, "be they at the scale of a house, an institutional building, or an entire city." [49] Accordingly,

Free choice/remote contact

46 Kahn, "Order Is," p. 58.

47 Kahn, quoted in Wurman, *What Will Be Has Always Been,* p. 257.

48 Kahn, *Conversations with Students,* p. 57.

49 See Brownlee, "The Houses of the Inspirations," p. 110.

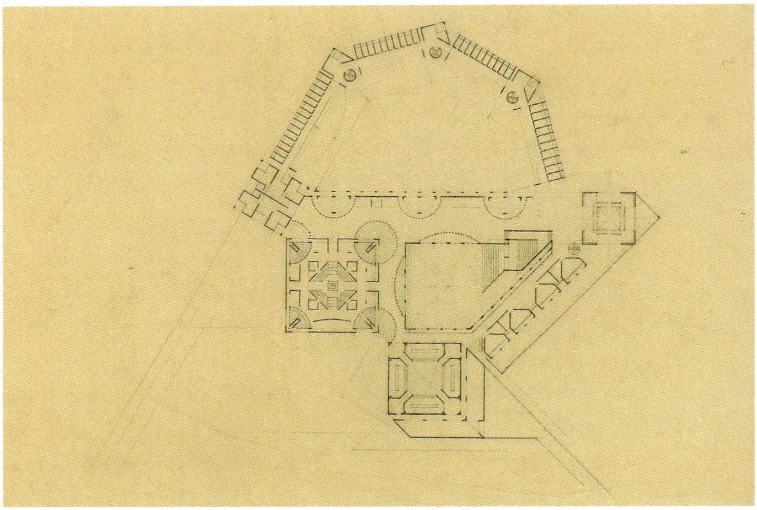

**26** Plan variation, June 1966, Louis Kahn (attributed)
**27–28** Plan variations, June 1966

all variations drawn here share a grainy combination of courtyards and galleries in order to increase both the number of interfaces and the types of possible relationships between spaces. If the version chosen to show to the sisters was judged to be superior to the others, one likely reason is how it fulfills the Kahnian imperative of choice, of remote rather than direct association. In the presented version, for example, the school rooms huddle together as if in dialogue, forming their own sub-court which in turn gives on to a larger court—a situation richer in possibilities of association than the linear disposition of those spaces as shown in figures 26 and 27. In the preferred version, the dependence on conventional single-loaded galleries has been held to a minimum. The position of the library in plan makes it a mediator between the school and the rest of the convent. In addition to its promising frictions and gaps between uses, this version seems to find the best balance between the solitary realm of the cells and the communal forum; as in the original "Form" drawings, each half of the program is given equal weight in the plan.

**Elevations: A "brick order"**

Four elevation studies were prepared for the first scheme, three by Kahn and one by Polk. **Figs. 23–25** Showing the north façade only, the drawings reveal the communal buildings as an expressive wall against the forest, each figure scaled to announce itself from a distance. If in the first discussions Kahn seemed set on stone, the buildings were now conceived of in brick.[50] Of a similar "brick order" to that of the contemporary Indian Institute of Management and the hostels at Dhaka, their flat arches and great circular voids lend the monastery an imposing face.

Kahn's rediscovery of brick—that most "unmodern" of materials—had not by chance accompanied his late blossoming as an architect, well serving his desire for gravitas and resistance, for discrete and directly constructed spaces, for grainy, light-reflecting opacity. More so than an enclosure of concrete or steel, a handcrafted masonry wall seems to have evoked that fundamental sense of enclosure for which he strove. In search of that quality, he gradually developed something approaching a backward-moving morphological series: beginning with the nearly weightless "Renaissance" veneers at the Yale University Art Gallery and the Richards Medical Laboratories, moving over the folded "Gothic" shells at the First Unitarian Church, to the archaic bearing-wall tectonics of the later works in India and Bangladesh.

Aside from his long-term preoccupation with the material, Kahn's decision to use brick is understandable in this case: prevalent and

50 Meeting minutes, David Polk, July 22, 1966, Box LIK 10, Kahn Collection.

indigenous, it expressively accommodates both small- and large-scale spaces of the program within its constructive order. (Kahn, on the similar problem of the Indian Institute of Management: "You notice I made all these buildings answerable to each other, even though the scale of the house and the dormitory and the school is so different. Brick bearing walls, piers, and concrete floors are used throughout, the larger spans giving rise to arches and buttresses, the more modest spaces simple slabs on walls."[51]) This said, the resulting elevations do raise some nagging questions. Can Kahn's monumentally scaled Indian architecture—developed, among other things, in response to the extreme sun, heat, and scale of the Indian subcontinent—be so literally transplanted to the mild climate and delicate scale of this wooded Pennsylvanian landscape? As with his very first attempts with the floor plan, it is difficult not to sense that Kahn is dipping into repertoire or purging himself of something. Accusations of formalism would be—at least for the moment—difficult to rebut: the brick may, as Kahn claimed, "want to be an arch," but the resulting elevations, with their huge openings and shadowy depths, seem to express more for expression's sake than in a truly lucid response to the particulars of *this* context, climate, and program.

**July 22, 1966: The presentation of the first scheme**

On July 22, 1966, Kahn and Polk took the train to Media to discuss the first scheme with the congregation's building committee, for now consisting of Mother Mary Emmanuel, Sister Monte, Sister Irene, and Sister James. Reading between the lines of Polk's extensive meeting notes, one can sense an atmosphere of friendly affirmation colored with subtle undertones of resolve: the sisters would prove to be agreeable, yet by no means submissive partners for Kahn in the following months.[52] They were generally appreciative of Kahn's interpretation of their program, approving of the disposition of the building on the site and of the individual parts to each other. They responded enthusiastically to the architects' suggestions regarding the relationship of the cells to the forest (Kahn: "the cell should express the dignity of the individual"), the strong connection between chapel and refectory, and the idea of the tower as a threshold and "special place" of entry. Kahn was off to a good start.

The clients were less enthusiastic, though, about the distance between school and cells, feeling that each rank of sisters should have its own schoolroom as a part of their living quarters, more strongly segregating the groups and making the woods a more active part of the convent. Although he immediately suggested how the schoolrooms

51 Kahn, "Not For the Faint Hearted," p. 124.

52 Meeting minutes, David Polk, July 22, 1966.

might be integrated into the cloisters, Kahn would fail to follow up on this, most certainly as it opposed his bi-polar, private-communal "Form" diagram. The proposed balconies for the cells were immediately rejected; brick was acceptable as a building material, but Polk noted that the sisters "hated" efflorescence. Regarding the refectory, the sisters maintained that "meals were now a social as well as a religious experience," and that many small tables would be more appropriate than the four great slabs drawn in the plan. Kahn protested, saying that the smaller tables would "make the place feel like a restaurant rather than a dining hall." Sensing, perhaps, that the sisters' sense of ritual might not live up to his own idealized images of convent life (there had already been requests for recreational facilities with swimming, badminton, basketball, and tennis, which would soon be followed by wishes for further modern comforts such as air conditioning and intercoms), Kahn expounded on "the presence of the chapel—the sense of ritual, not convenience, a feeling of exaltation." He must have harbored the greatest of expectations for the Dominican nuns: who, if not they, would be willing to trade comfort for architecture? In the coming months the sisters would not always live up to his romantic visions, though, and the cleft between his medievalist visions of monastic ritual and theirs of an active modern religious life would reopen regularly. On the particular subject of the refectory tables, Kahn stubbornly stood his ground, designing over the following months an entire spectrum of fixed tables and seating arrangements: T-formed, semi-circular, clover-leafed—seemingly anything but the despised "cafeteria style."

Agreeing on a follow-up meeting at the end of August, the architects left the sisters with a copy of the standard AIA contract and a fee schedule. Although Polk had already prepared a summary of the areas, Kahn hedged when asked by the sisters about the costs of his plan, stating that it would be more profitable to discuss costs after they had "brought the project closer to a true expression of their needs." Polk laconically concluded his notes, "The sisters do not seem overawed by the size of the project." Perhaps he was thinking what the sisters should have been: that a bit of awe would have been particularly appropriate in their case. The project on the table measured a proud 160,660 square feet (14,456 $m^2$), excluding basement.[53]

53 Calculations by architects on office blueprint, Folder 030.I.C.700.012. Dividing the $1,500,000 budget by Kahn's 160,000 square feet gives less than $9.50/square foot. Considering that Kahn's office would use prices from $25/sq. ft. for the cells to $50/sq. ft. for the chapel in their later estimates, the proposed scheme would have easily cost three to four times the sisters' budget! Source of prices: DMH Project files, Box LIK 10, Kahn Collection.

### The Second Scheme: August–September 1966

While the June meeting was largely affirmative, it did not take long for the first harbingers of difficulty to cloud the optimistic beginning. In September, Mother Emmanuel, likely developing a sense for the project's true dimensions, wrote Kahn to express her concerns and to remind him of the congregation's limited budget. High interest rates and inflation had added considerably to the burden of financing such a large project during the mid-sixties, and without a reliable cost estimate, she was uncertain of how to go forward.[54]

**Compacting the plan**

After receiving Mother Mary Emmanuel's letter, Kahn and Polk soon began to reconsider their design. Attempting to press the first plan's parti into a more compact package, the architects developed a second scheme over September. **Figs. 29–30** The monastery's position and orientation on the site remain the same, but now responds to the sisters' suggestion that the combined main and service entrance drive now lead in from Bishop Hollow Road. This lessens the sense of extended threshold when compared with the earlier approach through the orchard. Gone as well is the elegant separation of visitor and service access. On the other hand, the new monastery now has its own address, no longer accessed by driving past the manor house. On this point Kahn and the sisters were in agreement, and the new route of approach would remain for the duration of the design.

In response to the new approach, the entry tower—now octagonal in plan—shifts from the west side of the complex to the east. In an attempt to tighten up the plan, a narrower main gallery skewers through the tower, connecting the communal spaces and terminating in the school and the living quarters. The first version's generous system of cloisters has been compacted by pressing the building blocks tightly against each other; gone are the figure-ground obscuring "hollow columns" and "water gardens" of the earlier scheme. The direct relationship between chapel and refectory—favored by both architect and the sisters—remains. An intriguing moment in the plan is the chapel, where a square rotated within a square creates *poché* for ancillary spaces such as confessionals and sacristy as well as connecting neighboring rooms. Whereas in the previous version the governing geometry may be derived from both program and relationship to the topography, here an "irrational" geometry takes over in which both internal parti and external relationships are considerably less lucid than before.

**Order and inconsistency**

While this squeezing has wrung almost 35,000 square feet (3,252 m²) out of the plan (now measuring 131,600 square feet [12,226 m²] and

54 Letter, Mother Mary Emmanuel to Louis Kahn, September 7, 1966, Box LIK 10, Kahn Collection.

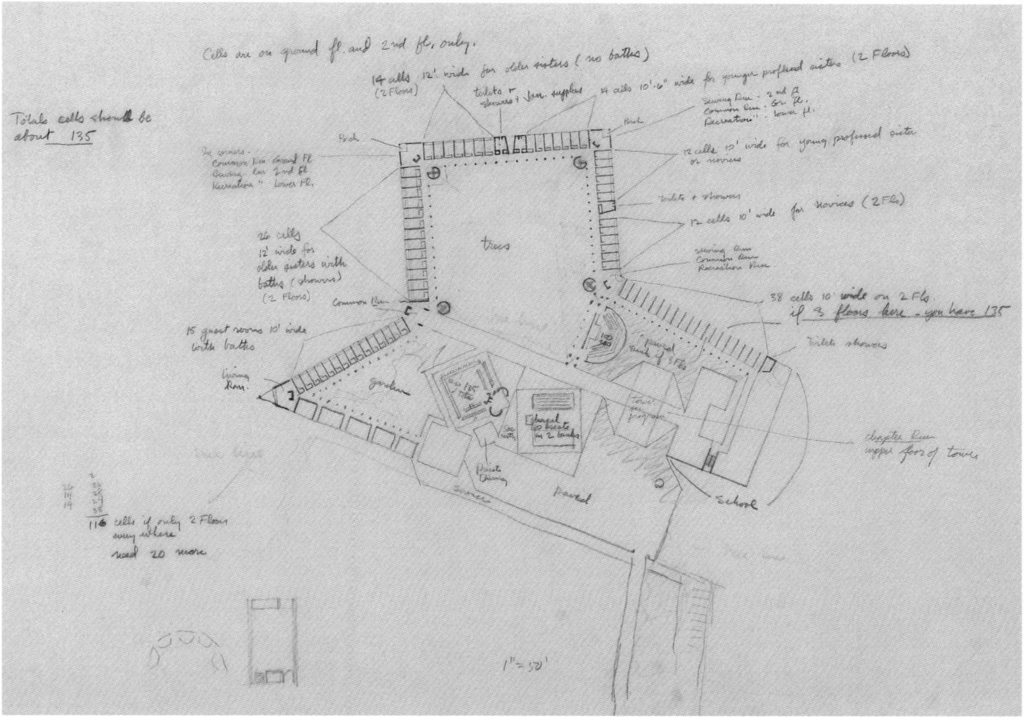


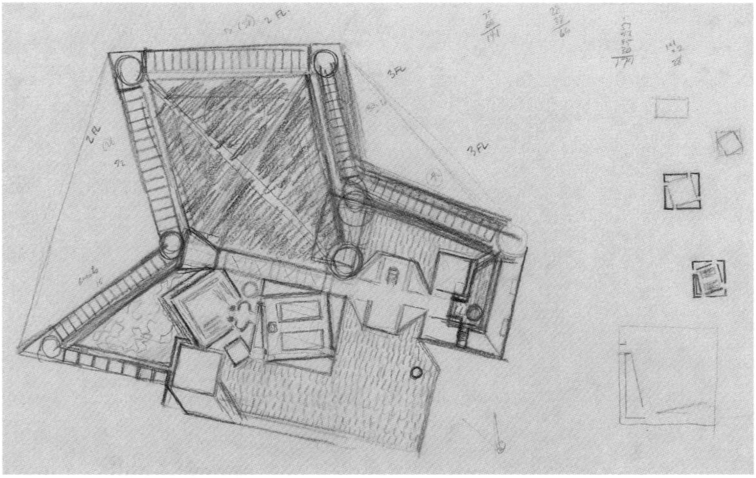

**29** Plan with notes, September 1966, Louis Kahn
**30** Plan, September 1966, Louis Kahn

estimated by the architects to cost $3,999,000[55]), it is difficult not to sense more probing than progress in this attempt. In reading the plan as a "Forum of Availabilities," it is apparent that, in contrast to the previous scheme, associations tend to be "direct rather than remote," unfolding along a mostly linear circulation system. Troubling, too, is how the ring of cells has been extended to include a guest wing, the schoolrooms, a kitchen, and secondary rooms. It is not only that the resulting figure is more than a little ambivalent—both in its response to context and for the spaces created inside—but that this extension considerably muddles the formal clarity of the parti. Whereas in the first scheme clarity and tension result from juxtaposing the small-scaled spatial order of the cells with the larger-scale common spaces, this has now been compromised by mixing large and small room types. Accordingly, the architects seem to be especially at a loss when it comes to integrating the school, finally leaving it unfinished in plan.

### The Third Scheme: October–December 1966

**The corner as connector**

Discontent with their efforts and advancing quickly from the second scheme—which would be neither polished nor presented to the congregation—Kahn and Polk continued to develop their plan. **Figs. 31–32** A new, third scheme is the first which calls into question the important, but expensive, main circulation gallery. Instead of being able to reach the individual communal rooms by circulating along that spine, the buildings themselves now begin to *become* the spine. This collision of bodies, the corners of which give way to create circulation within the plan, had been "discovered" previously by Kahn in Erdman Hall at Bryn Mawr College (1960–65) and the Fisher House (1961–67). Here, though, the collisions are handled with an easy casualness hitherto unknown in Kahn's larger projects.[56] A collaged plan, dated October 9, 1966, gives insight into a working technique that may have encouraged this freedom. **Fig. 31** The pre-established shapes and sizes of the various spaces have not—for the time being—been called into question, but rather the connections between them and how they are to be grouped. By cutting out the readymade rooms from a blueprint and repositioning them on paper, Kahn was able to shift, butt, and adjust the bodies in plan until—as if through the alternating pulls of attraction and repulsion—they had "found" their desired resting

55 Office blueprint with area calculations and cost estimate, Folder 030.I.C.700.007, Kahn Collection.

56 Kahn's first "informal," non-orthogonal planning in a large-scale project seems to date from 1951 in an unrealized sketch plan for the Mill Creek Housing project in which housing blocks stand at irregular angles to each other, producing oddly shaped courts (LIK Box 60, Kahn Collection). Eugene J. Johnson points out that this sketch was made by Kahn while at the American Academy in Rome directly upon return from a trip to Delphi, where he had experienced the non-orthogonal planning of the Greek sanctuary first hand. Lewis and Johnson, *Drawn From the Source*, p. 88.

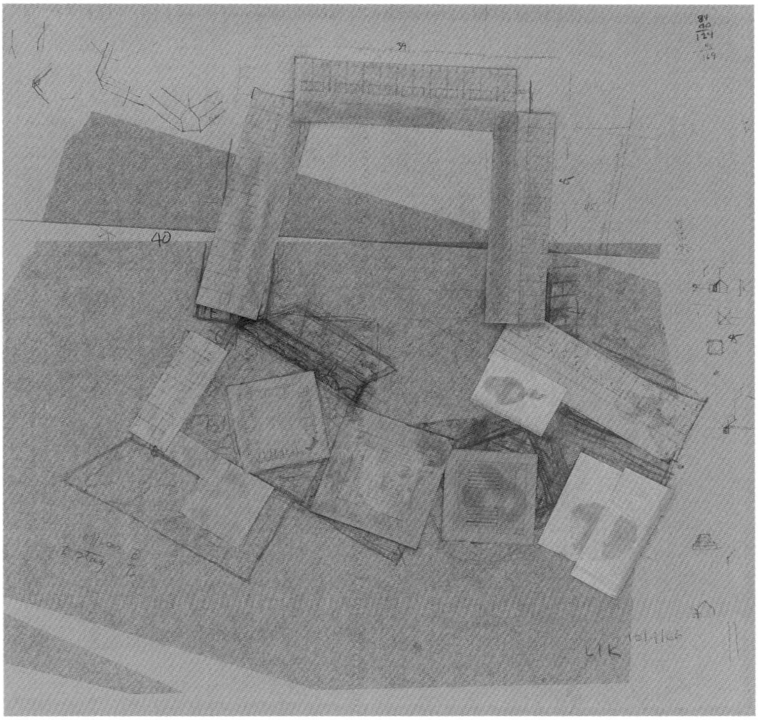

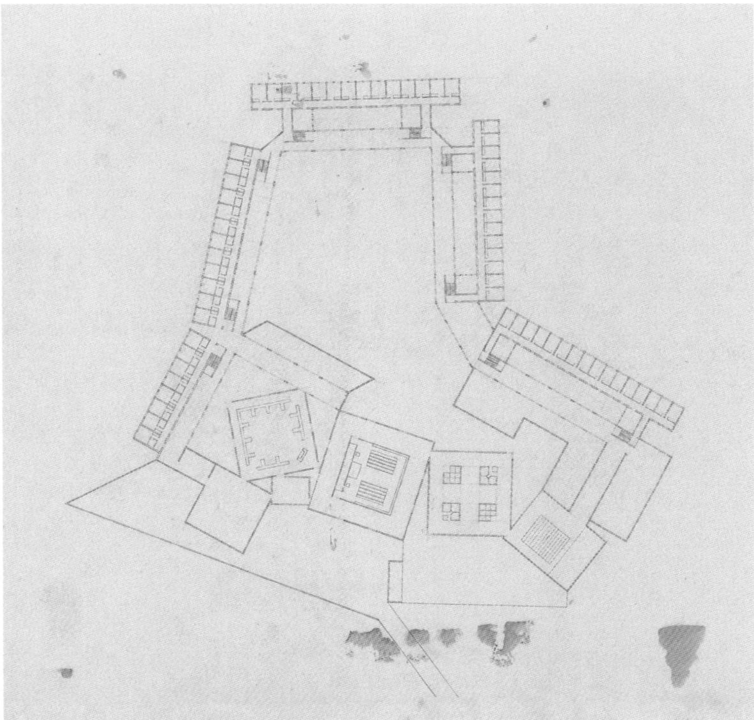

**31** Collaged plan,
October 9, 1966, Louis Kahn
**32** Plan: first floor,
October 1966

**33** Model, October 1966

places, where they could finally be pasted into place. This freehand collage method is, on the one hand, a means to expedite the generation of variations (even quicker than Kahn's favorite charcoal-on-yellow tracing paper), and, on the other hand, encourages these groupings to occur at those odd angles which would not necessarily be generated if drawing freehand or working with T-square and triangle.

**"Bricolage"**

It is difficult not to be drawn into speculation by Kahn's compelling collage, the only drawing of this sort to be found in the Kahn Collection.[57] What, one may ask—beyond the quickness of its method—motivated him to this new technique? And what was behind the quirky geometry that had slowly taken over the schemes? In search of influences it is tempting to look at Kahn's contemporary work with the sculptor Isamu Noguchi for the Levy Memorial Playground in New York (1961–66), in which Noguchi's earth forms and sculptural objects played against Kahn's architectural fragments in a collaged landscape, a collaboration which, according to Harriet Pattison, may have encouraged a sense of free play in his work.[58] A deeper current to consider might be his lasting fascination for that master *bricoleur* of the modern, Le Corbusier. Then there were the profession's recent rediscoveries of historical models which lay heavy in the air: John Soane's Bank of England, or the meetings of accident and planning at Delphi, the Athenian Acropolis, or the Villa Hadriana.[59] We also know from Vincent Scully that a reproduction of Piranesi's etching of the Campus Martius in Rome, with its tumbled collage of monuments, hung at this time on the wall above Kahn's desk in his Walnut Street office.[60]

Certainly, all these—and a myriad of other—images were present in Kahn's well-stocked visual treasury. Still, simple source hunting will not bring us very far with Kahn; the lessons of the past may have revealed essence and given guidance, but were not there to be mined as academic quarries. I suggest that the more fruitful way

57 While there are examples in which entire buildings have been cut out in order to compare sizes or to reposition within a site plan (Dhaka: see *The Louis I. Kahn Archive: Personal Drawings,* vol. 7.), this seems to be the only example of the collage technique used to design a *single* building by shifting and spacing the cut-out shapes of the individual rooms.

58 Interview, author with Harriet Pattison, Architectural Archives, University of Pennsylvania, October 21, 2004.

59 The extent of Kahn's knowledge of Hadrian's Villa and of its use as a model for his own work is open to speculation. According to his associate Thomas Vreeland, Kahn had often mused on the Villa as a "place of the immeasurable," and Vreeland had in 1960 actually directly traced a portion of it as a plan generator for the troublesome Salk Meeting House design, apparently receiving enthusiastic approval from Kahn, who did not immediately recognize the fragment (see Friedman, "Salk Institute for Biological Studies," p. 335). In an interview with Vincent Scully, though, Kahn denied any direct quotations in his work (see Wurman, *What Will Be Has Always Been,* p. 117). Whatever his knowledge, the Villa Hadriana and other historical models were certainly "in the air" around Kahn. Perhaps not incidentally, Charles Moore, Kahn's teaching assistant at Princeton in the late fifties, was one of the first among late-twentieth-century American architects to reappraise Hadrian's Villa in written form (see Moore, "Hadrian's Villa," pp. 16–27).

60 Scully, *Louis I. Kahn,* p. 37.

to continue our questioning is on a project-immanent rather than precedent-based level.

**Space as "Spacing"**

An earlier quotation may give insight into Kahn's thinking here. Speaking of the DeVore House (1954–55), he remarked, "In searching for the nature of the spaces of a house, might they not be separated by a distance from each other theoretically before they are brought together? A predetermined total form might inhibit what the spaces want to be." [61] In this method there can be no preconceived shape, as the planning consists of first establishing the individual spaces required by the institution; the rooms are then assembled as to make apparent the nature and strength of their relationships. By establishing their relative powers of attraction or repulsion, they make visible their roles and thus show what the institution really "wants to be." [62] Or, to again listen to Kahn: "The rooms talk with each other and they make up their minds where their positions are. And they must aspire, each room, to be as all-comprising, as all-rapport, with its nature.... If you name a room before it becomes a room, it dies; because it becomes just another item." [63]

**Irregular geometries**

While all this may explain Kahn's conception of a plan as a series of discrete "locales" and their respective "spacings," it does nothing to explain this particular plan's irregular geometry. Historical or contemporary influence aside, one may ask if there is a project-immanent logic that exempts this plan from Kahn's "Euclidian imperative," that regular and quite rigorous geometric order which had informed his larger projects until then. One possible explanation: Kahn had discovered with Erdman Hall that the square's corner—and thus a new sort of diagonal planning—was the key to "letting the rooms find their own connections." [64] One impetus for the irregular, as opposed to regular, diagonal collisions in the new monastery plan may lie in the program's varied "grain," in the varied sizes of its individual rooms—from small to large (with the exception of the cells) with little repetition. In contrast to, for example, Erdman Hall or the Indian Institute of Management, the program for the Dominican Motherhouse does not allow for a "meaningful" serialism generated by repeatable, regularly sized elements. Polk seems to have already established this fact in his early exploratory sketches. **Fig. 20** An irregular geometry was one way of dealing with this, allowing for multiple collisions to occur between the different pieces without drawing them into an ill-fitting

61 Kahn, quoted in Ronner and Jhaveri, *Louis I. Kahn: Complete Work,* p. 70.

62 See Devillers, "The Indian Institute of Management," p. 60.

63 Kahn, quoted in Wurman, *What Will Be Has Always Been,* p. 232.

64 Ibid.

geometrical corset: the Achilles heel of many of Kahn's mid-fifties and early-sixties plans.

Independence and inflection

The irregular geometry additionally underscores the *independence* of each fragment—moving away from serialism toward an individual character of parts. If until now Kahn had employed such ordering devices as symmetry, serialism, or organic growth metaphors to unify the elements of his plans, he begins to consistently employ here for the first time what Robert Venturi called, in his contemporary *Complexity and Contradiction in Architecture,* the principle of "independence and inflection," in which discrete parts gesture beyond themselves to a "difficult" whole:

"Gestalt psychology also shows that the nature of the parts, as well as their number and position, influences a perceptual whole and it has also made a further distinction: the degree of wholeness can vary. Parts can be more or less whole in themselves, or, to put it in another way, in a greater or lesser degree they can be fragments of a greater whole. Properties of the part can be more or less articulated; properties of the whole can be more or less accented. In the complex compositions, a special obligation toward the whole encourages the fragmentary part or, as Trystan Edwards calls it, the term, 'inflection.'

"Inflection in architecture is the way in which the whole is implied by exploiting the nature of the individual parts, rather than their position or number. By inflecting toward something outside of themselves, the parts contain their own linkage: inflected parts are more integral with the whole than are *un*-inflected parts. Inflection is a means of distinguishing diverse parts while implying continuity. It involves the art of the fragment. The valid fragment is economical because it implies richness and meaning beyond itself. Inflection can also be used to achieve suspense, an element possible in large sequential complexes. The inflected element can be called a partial-functioning element in contrast to the double-functioning element. In terms of perception it is dependent on something outside itself, and in whose direction it inflects. It is a directional form corresponding to directional space."[65]

The concept of inflection is applicable not only at the formal level, but is programmatically inherent in Kahn's ideal that in a "society of rooms" "the rooms relate to each other to strengthen their own unique nature."[66] What is captivating in this plan is how squares—static

65 Venturi, *Complexity and Contradiction in Architecture,* pp. 88–89. It is instructive to note that while in his book Venturi demonstrates the principle of inflection with the *façade,* with Kahn that principle tends to be most active in *plan.*

66 Kahn, "The Room, the Street and Human Agreement," p. 264.

and "closed" geometrical forms—have been engaged as open, "partial-functioning" elements.

Kahn's original bipolar "Form"—though weaker than in the first scheme—is fundamentally intact: the equipoise between the realm of the sisters' cells and that of the public and communal rooms still remains. The number of pieces in the composition remains likewise largely the same. The four bars of cells still dig into the mild slope of the hill, connected by a new version of the cloisters and sunken courts with doubled corridors and generous (and costly) arcades. A fifth bar of guest cells has been added, forming a small court together with the refectory and service rooms. At the request of the sisters, a small guest dining room has been added to the program. The compact bundle of communal rooms wedges upward into the cloister, prying apart its arch in an effort to densify the plan while maintaining the desired legibility of the convent's two realms. This third variation shares the formal inconsistencies of its predecessor, as schoolrooms, kitchen, and service rooms merge in formal dissonance with the outer ring. As in the previous scheme, school and auditorium are the most noncommittal moments in the drawings.

**The elevations**

Kahn now blocks out elevations in iconically childlike drawings, abandoning the cubic, Ahmedabad-inspired forms of the first scheme for a more figurative language. Figs. 34–37 The roofs—thin, folded plates in the form of multiple gables—repeat "house" over and over again, or evoke some kind of elementary gothic architecture. Large, circular cutouts still perforate the walls, now inviting us to see in them colossal rose windows. Each "house" is formally related to yet distinct from its neighbors. The entry tower is perhaps the most striking—tapering as it rises from its broad base to reach the same height as the chapel—at once squat and vertical, as much ziggurat as tower. In a whimsical visual pun, its silhouette echoes the bells drawn in its belfry. The section through the monastery Fig. 38 intimates how the thin doubled walls, folded and perforated to the point of fragility, make a light-and-shadow box of the chapel, and how the chapel and the wings of the cells embrace the top of the hillock.

**The presentation of the third scheme**

On October 10, 1966—six months after beginning the project—Kahn and Polk presented the drawings of the third version along with a plastiline and cardboard model in Media.[67] Fig. 33 As part of their presentation, they included a site plan of the first scheme overlaid with a paper cutout of the current scheme to demonstrate the considerable reduction in area.[68] In Polk's meeting notes we can read

67 Meeting notes, David Polk, October 10, 1966, Box LIK 10, Kahn Collection.

68 Collage plan in archive of the Dominican Motherhouse, Elkins Park, PA.

that the sisters approved of the architects' means of reduction, including the elimination of the main gallery: "The Sisters liked the easy but strong relationship between the major elements themselves and between those elements and the cells."[69] Kahn was now able to convince the commission that it was indeed best to keep the classrooms separated from the cells, preserving the two-part parti. While the architects apparently had little difficulty gaining approval for their specific design decisions, the sisters again aired concern over the cost of the project. (Astonishingly, the architects had still not outed themselves on this ticklish theme.) Even without an architect's estimate, by now it was clear to the sisters that the project on the table was most certainly beyond their means. Taking matters into their own hands, they suggested that the monastery might be realized in stages. A first stage of building might include: cells for a total of seventy-four postulants and novices, visiting parlors, common rooms, a kitchen, and the refectory. Kahn, obviously not keen at the prospect of having to realize the project piecemeal but certainly aware of the discrepancy between the size of his design and that of the congregation's budget, spoke "of the need for that which is built to invite construction of the whole. The beauty of the whole must be in the part. Thus the inclusion of the tower and possibly the auditorium, which might also be used temporarily as the Chapel, in the first stage of development should be considered."[70] In what amounts to his first admission that his design was not immediately buildable for the sisters' budget, Kahn suggested the possibility of indicating future construction in the form of gardens, a sort of topiary plan which could be filled in with the real buildings as the necessary funds became available.

**Inseparable parts**

But—crutch of a topiary plan aside—just how *does* one design an artifact so that the "the beauty of the [unfinished] whole be in the part"? At this point we—and Kahn—are faced with a fundamental question of method. If architectural design is manifestly a "top-down" operation of conceiving of "wholes," then to what degree can this wholeness be achieved through the apparently "bottom-up" procedure of accumulating parts? In spite of statements that might lead us to think otherwise—such as earlier proclamations about "growing" a plan—the evidence of his oeuvre shows that in the end Kahn never surrendered his allegiance to the whole.[71] And in the case of the Motherhouse, his reservations were not only of a formal order;

69 Meeting minutes, David Polk, October 10, 1966.

70 Lewis, "Dominican Motherhouse," p. 387.

71 In a letter to Kahn after an office visit, the young Colin Rowe stated, "You deplored composition because it appeared to be no more than a manipulation of forms for the sake of effect. You wanted to grow a building." Letter, Colin Rowe to Louis Kahn, February 7, 1956, Box LIK 65, Kahn Collection.

**34** Chapel, tower, school, October 1966, Louis Kahn
**35** Tower, chapel, refectory, October 1966, Louis Kahn
**36–37** North elevation, October 1966, Louis Kahn
**38** Section looking east, October 1966, Louis Kahn
**39** Section: cell and cloister, October 1966

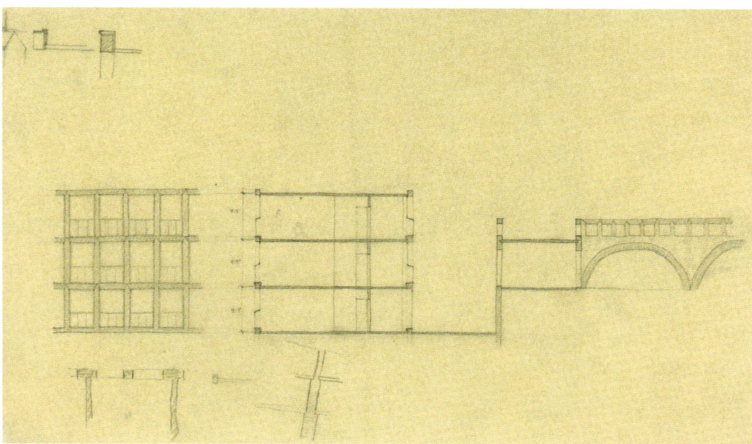

for him the institution envisioned gained its full meaning only with the presence and interplay of all its constituent parts. He obviously feared that, like the only partially realized designs for the Salk Institute or the Fort Wayne Fine Arts Center, an unfinished monastery would remain forever a fragment of the intended social vision: "Form is that which deals with inseparable parts. If you take one thing away, you can't have the whole thing. Nothing is ever fully answerable to that which man wants to accept as a part of his way of life unless all its parts are together."[72] Perhaps in an effort to convince the sisters of this necessity (perhaps, in a worst-case scenario, to at least end up with an attractive presentation for future publication), Kahn requested that the sisters invest in a "fine wood model" of the complete scheme.

This tension between "top-down" and "bottom-up" methods of design—manifest throughout the modern as the tension between "rationalist" and "functionalist" morphologies and explicitly installed as the twin poles of the creative act by Kahn in his "Form-Design" dichotomy—is neither a question of budget, nor is it peculiar to the Dominican Motherhouse, rather it is a principle source of the characteristic charge in all of Kahn's mature work.[73]

At this uncomfortable impasse the meeting ended, with the next meeting scheduled for October 25th. In addition to clarifying the question of the project's costs, it was agreed that by then Kahn and Polk would prepare studies of the individual cells at a larger scale. **Figs. 40–43**

**Money trouble**

Within a few weeks, in a letter dated November 18, 1966, the sisters received the long-awaited cost estimate together with a fee proposal from Kahn.[74] The third scheme, now measuring 147,061 square feet (13,662 m$^2$), was estimated—using a differentiated price-per-square-foot basis—to cost approximately $3,500,000. Kahn now tellingly spoke of the whole no longer as a "building" but as a "master plan," indicating the possibility—which for the sisters would have been a necessity—of realizing the monastery in stages. Whether in parts or as a whole, this sum was worlds away from the $1,500,000 the congregation had imagined they would spend for their new home. Mother Emmanuel answered Kahn with a letter dated December 16, letting him know in

72 Kahn at Yale (undated) speaking about the Fort Wayne Fine Arts Center, in Wurman, *What Will Be Has Always Been,* p. 13. Two (for Kahn unforeseeable) events have demonstrated "after the fact" the tension between the configuration as a "whole" and as a "conglomeration of parts" in Kahn's work. The failed attempts to convincingly extend the Kimbell Art Museum (1986, Mitchell Giurgola, arch.), and the Salk Institute (Anshen and Allen, 1995), have intimated that the apparently "unfinished" orders of those buildings were, in fact, only apparently so.

73 Adolf Behne was the first to draw attention to this split in modern architecture. In *Der moderne Zweckbau* (*The Modern Functional Building*) of 1926, he coined the term "functionalist" to describe a unique, tailor-made architecture based on well-defined functions, while the term "rationalist" was used to refer to the development of repeatable, type-based solutions. For more on this tension within Kahn's work, see Bottero, "Organic and Rational Morphology in the Work of Louis Kahn."

74 Letter with enclosed cost estimate, Kahn to Mother Mary Emmanuel, November 18, 1966, Box LIK 10, Kahn Collection.

friendly but no uncertain terms that the design was both in terms of means and cost far beyond the pale.[75] In an effort to guarantee that her architect stay within the bounds of their modest resources, she followed up her letter on December 27, 1966, with a typed, reduced program and now named a budget (written in boldface across the top of the first sheet) of $1,000,000.[76]

*My dear Mr. Kahn,*

*Since our last meeting in Media our little group has discussed frequently our building program and the suggestions that you have made. Much as we admire the plan we are agreed that it is not practical for several reasons.*

*1.) Our funds are limited (though our desires are not) and we do not have the money that the series of buildings would require. Perhaps we asked for more than we could afford or may need in the immediate future. At any rate we do not wish to be involved in such an extended program.*

*2.) Even if the necessary money were available, we would hesitate long before committing ourselves to spend so much in wide, exterior covered, cloister walks with high brick walls and numerous arches. This seems utterly inconsistent with a life dedicated to voluntary poverty.*

*3.) What made us actually reconsider the plan was the realization that the cost of the refectory alone would be in the neighborhood of $270,000.*

*4.) The Dominican Order is an apostolic order. Its spirit is one of action flowing from contemplation. The plan as you have developed it is geared more to a Trappist or Carmelite spirituality, where contemplation and solitude are their own end.*

*Could a single building be planned that would include all our basic necessities that would cost in the neighborhood of one million dollars? We need housing for about 50 Sisters now. Can we provide for them and permit future expansion to remain possible?*

*We deeply appreciate all the time and ability you have given to our problem, Mr. Kahn. If we have permitted ourselves to be carried away by your plans it is because they appeal to us very much. But be sure now that such expensive building does not suit our needs nor our funds.*

*I realize that my message must be a disappointment to you as it is to me. However, I would appreciate hearing from you about further possibilities.*

*Respectfully yours,*
*Mother Mary Emmanuel O.P.*

75 Letter, Mother Mary Emmanuel to Kahn, December 16, 1966, Box LIK 10, Kahn Collection.

76 Letter with program, Sister Mary Emmanuel to Kahn, December 27, 1966, Box LIK 10, Kahn Collection.

**40** Cell: plan, October 1966, Louis Kahn
**41** Cell: interior, October 1966, Louis Kahn
**42** Cell (professed): plan, October 1966, Louis Kahn
**43** Cell (young professed): plan, October 1966, Louis Kahn

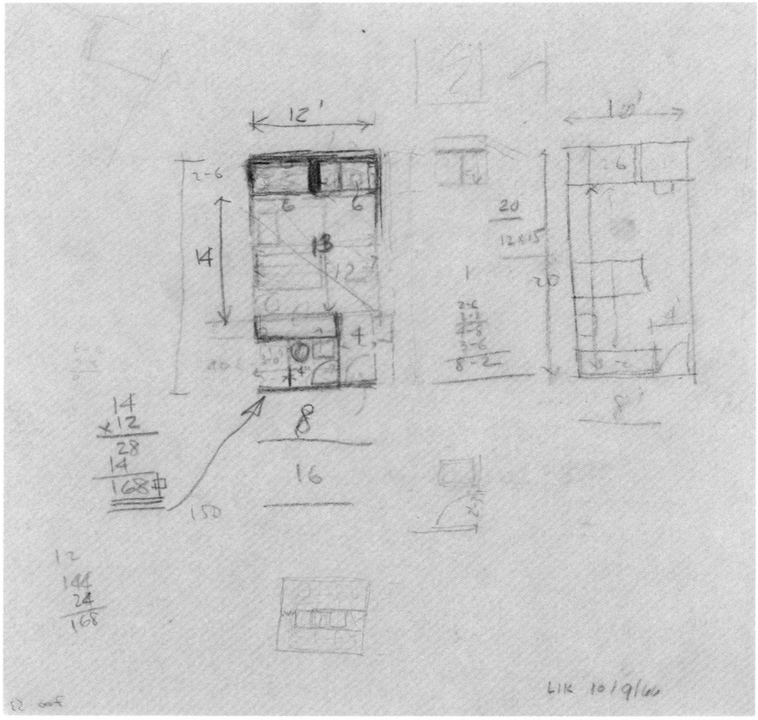


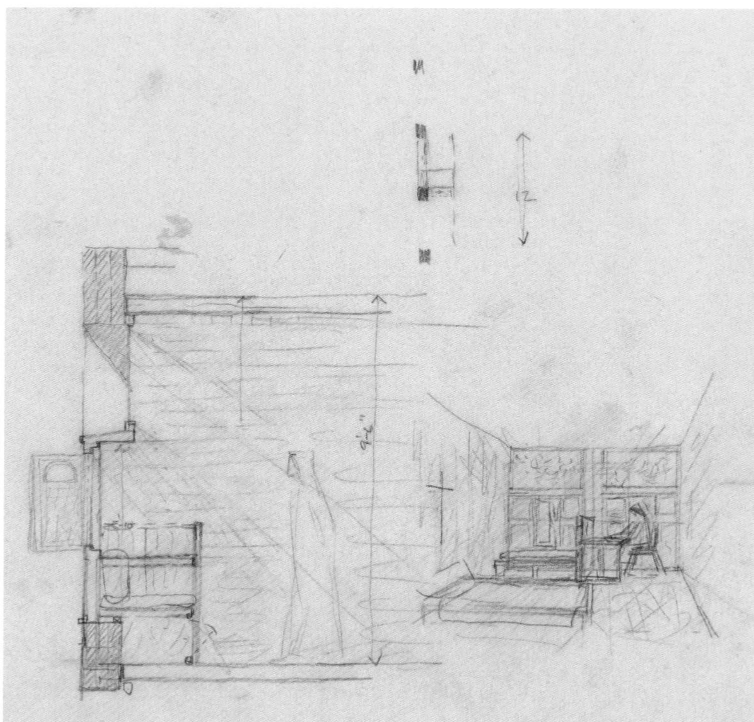

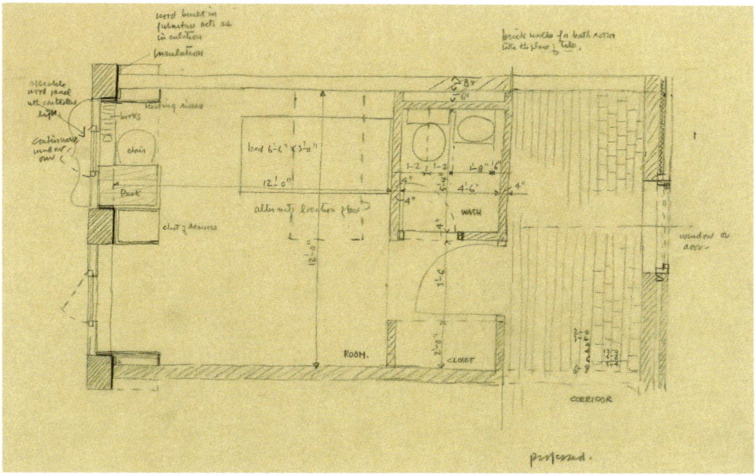
Insulation
heating risers
chair
Book
bed 6'-6" x 3'-0"
12'-0"
WASH
4'-6"
ROOM.
CLOSET
CORRIDOR
window or door
professed.

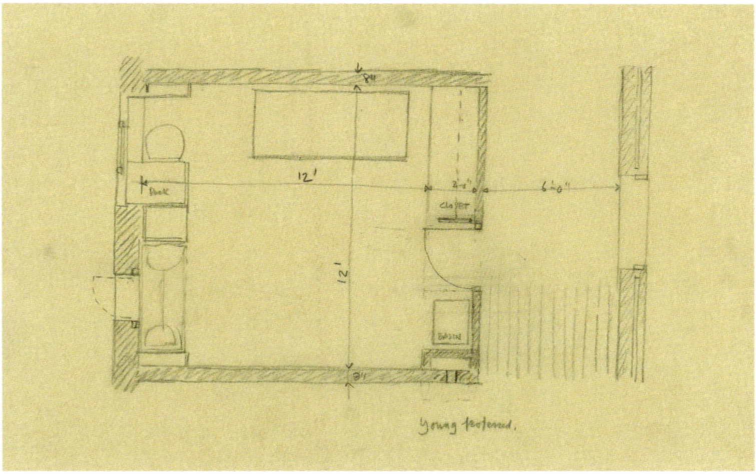
12'
Book
6'-0"
CLOSET
BASIN
Young professed.

A bubble bursts

If Kahn had beguiled the sisters into joining his "Trappist dream" over the previous months, planning an ideal monastery within a financial vacuum, this dreaming would suffer a cold awakening with Mother Emmanuel's letter. In retrospect, one might question Kahn's wisdom (and professionalism) in dealing with his clients: he knew months earlier of the project's costs, yet failed to reveal them to the sisters, in spite of their regular queries. Was he confident that that they could secure funds for their project after realizing what was possible? (This had been the case with other projects, and didn't the church have its share of sponsors and secret coffers?) Was he as yet incapable or unwilling to let the modest budget steer his thoughts on "Monastery"? Did he need to develop an ideal version of his "Form" diagram before distilling it into its more affordable essence? Just how much bluffing, how much necessity, and how much wishful thinking were at play here is impossible to ascertain from our distance. Kahn had often attempted to explain what he considered to be the difference between "economy" and "financing," and an excerpt from his address at the 1959 CIAM Congress in Otterlo might give insight into his thinking on budgets and institutions: "A school or a specific design is what the institution expects of us. But School, the spirit school, the essence of the existence will, is what the architect should convey in his design. And I say he must, even if the design does not conform to the budget."[77] But this kind of lectured idealism does have its limits for an architect passionate about building, and one thing must have by now been abundantly clear: although the sisters had been the most patient of clients, there was now a real danger of either losing the project entirely or of only realizing a fragment of the desired scheme if he did not soon bring costs within their means. Mother Emmanuel, too, had by now understood the difficulty of designing so much monastery for so little money. In her revised program of December 27, she now sacrificed forty-five cells—reducing the required to seventy-five—in addition to making various other reductions in order to cut costs.[78]

## Sketching: January–February 1967

Sketching towards a new form

Mother Emmanuel's critique of the third version, together with her reduced program and budget of December 27, would now push the project in a new direction. Acting directly on the communiqués from December, Kahn and Polk would, by February 1967, dramatically distill and densify the project. A series of sketches from these weeks are compelling evidence of the architects' struggle to compact the

77 Kahn, "Talk at the Conclusion of the Otterlo Congress," p. 42.

78 Typed modified program from DMH congregation, December 1966, Box LIK 10, Kahn Collection.

plan. Although undated, it is possible to assume an "operational" chronological order for the sketches based on the context of the design thus far.[79]

In what we may assume to be the first of these sketches **Fig. 44**, the third scheme has been streamlined and reinterpreted as a regular pentagon, with two of its sides given to communal spaces and three to cells. Kahn must have realized immediately, though, that the long periphery of the building meant no significant savings in terms of area; in addition, the strongly linear circulation could have hardly appealed to him. (See "remote vs. direct association" in scheme two.) Elaborations of this scheme (by Polk?) **Fig. 45** are no more convincing, the strong geometric figure anathema to both the particulars of topography and to the architects' previous attempts at organizing a loosely informal "society of rooms." In second and third variations **Figs. 46–47**, cells and communal spaces flatten to press up against each other on either side of a narrow, crescent-shaped court in attempts to minimize the circulation space. While the individual parts remain largely the same, any sense of a balanced Gestalt is lost while the relationship between the topography and the plan becomes increasingly uncertain. It is more than a little tempting to read in the hasty charcoal strokes of these sketches Kahn's impatience with his own efforts. Additionally, in his push towards compactness he seems to be indulging in some wishful thinking: it is not really clear how he expected to fit all of the required cells into these versions, even if they were to be a full three stories tall. (Figure 47 has, for example, been notated with "60 cells on 3 levels.")

Drawings have a life of their own and an observer may find it difficult to judge to what degree the drawing tool has been led and to what degree it has done the leading. With the series of sketches at hand we seem to have reached one of those passages where charcoal strokes play quickly back upon themselves to generate further and still

79 It is at this point of the narrative that reconstructing the path becomes most difficult. Whereas virtually all other steps may be chronologically verified either by dated plans, project files, and/or by the context of other drawings, in terms of both attribution and chronology, these undated and unsigned sketches represent the most speculative passage. A note on attribution: although none of these sketches have been filed among those eighty-five project drawings which have been "definitively" identified as Kahn's, the "handwriting" of most of them does seem to indicate that they belong to him. We have, then, either a case of Kahn's drawings having been filed in the office drawing portfolios, or of Polk sketching in a Kahnian manner, leaving us to find contentment with a picture of both Kahn and Polk pushing the project forward together. And a note on the drawings' chronology: while Ronner and Jhaveri have placed figures 44 and 46 as intermediate steps between the schemes of June and September 1966, I propose that at least three facts speak for the chronology presented here: first, the unity of handwriting and medium in all the sketches in question; second, that the proposed chronology best matches the architects' and sisters' goal of compacting the project (figures 44 and 46 indicate considerably fewer cells—a maximum of sixty: see Kahn's note on figure 47, "60 cells on 3 floors"—than the schemes of September and October, indicating that they were almost certainly drawn after Mother Emmanuel's reduced program with seventy-four cells from December 27, 1967); and finally, the fact that the proposed chronology describes a plausible development within the scope of the project. Because the tendencies illustrated by the sketches are long-term, I propose that the general argument presented here in form of a narrative remains feasible even with allowance for certain deviations from the presented chronology.

**44** Plan, January/February 1967, Louis Kahn (attributed)
**45** Plan, January/February 1967, David Polk (attributed)
**46** Plan, January/February 1967, Louis Kahn (attributed)
**47–49** Plans, January/February 1967, Louis Kahn

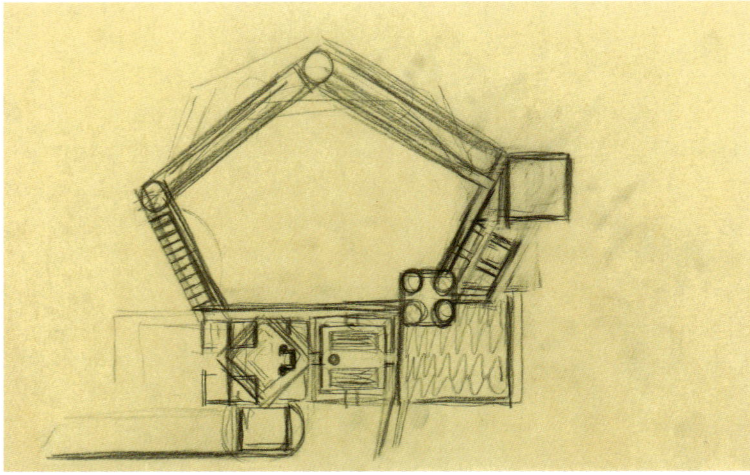

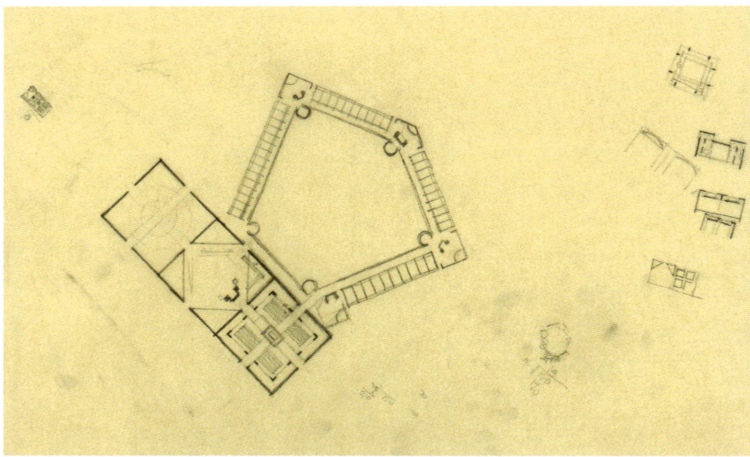

**50** Plan, January/February 1967, Louis Kahn
**51** Plan with site, January/February 1967, Louis Kahn
**52** Plan with site, February 1967

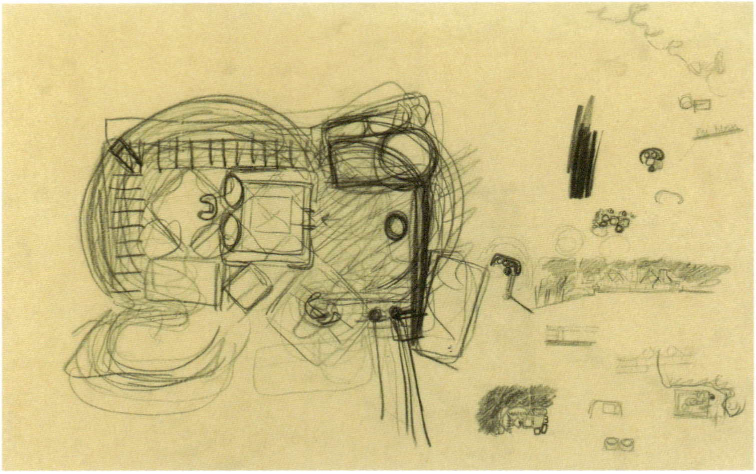

further drawings. As a result of this repetitive, self-forgotten shifting and probing, something unexpected falls into place. In a new variation Fig. 48, the communal rooms are no longer held in equipoise to the cells across a court, but have been neatly assembled—like pralines in a box—within the rectangular space formed by those cells. The entry tower—until now a constant—has been abandoned in favor of an entry court. While the reward for this change of tack is a promising new take on a vexing problem, the diagram is still mute in regard to its (undrawn) context. Apparently sensing potential in this variation, Kahn now proceeds to adapt it to the specifics of the site in successive attempts. Figs. 49–50 The figure is pressed tightly together, rotated ninety degrees counterclockwise (the square chapel allowing for rotation in any direction while maintaining liturgically correct orientation) and fitted into a forest clearing across from some sort of place of arrival. Several tiny diagrams on these sheets show Kahn's concern for fitting the plan both to the topography and to a space "excavated" from the arboreal mass. In further developments, Kahn continues to explore the interaction between figure, site, and program. Finally, the regularly shaped pocket in the forest is now almost equally filled with the monastery to the west and a clearing to the east. The threshold/tower has now returned to the composition, straddling the border between these two realms. Fig. 51

### The Fourth Scheme, First Version: The Plan of February 16, 1967

Out of the previous weeks' struggle, a drawing dated February 16, 1967, emerges as a significant breakthrough. Fig. 52 The emphatically dualist interpretation of the program, with its two distinct realms held in equipoise across an open center—a constant of all previous schemes—has now been called into question after nine months of work. The cells, until now articulated according to the sisters' four-tiered hierarchy, now form a three-sided, open rectangular frame which is staked out at its four corners by the living rooms. Into the open arms of this regular frame the plan now implodes, the communal rooms being drawn as if by force into what had previously been the open cloister. What is remarkable is how the contrast between the simple shapes and their seemingly spontaneous collisions within the orthogonal frame gives the plan a hitherto unknown internal tension, as if the several buildings of the previous plans were striving—without quite succeeding—to become the "single building" Mother Emmanuel had envisioned. The elaborate system of arcades and galleries which had been so unmistakably criticized in Mother Emmanuel's letter has now all but disappeared, the building blocks straining, as Kahn would describe, "to find their own connections."

**Inversions: Form and landscape, rotation and closure**

If the first three schemes represent a progressive series of variations based on a group of constant premises, the new scheme may in many respects be seen as a series of inversions of those premises. Changed, for example, is the relationship of the plan's figure to the forest and to the site's topography. Whereas the earlier schemes had used the edge between woods and meadow as a line of demarcation between the monastery's private and communal realms, the new configuration forms concentric rings moving out from the center of the clearing to the forest's edge. The orientation of the ensemble has changed as well: by rotating the whole ninety degrees counterclockwise, a wing of cells now closes the figure to the north, strengthening the impression of a man-made clearing in the forest. (The previously unchallenged parameter of direct sunlight for all cells was sacrificed in order to achieve this.) Instead of first experiencing the monastery in its frontality, one now approaches the tower obliquely, slipping in along the edge of the clearing in order to find oneself at its center.[80] A crescent-shaped pond brackets the clearing to the north. Where the previous schemes had held the top of the hillock open, nestling the cells into the brow of the hill with a series of (expensive) retaining walls and sunken gardens, the new scheme exaggerates the existing topography, building up from ground level and placing the tallest buildings—the tower and the chapel—on the crest of the hill. Geometrically as well, the new scheme is an inversion of the first scheme, in which the freely floating cells were juxtaposed to the orthogonal communal spaces; now it is the cells that form the orthogonal counterpart to the informally ordered communal spaces.

On March 2, 1967, shortly after submittal of the new plan, David Polk sent Mother Emmanuel a summary of areas together with an estimate of construction costs.[81] The complex had been dramatically reduced to 50,171 square feet (4,660 m$^2$) including basement and mechanical spaces, and was now estimated to cost $1,593,000, with landscaping. In his accompanying letter Polk assured the prioress that the project could be built for $1,500,000. Relieved that the architects had so dramatically reduced area and cost—cutting both by well over half—the sisters reinstalled the original budget of $1,500,000. The architects could breath deeply again: their project could continue.[82]

**A modified "Form," a new equilibrium**

The step to the fourth and final scheme was undoubtedly the most radical in the process to date, transforming the very hypothesis of the original "Form" diagram. At its presentation on February 16, 1967, the

80 For a discussion of movement and diagonal planning in Kahn's work, see Brownlee, "Turning a Corner With Louis I. Kahn," pp. 48–58.

81 Letter with cost estimate, David Polk to Mother Mary Emmanuel, March 2, 1967, Box LIK 10, Kahn Collection.

82 Interview with David Polk, October 20, 2004.

sisters praised the architects, not only for meeting their budget, but, tellingly, for finding a scheme more appropriate to their institution.[83] By superimposing public and private realms, by eliminating halls and galleries and forcing spaces to meet in severely unmediated fashion, the new plan suggests a substantially different environment than the previous schemes, one in which the monastery's various activities—contemplation, worship, learning, assembly, even cooking—are given nearly equal significance and bound together in a vision of community in which the distinction between private and communal lives has begun to erode. Reading Polk's meeting minutes, it is surprising to sense the confidence with which the sisters accepted this unorthodox plan. Was their trust in Kahn that great? Did they really understand the drawing on the table? There is another interpretation: perhaps they understood the plan's boldly unmediated quality to be in the spirit of the Dominican rule of voluntary poverty, in harmony with a vision of community which was, in spite of its internal hierarchies, fundamentally egalitarian. Whatever the case, the sisters must be credited for their insight and courage in approving such an unconventional—and as of yet schematic and unresolved—plan.

In retrospect, they may have sensed in the germinating plan an attempt to make spatially manifest the equilibrium called for by their order's ideal of spiritual life:

"That which characterizes the Dominican Brother [Sister] is the concord, the harmonious synthesis, of virtues, apparently the most contrary: gentleness with energy, love of study with love of action, genius for contemplation with the spirit of organization.... The Order's spirituality is complex and made up of many elements, but they are unified in a single goal that is sublime. All its constituents lead to a contemplation which seeks to fructify in the apostolate.... The spiritual life of the Friars [Sisters] is delicately balanced and, for those who are less than saints, hard to live. If thrown off center its constituents destroy themselves—the priestly element becomes 'parochial,' mired in local interests; the monastic element becomes 'monkish,' considering the apostolate a distraction; the doctrinal element becomes 'bookish,' having little to do with the salvation of souls; the apostolic element becomes 'activistic,' spending itself in feverish activity.... An apostolic message that has not been shaped in the sanctuary, the choir, and the cloister is never complete."[84]

83 Meeting minutes from February 13, 1967, Box LIK 10, Kahn Collection.

84 Hinnebusch, *Dominican Spirituality*, p. 123.

More than the previous versions, this new scheme—with its multiple juxtapositions and diminished hierarchies—may be read as an attempt to make palpable the delicate balances and desired synergies between the individual constituents of Dominican life. As if to underscore this, Kahn added to the sisters' comments that the architects' challenge was now the development of the individual spaces and their connections so that they were to become "truly equal in terms of their quality."[85]

**A methodic search, "re-search"**

That Kahn would spend several months working through the consequences of his first "Form" diagram before modifying his stance may seem extreme, yet is emblematic for his manner of developing an idea. Seen within the scale of his entire career or that of a single project, Kahn's moving forward was a methodical and purposeful searching, a building upon that which came before, rather than an introduction of a plethora of new impulses or themes. In this economy of ideas, a hypothesis or theme—once introduced—will be explored in all of its consequences before it is abandoned or modified. What appears to the outsider as stubbornness or a paucity of ideas may instead be seen as the hidden strength of the work, for it is precisely this quality of sustained attention to a limited number of themes, of holding an idea firmly while working upon it, which lends the activity of designing a character approaching that of "re-search" in the original meaning of the word.

**A deeper understanding**

While much theory and criticism emphasizes the volitional power of the architect and downplays the role of contingencies, it is instructive to note that this is not the only occasion that budget had obliged Kahn to modify a hypothesis or to distill a more succinct essence. In spite of what he had to say about his disregard for budgets, the Exeter Library, the Kimbell Art Museum, and the Yale Center for British Art are all happy cases in which less (money) equals more (elegance of final concept). This said, Kahn *had* indeed been in dialogue with the sisters for several months, months that had served to deepen his understanding of their life and order. It is reasonably safe to assume that of comparable significance to budget in the genesis of the new scheme was an increasingly complex view of monastic life, one gradually eclipsing those stereotypes at the outset of the project.

85 Meeting minutes from February 13, 1967, Box LIK 10, Kahn Collection. In a remarkable parallel to Hinnebusch's text on Dominican life (and Kahn's design) is a discussion in Kahn's Master's Studio at the University of Pennsylvania from 1961, in which the problem of a monastery had been assigned: "An Indian woman gave the first remark of significance./She said, 'I believe that this place should be so that/everything stems from the cell./From the cell would come the right for the chapel to exist./From the cell would come the right for the retreat/and for the workshops to exist.'//Another Indian student/(their minds work in most transcendent ways)/said, 'I very much agree,/but would like to add/that the refectory must be equal to the/chapel,/and the chapel must be equal to the cell,/and the retreat must be equal to the/refectory./None is greater than the other.'"

## The Further Development of the Final Scheme: February 1967–December 1968

### The Plan of February 16, 1967

A difficult proposition

Ten months had now passed since beginning the project. The plan's new hypothesis—that established monastic ritual and modern informal religious life might both be done justice in a unified spatial gesture, in a single "big house" as it were—is a challenging one. The proposition of the unorthodox plan brings, coupled with its promise of becoming a "society" of equally significant spaces, its share of functional, spatial, and formal difficulties. Kahn's proposal largely attempts to do without that helpful repertoire of mediating architecture—corridors, galleries, halls, and courts—which he knew so well from his neo-Beaux-Arts training. To renounce this "architecture of connection" raises first of all functional questions. How, for example, does one move through the plan without disturbing the sanctity of the chapel, the concentration of the classrooms, a gathering in the auditorium? How to mediate between spaces if not with corridors? If there is no longer a "back door" to the complex, how to separate access to the valorized public spaces and the profane service spaces? Furthermore, if—as we have heard Kahn declare—it is precisely this "architecture of connection" which "gives the man walking through the building a feeling for the entire sense of the institution," how to reach a sense of coherence in the plan without it? Can the subtle hierarchies in the program be done justice by a plan in which the distances have collapsed? And then, formally and spatially, to what degree are the individual parts autonomous, to what degree do they consolidate within a single whole? These questions are by no means trivial—they will occupy Kahn and his assistants for several months to come.

Suspending judgment

Inherent to this method of functional bricolage is that each element may be developed independently—the potential being, in Kahnian terms, that the "existence will" of each space may develop freely into what it "wants to be," uninhibited by a totalizing form or structural unit. Taken to its extreme, this method of "growing" and then assembling individual spaces might produce works that would transcend the designer's existing preferences or prejudices. A suspension of judgment is required of the architect, who to a certain degree becomes a spectator of his own work, the potential reward being results that surprise their maker by transcending the limits of his will and imagination. The craftsman is never cleverer than his craft; or, according to Kahn, "Order is not what you want it to be."[86] Or again,

86 Kahn, quoted in Wurman, *What Will Be Has Always Been*, p. 235.

"From what the space wants to be the unfamiliar may be revealed to the architect. From order will derive creative force and power of self-criticism to give force to this unfamiliar."[87] In this sense, the Motherhouse must be the most literal and extreme illustration of Kahn's setting a process of discovery in play toward a house that is a "society" of quasi-independent rooms, each engaged in finding out "what it wants to be" while it at the same time "talking together and making up their minds where their positions are."

**Open questions**

And yet, closer study of the plan of February 16, compelling as it may be within the context of the project's development, offers more promises to what it might become than convincing answers to how its self-imposed conflicts are to be resolved. The plan has been drawn in a manner that fixes intent while leaving much open—functionally, formally, and spatially. Functionally, circulation and adjacencies are difficult to imagine in several instances. The axial link between chapel and refectory directly behind the altar undermines the sanctity of the holiest of holies, the passage to the cells via the auditorium means a compromise in both the usability of that space and the accessibility of the cells, the use of an institutional kitchen as a connective space between private and communal rooms would certainly stretch even the most liberal of clients' sense of decorum, while the adjacency of the main entrance and the service court entrance—the crossing of garbage cans and visitors in plan—is a banality over which even an architect of Kahn's stature may stumble. For the time being, the question of vertical circulation has been left completely open: not a single stair has been drawn.

Formally, too, the architectural consequences of "letting the rooms find their own connections" are as yet unresolved. Whereas certain rooms naturally "find their connections" through direct collision with their neighbors, others need "adapters" in order to make those connections work—an additional, superfluous, architectural order is thus called into play. Spatially, the oblique entry approach toward the tower tends to direct movement either toward the chapel, or to unintentionally deflect it toward the service court. A multitude of sketches exist from the design phase that begins here, testimony to the difficulty of the topological puzzle Kahn had proposed for himself. Figures 53 to 56 illustrate some of Kahn's many attempts to organize and connect the core spaces during the following weeks, and out of these attempts would begin to crystallize the plan variations detailed below.

87 Kahn, "Order Is," p. 59. To which Gertrude Stein might have countered, "The inventor because he does not know what he is going to invent inevitably the thing he makes must have its ugliness" (about Picasso).

### The Plan of May 1967

The entrance to the tower has been displaced ninety degrees, now more graciously greeting visitors. **Fig. 57** This has the added advantage of pushing the service entrance into a secondary position, out of sight and traffic flow. Unfortunately, this is done at the cost of transforming the central court—in the last version a small *hortus conclusus*—into a service court. Kahn must have been uneasy with this; even in a "nonhierarchical" plan, a service court occupying the geometric center—and sharing a wall with the chapel at that—would have certainly violated his sense of propriety. In addition, the schoolrooms, auditorium, and north wing of cells are now cut off from having direct access from the main entrance, resulting in either "open air" circulation or extremely long routes through the building.

The octagonal shape of the refectory—a recurring motif in classicist and Beaux-Arts plans—is a device that allows this space to elegantly turn the corner in plan. The schoolrooms have consolidated to form a hammerhead block at the head of the northern wing. As with the schemes of October and November 1966, a question of "order" or syntax is raised: the larger, communal room-type in discord with a periphery formed by smaller cell types. Again, Kahn seems aware of this contradiction and hesitant to commit to it—the schoolrooms are left unfinished in plan.

**Subtle geometries**

There is a subtle yet important change in the geometry of the plan: whereas in February's version the core spaces float freely within the frame of the cells, apparently unbound by geometrical rule, they have now—with the exception of the tower, which is tilted approximately thirty degrees away—locked into the same grid. It is instructive to note that this geometric cleansing has at the same time increased the tension in the plan, the volumes of the communal spaces rotating now in unison to "pull" against the orthogonal frame that contains them. Kahn knows meaningful dissonance exists only in the context of order. As if aided by the simplified geometry, the core spaces no longer need "adapters" to find their connections. Although still functionally flawed, formally, at least, the plan has taken a step toward possible resolution.

### The Plans of June 28 and August 7, 1967

**Internal network of paths**

A drawing from June 28, 1967 **Fig. 59**, based on a sketch from Kahn **Fig. 58**, is the first large-scale drafted floor plan of the final scheme (1/16 in. = 1 ft., approx. 1:200). This plan is further elaborated in a large (1/16 in. = 1 ft.) site plan and elevations for presentation to the sisters and Father Phelan in Media on August 7. **Fig. 60** The tightly drawn, pencil-on-vellum plans are, for the first time, a commitment to investigate

**53** Core: plan, for June 28, 1967, Louis Kahn
**54** Core: plan, Spring 1967, Louis Kahn
**55** Core: plan, for June 28, 1967, Louis Kahn
**56** Core: plan, Spring 1967

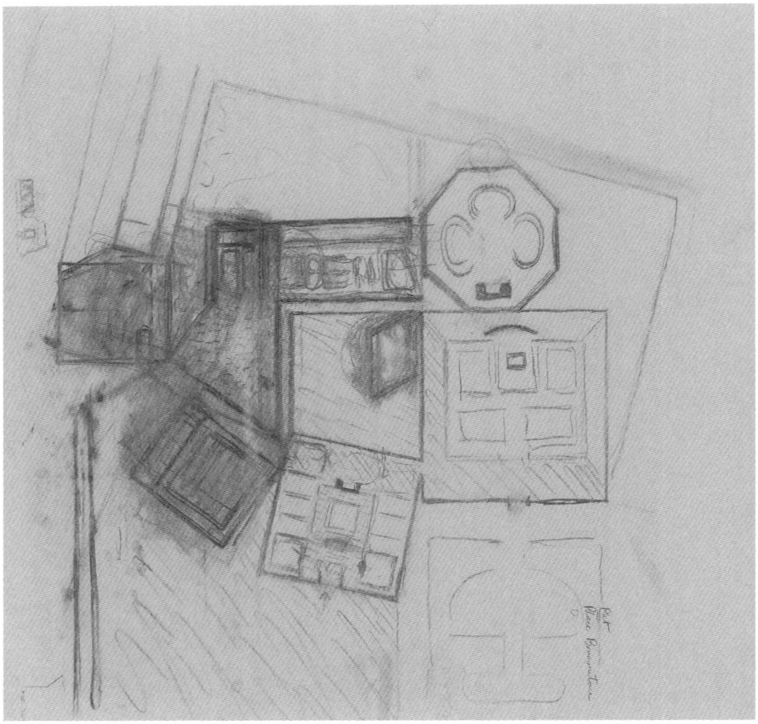

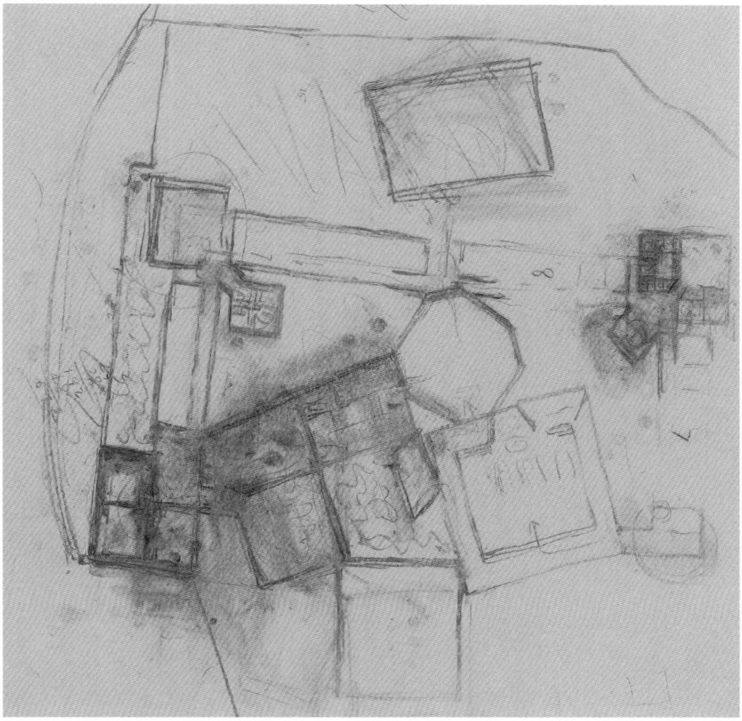

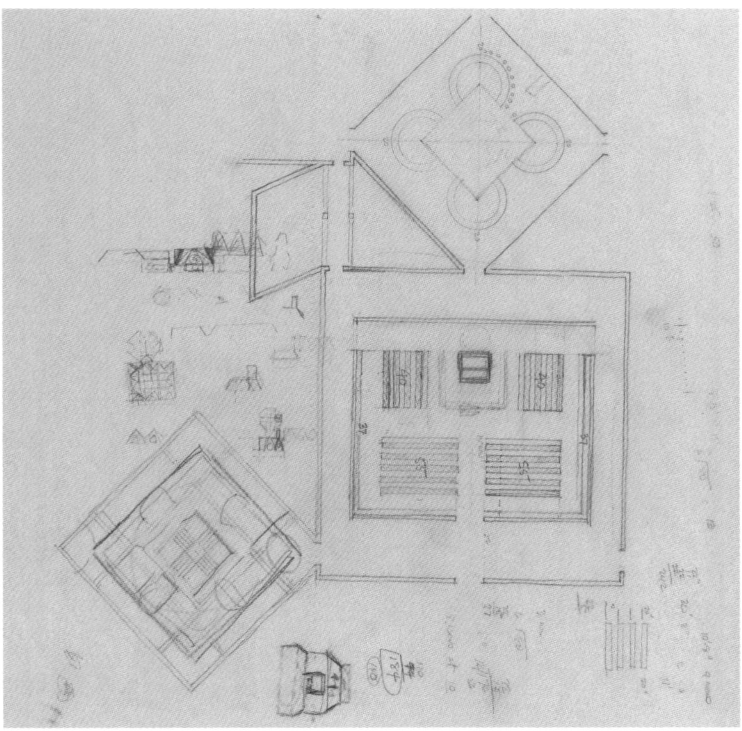

**57** Plan with site, May 19, 1967, Louis Kahn
**58** Plan fragment, for June 28, 1967, Louis Kahn (attributed)
**59** Plan: first floor, June 28, 1967
**60** Plan with site, August 1967

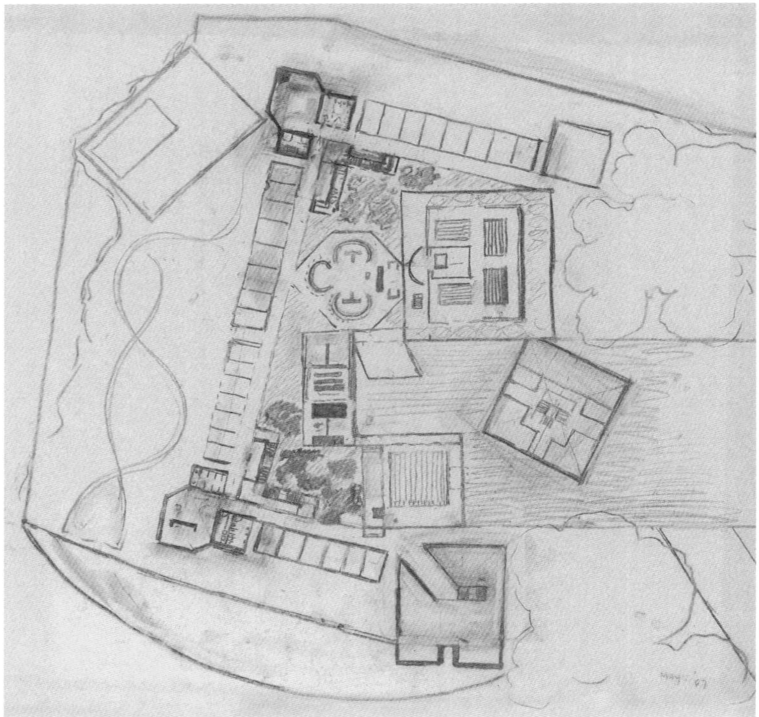

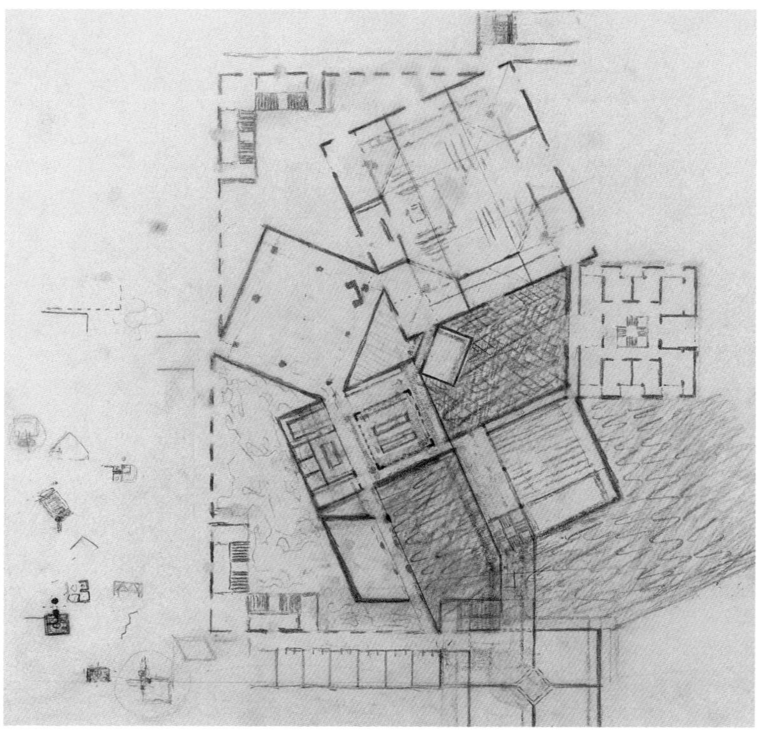

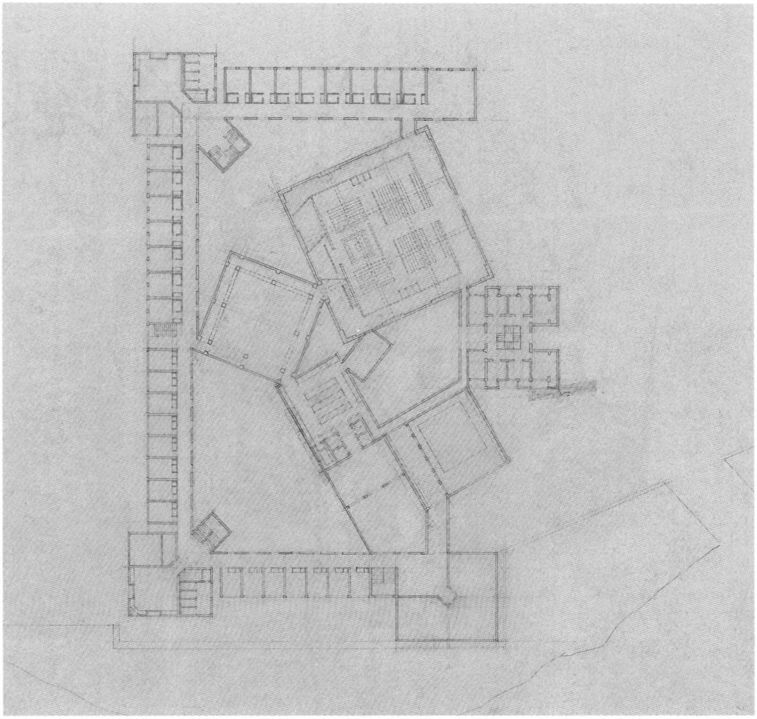

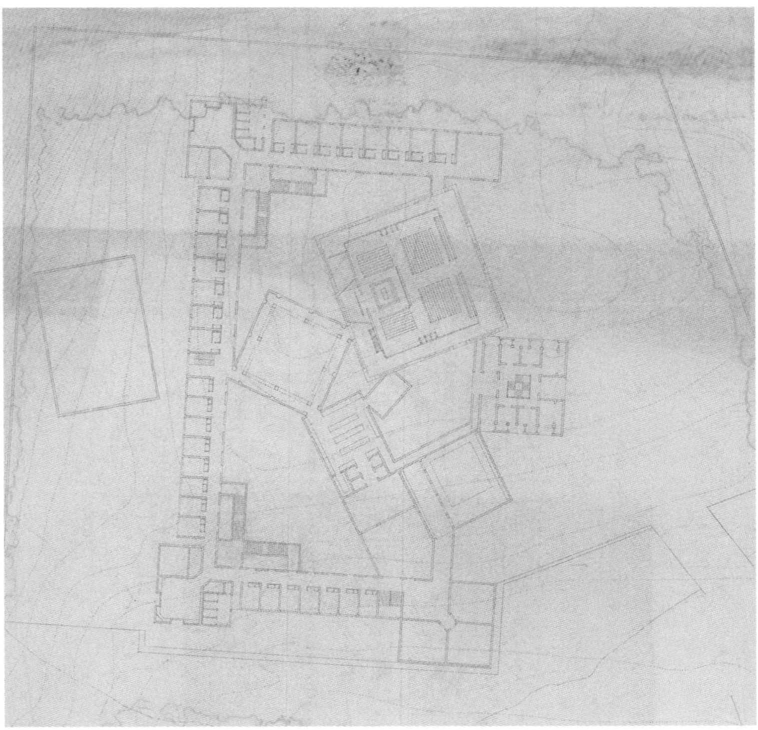

**61** East elevation, August 7, 1967, Louis Kahn

MOTHERHOUSE
LIK, AUG

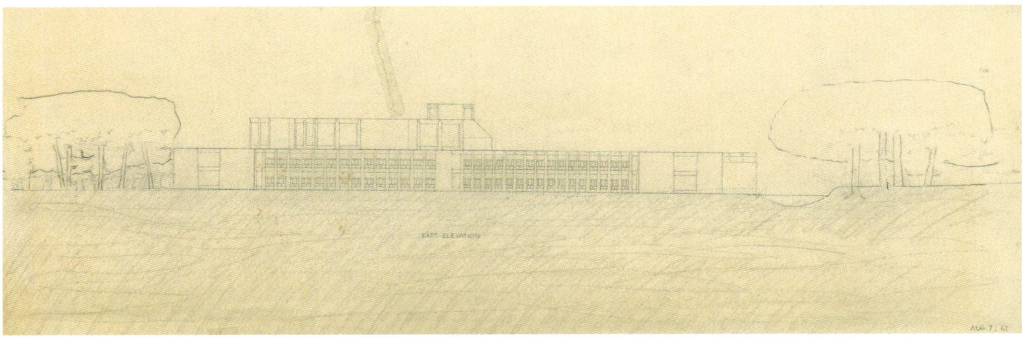


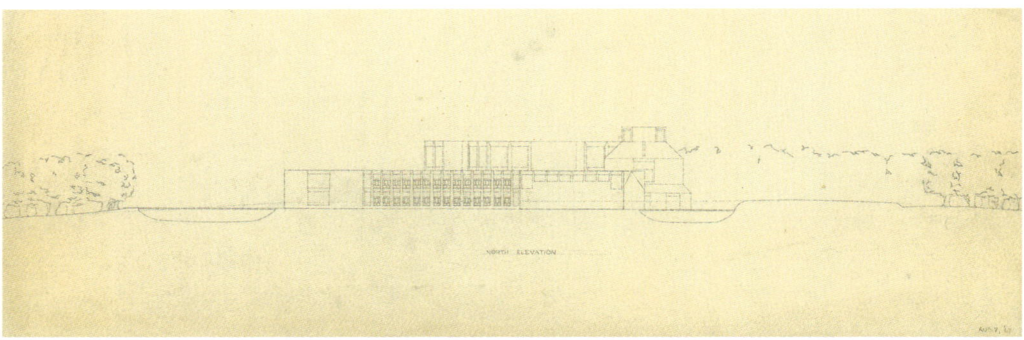


**62** South elevation, August 7, 1967, Louis Kahn
**63** East elevation, August 7, 1967
**64** North elevation, August 7, 1967

a scheme in detail, intimating particulars of construction, consequences of the room collisions, and intricacies of scale. The disposition of the parts is largely the same as in May, with a few small, but decisive, changes. The auditorium has drifted to meet the tower, conveniently making space for a small service court and its entry. Freed of its service function, the central court is again a small garden around which the plan unfolds. Just as important, the new disposition of core spaces—for the first time linked together in a "continuous collision"—allows for an uninterrupted and non-hierarchical network of paths through the house. The most sensitive of these spaces—the chapel and the refectory—are double-layered, each with an ambulatory at once room and hallway. The tower is now parallel to the cells, staking out a reference frame within which the core spaces rotate. Again, the plan gains tension with increasing geometric rigor.

**Restraint vs. expression**

With Kahn's ample (1/8 in. = 1 ft.) and atmospheric charcoal sketches **Figs. 61–62** showing the way, the floor plan is accompanied for the first time by elevations from all sides. **Figs. 63–64** While the expressive "ziggurat" tower has remained, the other elements have been restrained. Gone are the multiple gables and circular arches, replaced by a more reticent and tectonically precise "brick order" of flat-roofed volumes, tapered pilasters, and jack arches. The contemporary Phillips Exeter Library (1965–72) is a close relative. Although these abbreviations may have originated in the architects' search for economy, it is not difficult to sense in the subdued prisms a response to the Dominicans' vow of poverty, to the delicate scale of the landscape, and to the complex floor plan, which causes considerable visual excitement in itself; to sense, in short, a search for appropriateness.

**Presentation of the plan**

According to the meeting minutes from August 7, 1967, the sisters again accepted the premises of the plan and, together with the architects, set a number of refinements for the next stage of designing. The school was to be combined with the auditorium by placing the auditorium on the upper floor; the library—until now, either a discrete element or included in the school or auditorium building—was to be moved to the second floor of the tower. Additional sitting rooms—now totaling eight—were to be added to the west end of the cells.[88] The liturgy and furnishing of the chapel were discussed with Father Phelan. For intimate worship, a small chapel (Kahn: "a religious place in the religious place") for thirty persons was to be added to the east of the sacristy; a confessional room, "an agreeable room for two people to converse," would replace the confessional booths. A private room for the priest was to be located above the sacristy. In accordance

88 Meeting minutes from August 7, 1967, Box LIK 10, Kahn Collection.

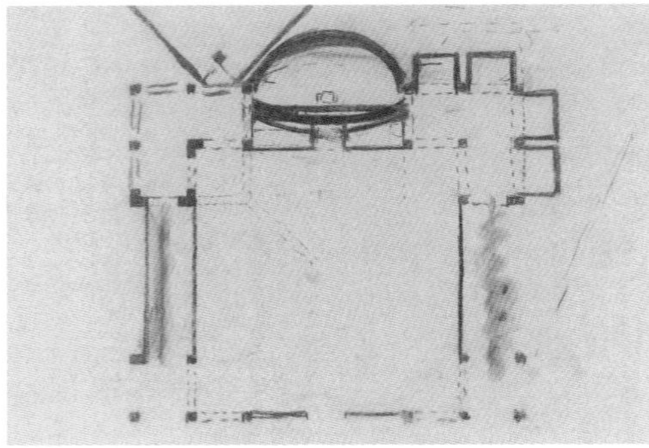

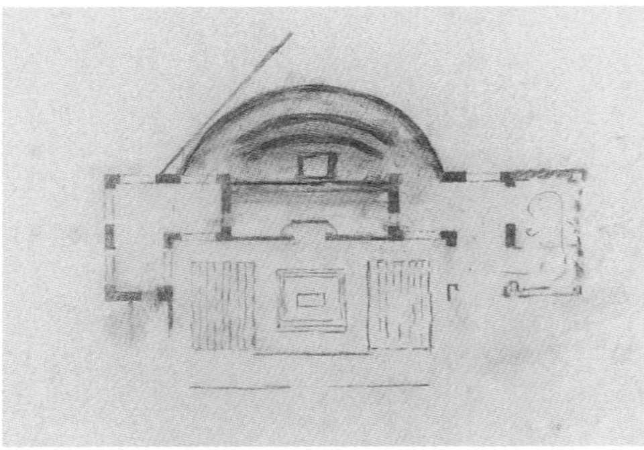

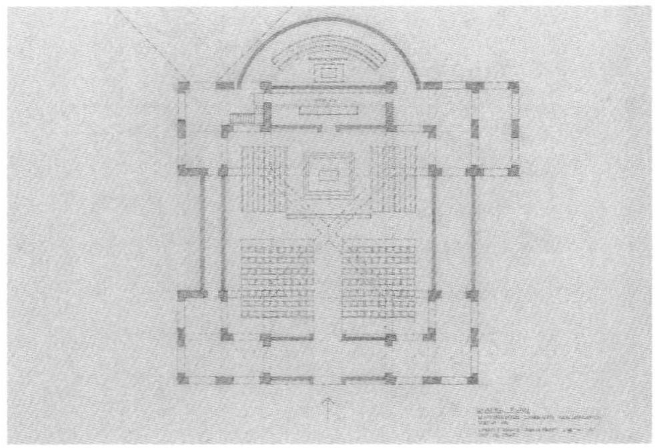

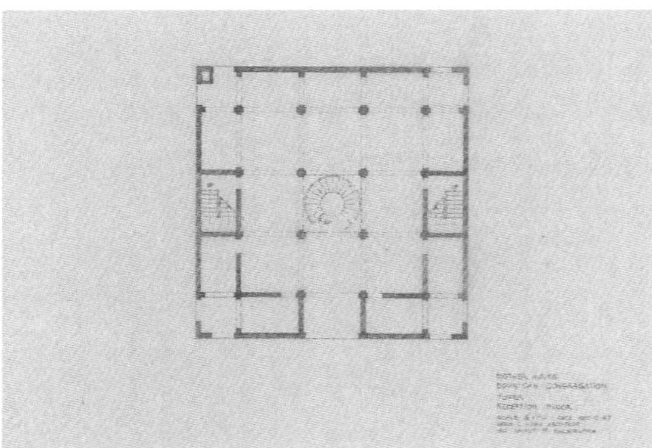

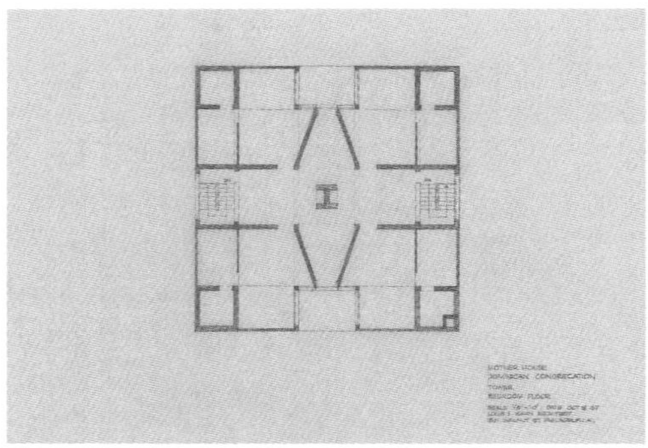

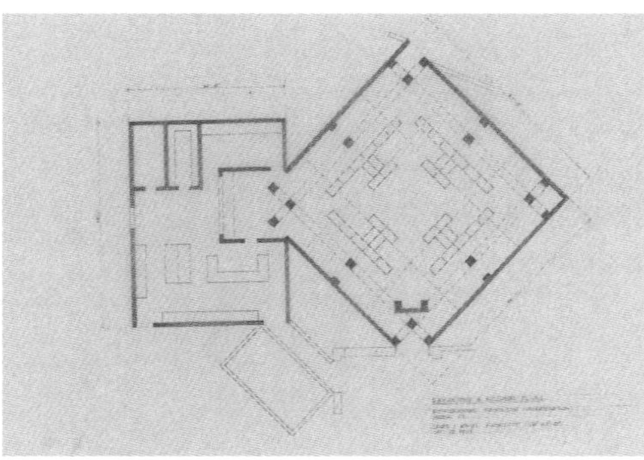

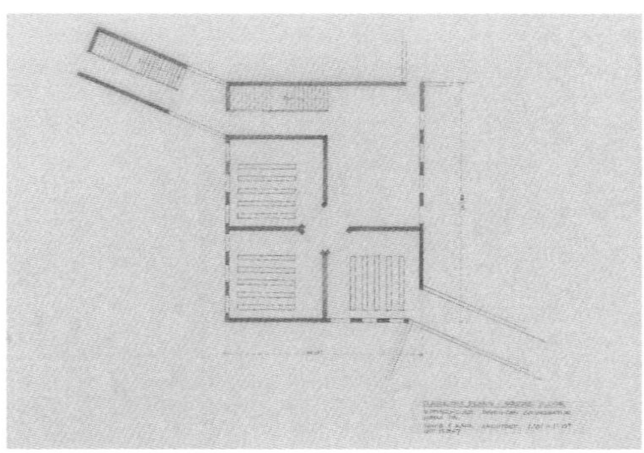

with the Dominican ideal of an "action religion," Father Phelan suggested that chairs would be more appropriate than pews, which would allow alternate seating arrangements and even other, non-liturgical uses.

Records from these weeks reflect the sisters' commitment. On August 7, 1967, almost a year and a half after their first meeting (!), Kahn and Mother Emmanuel signed an AIA contract for architectural services.[89] On August 24, 1967, Kahn wrote to the sisters, recommending four general contractors who might bid on the project: Joseph Farrell, Inc., builder of the Richards Medical Research Building; Mason & Cullen, Inc., builders of Erdman Hall; Unkefer Brothers, who had made extensive additions to an office building as planned by Kahn; as well as the firm of McCullough-Howard. In November, the office of Vinokur-Pace, a frequent consultant to Kahn, was officially contracted for structural and mechanical engineering.[90] The project, having barely survived the winter, was now gaining momentum.

**65–67** Chapel: plans, September/October 1967, Louis Kahn
**68** Chapel: plan, October 12, 1967
**69–70** Entry tower: plans, October 12, 1967
**71** Refectory: plan, October 12, 1967
**72** Classrooms: plan, October 12, 1967

### Fall/Winter 1967–1968: Densifying the Plan, Developing the Parts

The next months were spent exploring the individual spaces in terms of construction, spatial qualities, and interrelationships. Although Kahn had sown the seeds of construction early in the process with his sketches of the cells, the accepted scheme, the signed contract, and the addition of Vinokur-Pace to the team seem to have given the impetus necessary to step up the planning tempo and depth of detail.

Allowing each part of the monastery to develop into what it "wants to be" results in a project resembling as much several buildings as a single building. By mid-October, Kahn and his associates had drawn each of the core spaces in plan at 1/8 ft. = 1 ft. scale. **Figs. 65–72** The walls of these spaces—until now drawn as simple lines (planes)—have now "grown" a tectonic framework of pilasters, columns, and beams appropriate to their volumes and the loads in play. Columns and frame are used in turn to articulate use-space: defining galleries or rooms-in-rooms, establishing concave or convex thresholds at the collisions of the volumes. (A comparison with the unmediated transitions in the earlier plans shows how significant is this enrichment.) Chapel, tower, and refectory all profit from this tectonic fleshing-out, with such spatial highlights as the tower's third-floor room-fugue or the refectory's overlap with the kitchen. Only the school/auditorium lags behind: the attempt to combine the two uses is as yet unsuccessful (circulation leading through a classroom!) and the construction still schematic.

89 AIA Contract between Louis Kahn and Dominican House of Retreats and Catholic Guild, August 7, 1967, Box LIK 10, Kahn Collection.

90 Letter, Kahn to Mother Mary Emmanuel, August 24, 1967, Box LIK 10, Kahn Collection.

On drawings: the plan as generator

It is instructive to note that no sections or volumetric drawings accompany these latest studies. By this stage of the narrative, at the latest, it is abundantly clear that the architects have used orthographic *plan* drawings as their primary means of thinking spaces, with sections and elevations, perspectives and models used only sparingly in the process. (This is true not only of this project, but, with the notable exception of the section-driven Kimbell Art Museum, of virtually all of Kahn's works.) If Kahn's priority lies, as claimed, in the development of an institution's "Form," it follows logically that the plan will tend to become the generator of the scheme, laying out the parti in respect to the way that humans are likely to move and relate to each other—on the horizontal plane. But beyond its role as a socio-spatial diagram are other, generative dimensions of plan drawing, which must by now crowd into the foreground of our attention. In addition to its use as an agent for orchestrating mass and void (Kahn: "the rhythm of light—no light—light ...") plan notation—not unlike musical notation—is an instrument to both express and generate tension or repose, to describe phases of movement, pause, and rest. Alan Colquhoun has depicted, in his essay "The Beaux-Arts Plan," an experience of plan-as-partita that well fits Kahn's mature plans, the Dominican Motherhouse included:

> "When we 'read' a Beaux-Arts plan, we seem to be carrying out three operations at the same time, or at any rate in quick succession. First, we interpret the marks on the page as a Gestalt pattern. Second, we translate this into an imagined two-dimensional space which we experience sequentially—following the direction of narrow, bounded spaces, halting at square spaces, interpreting rhythmically arranged points as transparent boundaries, and so on. Finally, we translate this into three-dimensional volumes. From these interpretive steps we arrive at a coherent organization which does not gain its meaning from any but the most generalized functional attributions. It is in this generalized 'program' that one of the most striking analogies between the Beaux-Arts plan and the symphony lies."[91]

From plan to volume

Colquhoun's passage is compelling for several reasons, two of which will be explored later in the text: the "loose fit" between form and function, and the Gestalt qualities of plan notation. Colquhoun has additionally broached an intriguing theme: the "impulse" of horizontal

91 Colquhoun, "The Beaux-Arts Plan," pp. 50–65. In a manner related to Colquhoun's, Kahn spoke of the plan as a partita: "Open before us is the architect's plan. Next to it is a sheet of music. The architect fleetingly reads his composition as a structure of elements and spaces in their light. The musician reads with the same overallness." Kahn, "The Room, the Street and Human Agreement."

dimensions to unfold into three-dimensional space. From the Renaissance to the Ecole des Beaux-Arts, there existed wide consensus, either tacit or explicit, that a well-conceived plan is the seed of its own vertical dimensions: "Every three-dimensional form is born from its plan as a tree is born from its roots."[92] With the advent of slab-and-frame construction and with the resulting emphasis on the horizontal plane, modern architecture no longer upheld such a binding horizontal-vertical correspondence; on the contrary, such a correlation would have tended to upset the non-hierarchical horizontal space programmatic for so many moderns. Reflecting on this horizontal-vertical correspondence in orthographic drawings, it has been pointed out:

"Not all drawings take advantage of this capacity. Compare, for example, the plan of a building such as the Villa Madama and Mies' project for a brick villa. The understanding that the plan notation presumes volumetric control seems to be extant in the former, while missing from the latter. Though some would have difficulty with the assumption of the plan as the primary organizational device, and would choose an alternate point of departure, such as the section, there is still the potential to express the essence of volume in the two-dimensional drawing. The issue is that the drawing that depicts only two dimensions is capable of expressing the essence of volume and surface—indeed, the aesthetic intent."[93]

But how exactly? A nagging question at this point—for Kahn's plans do not simply "extrude" into three dimensions—is just how and to what degree *are* volumes "inherent" in these plans, and how do Kahn and his associates go about "growing" those volumes/spaces out of two dimensions? (Questions that further beg the question of the relevance of Kahn's plan-based method in the face of today's 3D-modeling capacities.) It is important to note that especially in this type of "labyrinthine" plan, the vertical dimension plays a major role in establishing hierarchy, orientation, and variety as one moves through the spaces. (A quality virtually missing, for example, in the labyrinthine plans of Le Corbusier, and in most structuralist and "mat" buildings of the mid-sixties.) Along with the positions and "spacings" which the individual spaces have "found" in plan, it is precisely this articulation of their vertical dimensions that establishes their relative significance within the whole. Kahn hinted at this: "Civilization is measured by

92 Barbaro, *La Practica della Perpettia,* 1568.

93 Graves, "The Necessity of Drawing," pp. 235–45.

**73** Parti sketch, March 7, 1968, Louis Kahn

the shape of your ceiling."[94] Having introduced the question of plan-section correspondence, we must admit that the drawings seen to this point shed only dim light on the architects' means of developing spaces from their plans. This remains, then, a point to return to as the schemes unfold.

### Intermezzo: Sketch of March 7, 1968

The development of a design is not a linear process. (Indeed, Kahn disliked the word "process" in connection with architecture: "Making architecture is not 'a process,' making beer is a process."[95]) Although from our privileged vantage point the forward momentum of the current scheme seems clear enough, with the energies of all parties apparently dedicated to its realization, a small sketch in Kahn's hand, dated March 7, 1968, seems to express second thoughts about that design. **Fig. 73** Once again, a "Form" diagram shows, as in the earliest schemes, the clear separation of private and communal realms. In contrast to the current loose conglomeration of discrete spaces, Kahn proposes a symmetrical composition with a cloistered grove at its center—a return to a conventional monastic typology. It is as if Kahn is stepping back to hold review: Is the current scheme just too difficult to work out? Is he still uncertain about the rightness of the modified "Form"? Does he have doubts about remaining within budget and seeking a still more compact solution? All this remains speculation, as he will inevitably stay with the present scheme. Still, such sketches are evidence of the doubt and uncertainty that are a part of designing, of an architect hesitating before committing himself completely, even this late in the development of an idea.

**The published scheme**

### Sketch of February 1968/Plan of April 22, 1968

The winter's studies of the core spaces coalesce into a comprehensive and evocative plan with Kahn's delightfully spacious ⅛ in. = 1 ft. scale charcoal drawing from February/March 1968. **Fig. 74** With a number of minor adjustments, this sketch is tautened in the associates' plan of April 22, 1968. **Fig. 75** Although this plan belongs to the intermediate steps, it has been by far the most frequently published of the Motherhouse variations to date, often presented as the "final design."[96]

94 Kahn, transcribed note of a studio discussion, University of Pennsylvania, December 5, 1960, quoted in McCarter, *Louis I. Kahn,* p. 133. Each discrete space is strengthened in its search for significance not only by finding the right place within the whole, but also by receiving its own *scale.*

95 Kahn, quoted by David Polk in interview with author, October 20, 2004.

96 An incomplete list of publications that have presented the plan of April 22, 1968, as the "final design," include Gast, Giurgola, McCarter, Saito, and *Monografías de Arquitectura & Vivienda,* special Kahn issue (2001). The reproduction used for these publications is based on an extremely large (⅛" = 1' 0") first floor plan. The other levels, though never published, had indeed been drawn in this scale.

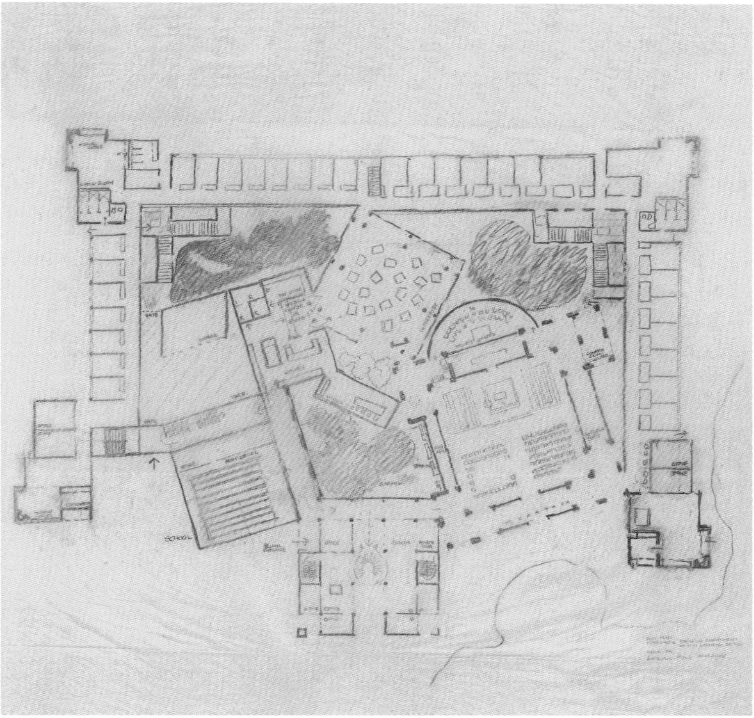

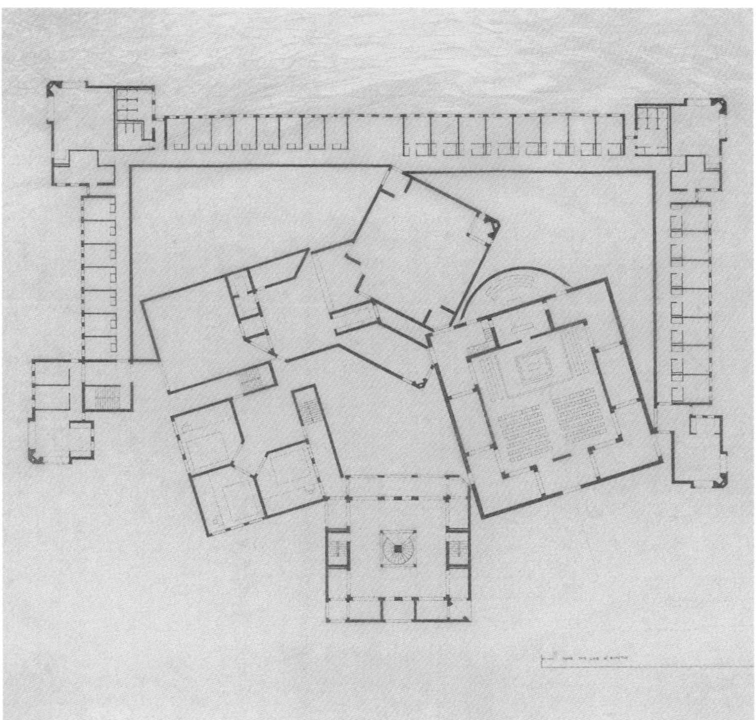

**74** Plan: first floor, February/ March 1968, Louis Kahn
**75** Plan: first floor, April 22, 1968

A clear spatial order

Kahn's sketch and the plan from April 22, 1968, validate the sisters' idea of placing the auditorium above the school. It is a stacking that simply makes functional sense, with the oft-frequented classrooms at ground level, the larger auditorium under the big roof upstairs. What is more generally demonstrated by this move is how, in a configurative art such as architecture, the modification of a single element may significantly affect the rest. The subtraction of one element from the plan's equation instantly relaxes the whole, ridding it of its formally and functionally most uncomfortable moments (the unresolved school, the kinks in the circulation, etc.). All communal rooms are now in the core, resulting—for the first time since June 1966—in a clear spatial order. Finally convincing is the ease with which the core spaces now "inadvertently" connect. The resulting circulation ring formed by the linked spaces echoes the outer ring of cells and galleries, increasing possibilities for traversing the plan. The tower now hosts three stairs: a central stair leading directly to the library on the second and third floors, and two additional stairs to the offices and guest rooms above. The new private chapel forms an apse-like appendage to the main chapel. The desired confessional room—present in Kahn's sketch—has been left out of April's plan.

The great wall of cells receives living rooms at each of its corners, with four chimneys anchoring the horizontal wings and staking the limits of building in the clearing. The fireplace remains a powerful symbol of dwelling for Kahn, showing "the presence of man in the building" and a moment of domesticity in his institutional buildings. (The monastery's seven fireplaces hint at the degree of domesticity desired here.) Although included in Kahn's February sketch, missing in April's plan are the stairs to the cells—only one has been drawn in the north wing. The draftsman has also filled in the windows of the cloister, drawing an unbroken wall to the courtyard. Ironically, these two "shorthand" solutions—never intended as being final—have belonged through their repeated publication to the plan's more "permanent" and enigmatic features. (Or are we to imagine that—building code aside—Kahn would have connected the upper floor cells with a single stair, would have considered long galleries without natural light? [97])

Elevations and sections

The elevations attest to the continued infighting between expression and reticence. **Figs. 76–77** The bell-shaped tower has become a carved block, appendaged with what seems to be an outrigger belfry. Continuing the "house" theme, chapel, school, and refectory are topped

97 Robert McCarter suggests that this was indeed the case and that the stairs were reinstated in the following version as a concession to the building code. See McCarter, *Louis I. Kahn*, p. 295.

**76** West elevation, April 22, 1968
**77** East elevation, April 22, 1968
**78** Section looking west,
April 22, 1968
**79** Section looking south,
April 22, 1968

80 Plan with site, April 17, 1968
81 Plan: first floor, Spring 1968
82 Plan with overlay, May 20, 1968

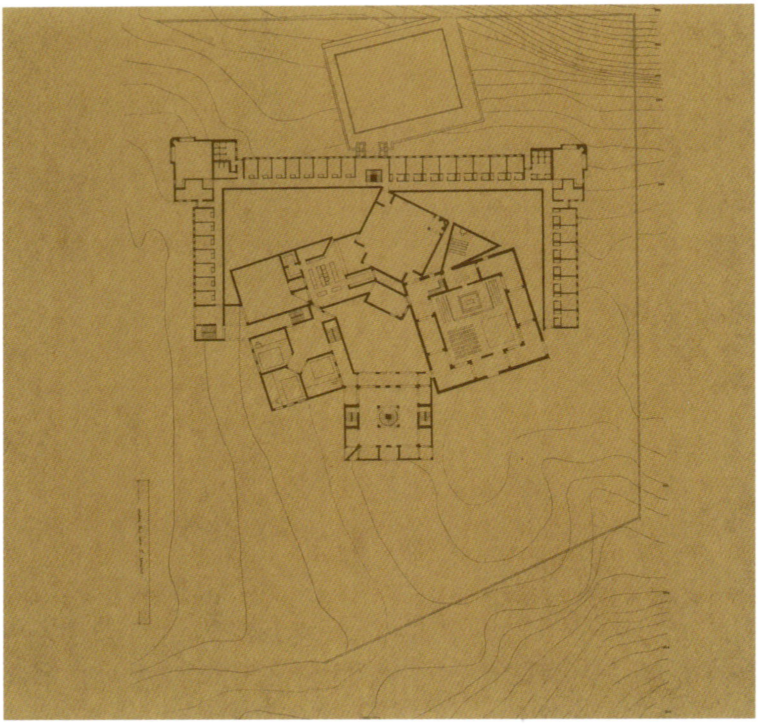

by giant fragments of hipped roofs—the school's roof chopped off dramatically on the courtyard sides, the chapel's roof clamped between giant hollow corner lanterns, which bring light rebounding into its interior. (The lanterns are closely related to the skylight monitors of the First Unitarian Church and the "hollow columns" of the mosque at Dhaka.) The façades are at once plastic and austere, the west entry somewhat sternly greeting the visitor with its brick prisms all but closed on their lower levels. Turning the corner toward the forest, the building transforms from a closed bearing wall structure on its entrance side to an open masonry frame. Accompanying the elevations, two sections through the monastery—astonishingly, the first to be drawn since the third scheme, and the very first to be drafted of *any* scheme—intimate the fall of natural light and the vertical modulation of space. **Figs. 78–79**

### The Plans of late April–June 1968

**Gestalt and plan**

By late-spring 1968, with the disposition of the parts apparently no longer in question, the architects turned now to the refinement of those parts and to the plan's context. The archive is rich with plans and prints from these weeks, for rather than working out minor changes by using tracing-paper overlays (which would have been the

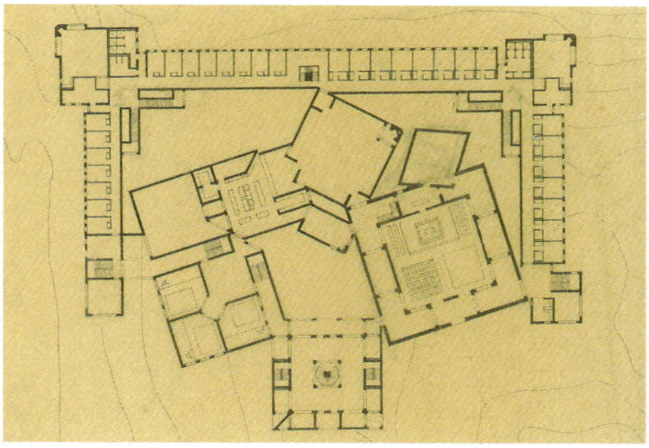

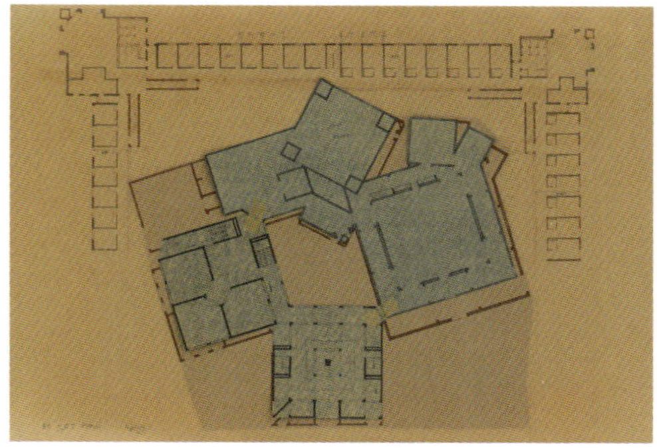

likely, economical method), entire plans have been redrawn to change a few details. Studying the different variations—which due to their minute differences are often difficult to order—one may gradually conclude that the reason for this considerable extra work lies in the architects' regard for the plan as an organic structure or Gestalt pattern, that changes in one part of the field call for counter-changes elsewhere in order to maintain equilibrium and a common syntax.

In what is likely the first plan after April 22 (courtyard stairs and windows are still missing) **Fig. 80**, two living rooms are removed; the small chapel is now triangular in shape and the pool has returned, accompanied by a garden wall that seems to have as its main function the intertwining of building and surroundings. In a second plan **Fig. 81**, the stairs have returned to the cell tracts, the small chapel is now a more usable diamond shape, and the pool has again disappeared. The plan dated May 20, 1968, which continues to refine the previous steps, is evidence of the architects' constant battle with the budget. **Fig. 82** Accompanying almost every scheme is a calculation of its area. Here, the consequences of shrinking the core spaces by approximately 10 percent are tested by pasting a reduced print of those rooms onto an existing plan.

**Finally: A comprehensive plan set**

The overlay of May 20 is based on a fully developed set of floor plans in which virtually all questions of form and use have been addressed. **Figs. 83–86** A true banquet for floor plan devotees, all parts and all levels have been thought through and drawn—we are finally shown the consequences of this extended, rigorous shifting and articulation of elementary plan shapes. The placement of library and auditorium in this "society of rooms" is now evident: their presence on the second level, their spacings to the ground floor. The multiple possibilities for traversing the plan are now apparent, the twelve different stairs exponentially deepening the plan's labyrinthine character. One might well imagine an inhabitant, setting out from her second-floor cell toward the chapel, to alternately choose a route over the library, the school, or the kitchen. Even without the use of sections, a filigree fugue of tectonics, light, and

**83** Plan: first floor, May 20, 1968
**84** Plan: second floor, May 20, 1968
**85** Plan: third floor, May 20, 1968
**86** Plan: roof, May 20, 1968

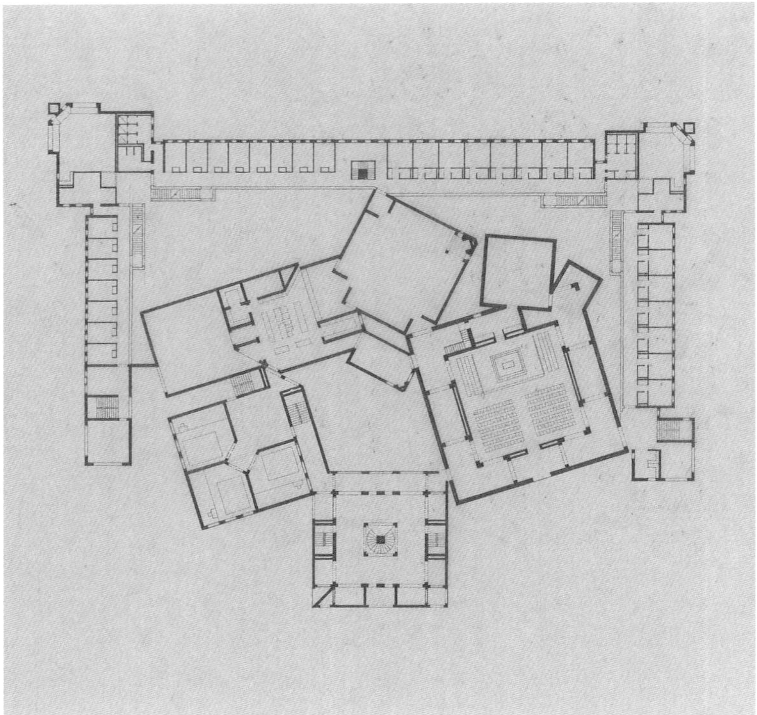

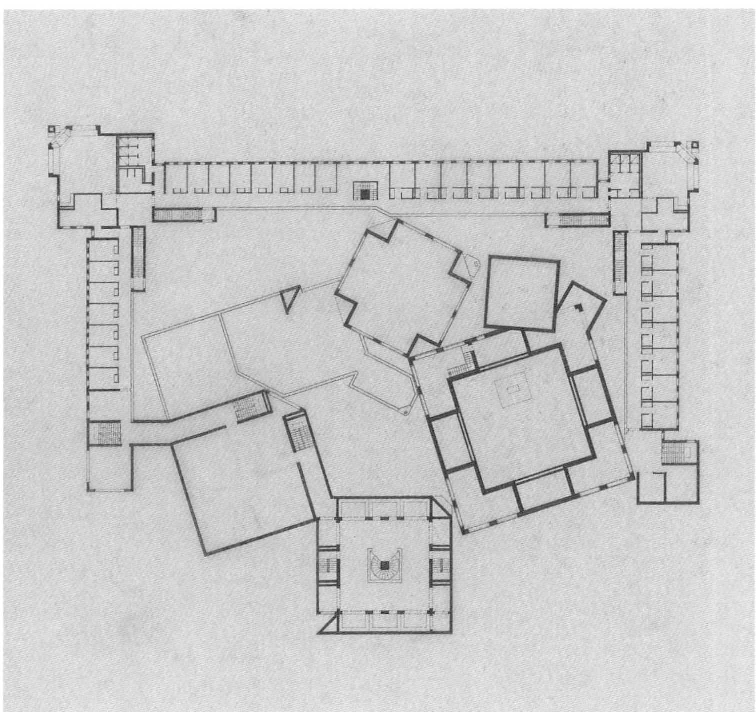

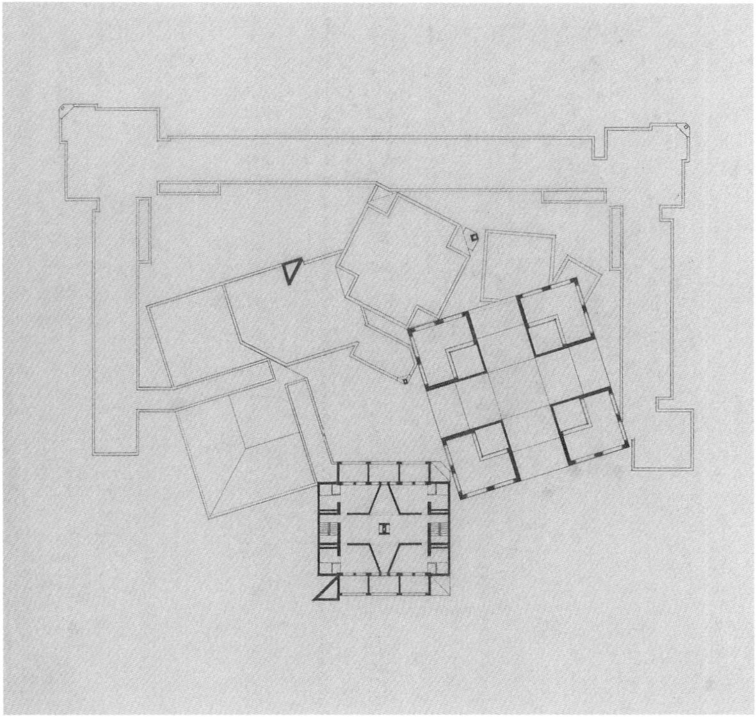

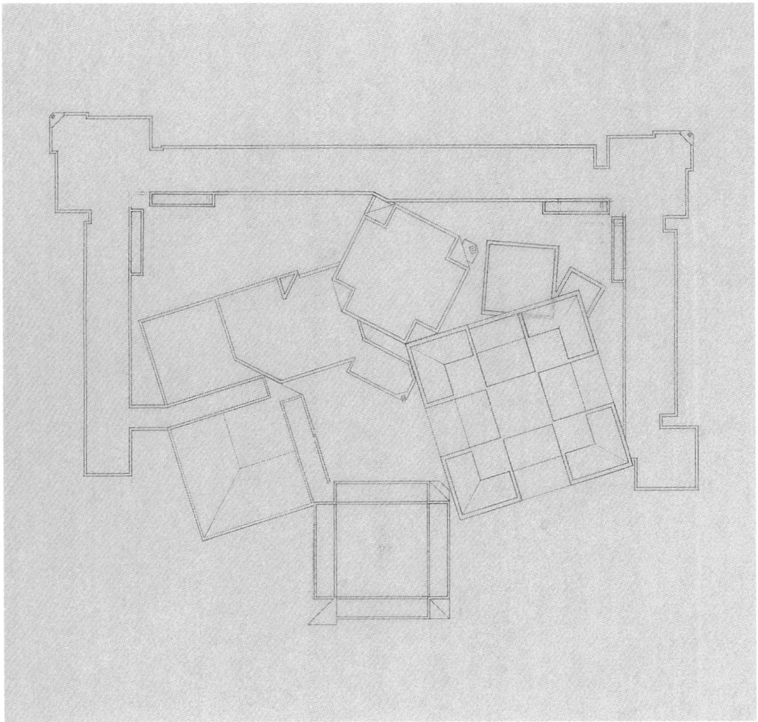

**87** Site plan, Spring 1968

Granite Block paving
Brick wall
Water Pool
Drive
Brick wall
Drive
1" = 50' - 0"

space is revealed to those literate in plan notation as the layered set unfolds vertically: the tower's ground-floor office spaces becoming on the next floors the library's double-height, top-lit book niches, and further upward the loggias of the guest rooms; the wall-folding superimpositions of cross and square in chapel and refectory becoming apparent in the upper levels. (The chapel admitting light over its corners, the refectory over the center of its gables, the thin, folded, light-reflecting planes, etc.) A spatial richness only hinted at in the published plan of April 22—conceived, but not yet shown—becomes undeniably manifest in these four plans. Here, at least in partial answer to the question of some pages back, is Kahn indeed "thinking" his extraordinarily three-dimensional spaces in a two-dimensional plan-partita.

**The composition in its context**

Not only are the internal spaces of the monastery now largely resolved, but for the first time in several months the floor plan is also drawn in a comprehensive site plan, showing forest, topography, and approach. Fig. 87 If, in following Kahn's taxing struggle with the plan, one has understandably lost sight of its context, it is once again apparent how integral the surrounding landscape is to the interior life of that plan. As the core spaces rotate within the frame of the cells, so rotates the entire monastery within the forest clearing. As if caught in the same centrifugal pull, forest and pieces of monastery have become separate parts of a single, turning movement. The space between the forest's edge and the building's volumes becomes almost palpable through this rotation, with each irregular piece of in-between charged by the movement. Forest and architecture at once reinforce and contradict each other, describing at the same time the stasis of a forest clearing and some kind of movement away from that center.

If we approach the monastery along the entry drive—which echoes the angle of chapel and school, geometrically anchoring the rotating composition to its site—it becomes apparent that the complex resists any attempt at experiencing it frontally. (The elevations viewed until now tend to let us forget this.[98]) We slip into the forest clearing obliquely, being allowed only partial views of our goal, as if our own movement toward the building sets it rotating away from us. Any symmetry which the plan suggests is relativized by its siting. Frontal views of one volume are accompanied by diagonal views of others, the unseen rest receding against the edge of the forest. The prismatic effect which we've encountered inside applies to the whole in its setting. Forest and architecture are thus conjoined, the whole experienced

98 An effect of the building on approach similar to Kahn's description of the perception of Erdman Hall at Bryn Mawr College: "The effect of the building as one approaches ... will be that of diagonal walls East and West. When the sun is rising, three walls will appear in light and three walls will be in shadow; and when the sun is setting, the walls previously in light will be in shadow." Quoted in Wurman, *What Will Be Has Always Been*, p. 5.

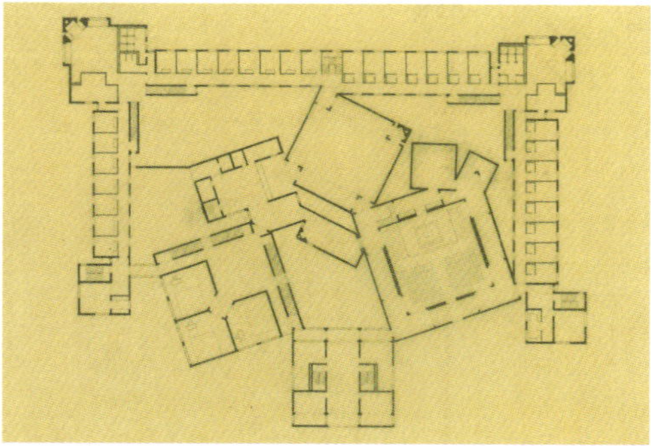

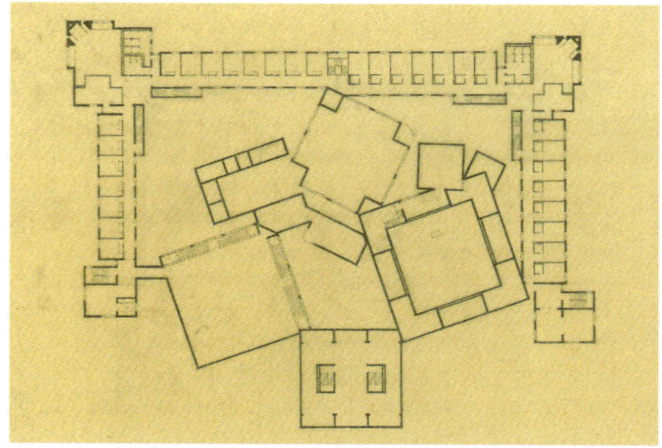

as if from the "inside"—even when outdoors. The explicitly "two" of interior and exterior are implicitly "one."

**88** Plan: first floor, July 17, 1968
**89** Plan: second floor, July 17, 1968

#### Plan of July 17, 1968

In spite of all efforts to the contrary, the budget continued to hover like Damocles' sword over the project. As the prospect of realization drew nearer, cost estimates increased in frequency and detail. In July, the plan—its first and second levels are drawn—is again distilled to reduce its area. **Figs. 88–89** The frame of cells is telescoped together at the central stair to reduce the circumference of the whole; the core volumes reduced accordingly to fit the smaller space formed by the cells. With these adjustments, an additional 1,539 square feet (143 m$^2$) could be wrung out of the plan. While this reduction brings increased elegance (the elimination of one stair in the tower, the new straight-run stairs in the school tract) and balance (an adequate termination of the north wing, an addition of an intermediate circulation space adjacent the kitchen), it also robs a certain spatial richness. Especially the tower suffers from the loss of its outer spatial layer when compared to the plan of May.

#### Plan of August 5, 1968: "Final" Version

**Towards construction drawings**

By August, the architects were finally on the threshold of the construction-drawing phase. The new plans—the last to be drawn as a set—have been refined in detail. **Figs. 90–93** The most obvious changes are the "hollow columns" that, in addition to adding weight and depth to chapel, tower, and school, serve as "servant spaces": ductwork for air conditioning and pipes. These tectonic/technical elaborations are used to spatially enrich the core: the outer corners of chapel and refectory are now supplemented by a re-entrant, inward-pointing movement. Thus turned back upon themselves, the stasis of the squares is challenged. Transitions between spaces are considerably more complex than in the roughshod collisions of earlier versions: thresholds

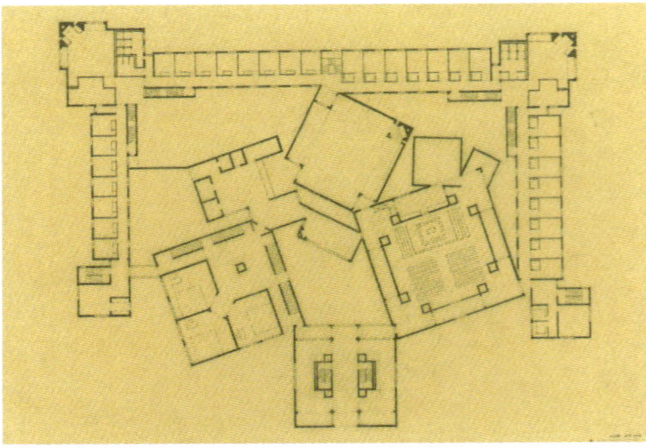

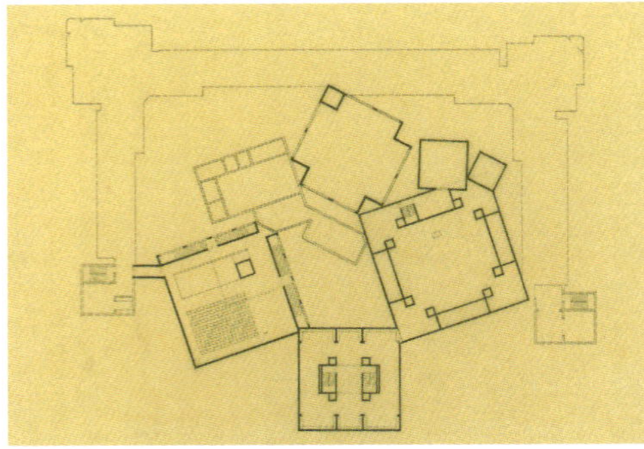

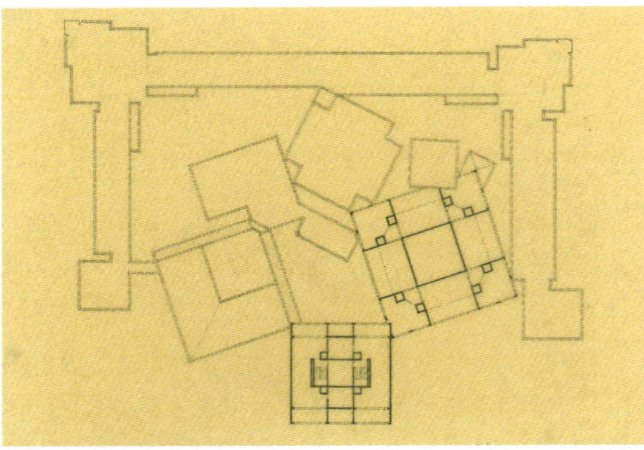

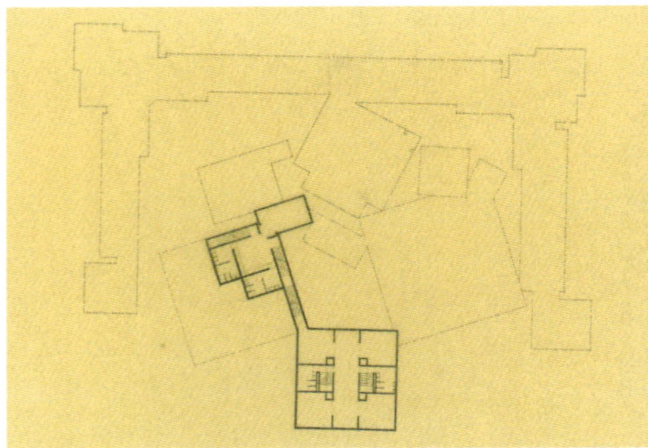

**90** Plan: first floor, August 5, 1968
**91** Plan: second floor, August 5, 1968
**92** Plan: third floor, August 5, 1968
**93** Plan: basement, August 5, 1968

are established, ceiling heights varied, spaces inflected both inwardly and outwardly, concaves answered by convexes.

The myriad decisions, large and small, the multitude of adjustments, rough and fine, are testimony to a paradox in this Kahnian paradigm of order. This apparently "free" composition—in order to reach a level of coherence and elegance above that of a banal conglomeration of parts—has required the greatest discipline in planning, a precision at least equal to that of Kahn's classical compositions. The months spent manipulating the plan are testimony to this fact. The parts, apparently tossed into place like so many dice, with resulting angles both acute and obtuse, are in fact precisely and subtly intertwined: in terms of geometry, constructive module, spatial sequences, and function. At this stage any attempt to move or even slightly re-dimension a relevant room would set off a chain reaction throughout the whole, disrupting its formal structure and making its multiple internal dependencies visible. The transitions that have been so laboriously constructed to appear incidental are anything but.[99] To have captured

99 Any attempt to digitally reconstruct the later schemes (such as the author's) using the planning module of the concrete blocks and the width of the cells as a grid will make the multiple dependencies within the plan immediately apparent. Indeed, in certain versions Kahn's associates were not beyond "stretching" the planning grid in order to formally resolve the connections.

the energy and tension of the first collage drawing in a formally resolved and completely functional plan is anything but trivial. It would at this point be worthwhile for the reader to linger in the spaces of this plan, to review the many steps taken, great and small, since the establishment of the final scheme in February 1967, in order to reflect on the distance traveled in this single scheme.

#### August 1968–March 1969: Final Development and Sudden End

**Towards a fine austerity**

The plan has now reached its final state: each of its building blocks will maintain its form and disposition for the duration of the project. In the following weeks details of construction are explored, always in regard to the sisters' austere budget. Although concrete block had been indicated as the main material in early sketches of the cells and had been used as the basis of the planning since then, Kahn had not given up hope of a brick construction. Brick details were drawn and estimated along with a more economical scheme using brick-sized concrete masonry piers and full-sized concrete-block filling, similar to the Tribune Review Building of eight years earlier. Concrete block proved far more affordable—over $400,000 less than brick—and was thus chosen for the final plans.[100] The concrete floor slabs of the core buildings and corridors are succeeded in the cells by more economical, almost primitive, wooden plank-and-beam floors; slate shingle roofs priced against less expensive lead-coated copper; windows and millwork were to be of white pine or—budget allowing—cypress.[101] The elevations and details from this final phase intimate what had become the convent's rough and reticent austerity—certainly a far cry from the exuberant baroqueness of the earliest scheme! **Figs. 94–95** The details, though, hint at how these "Dominican poor" concrete-block walls, defining all spaces interior and exterior, are transformed by architects' thought into something luxuriously ascetic. **Figs. 100–112** The concrete-brick pilasters and large block fillings tell of the walls' tectonics (Kahn: "A beam needs a column, a column needs a beam. There is no such thing as a beam on a wall." [102]) while scoring a delicate gray-in-gray rhythm across the façade. (Kahn again: "The joint is the beginning of ornament." [103]) Knowing Kahn's masonry work helps us imagine how—through craftsman's jointing details and the juxtaposition of elements from a limited palette of natural materials: lead, slate, cypress, or oak—the otherwise dull and grainy cinder

100 Source: handwritten cost estimates with variations for materials and construction, dated May 16, 1968, June 4, 1968, and August 13, 1968; typed cost estimate (four pages) August 15, 1968; meeting notes, November 12, 1968. LIK Box 10, Kahn Collection.

101 Ibid.

102 Kahn, "Silence and Light," p. 9.

103 Kahn, "Foreword," in Latour, *Louis I. Kahn: Writings*, p. 332.

**94** South elevation, August 5, 1968
**95** West elevation, August 5, 1968

Following pages:
**96–97** Core: section, August 5, 1968
**98–99** Entry tower: section, Summer 1968

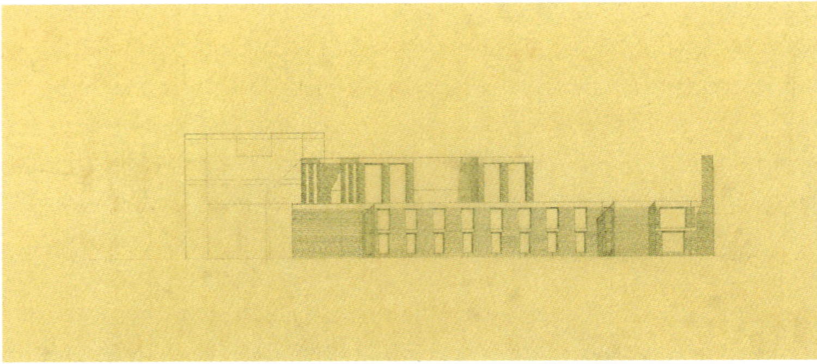

blocks were to come alive in the natural light which they were to catch and reflect.[104] This frugal meting out of costly materials and techniques in order to ennoble a budget-bound whole had been an effective tactic at the Tribune Review building and would become a major strategy for the National Assembly at Dhaka, which Kahn later described: "The concrete is made like rotten stone. The marble inset mixes the fine with the rough and the fine takes over." [105]

A detailed cost estimate of the design from August 5, 1968, prepared by Bill Gennetti and presented by Kahn to the sisters in November, stated a total construction price of $1,572,036, including landscaping, paving, and mechanical services for a convent that now measured 52,902 square feet (4,915 m²).[106]

**Towards realization**

The project was within reach of the congregation's budget and on course towards realization. A call for bidders was placed in local

104 The Tribune Review Building, with its pilasters of brick-sized concrete blocks and filling of full-sized blocks, employs a subtle combination of struck and pointed mortar joints, shadow joints, and strategically placed string courses to tell the story of its tectonics. The fine detailing, which encompasses the precast concrete roofs and beams, gives the building a striking dignity that belies the modest materials of its construction. As such it intimates to a certain degree what the materiality of the Dominican Motherhouse might have been.

105 Louis Kahn in conversation with Richard Saul Wurman, October 1973, in Wurman, *What Will Be Has Always Been,* p. 232.

106 Cost estimate, Bill Gennetti, dated August 13, 1968, Box LIK 10, Kahn Collection.

building periodicals and Kahn's office sent drawings to selected contractors for preliminary estimates.[107] In autumn meetings, details of construction and use were discussed: the merits of wood windows versus galvanized steel, kitchen equipment, seating arrangements in the chapel, final dimensions of classrooms, etc. In Media, on November 13, 1968, Kahn promised the sisters to complete design development preliminaries by mid-December; with an additional six-month head start for working drawings, and one and a half years for construction, they could move into their new convent within two years![108]

Here, on the threshold of realization, the sisters would stop short. In spite of all successful measures to reduce costs, money had remained a dominant theme at their internal project meetings. The architects had squeezed and cut where they could and there were now no reserves should the inevitable happen and costs begin to slowly inch upward again. A more economical means of construction than the bare concrete-block walls was hardly conceivable, and the distilled plan could be reduced no further without compromising aesthetic integrity or use. The sisters, reluctant to burden their future generations with debt, were acutely aware of this.[109]

**A great disappointment**

But budget problems, however real, were not the only or perhaps even greatest threat to the project. Changes had been at work within the congregation and the society around it that would put an end to the work. On the one hand, the number of new postulants had dropped steadily in the four years since beginning the project, calling the sisters' need for more space seriously into question. More important, though, were the Second Vatican Council's reforms to monastic life from 1965, the very year in which the sisters had initiated their project.[110] Their discussion and integration into the congregation had paralleled the long development of Kahn's design, which had ironically served as a catalyst for often heated debates on the virtues of traditional monastic life versus new opportunities for working in the world.[111] Eventually, the sisters began to see ever more of their seminary work and active religious life taking place outside of their convent—at churches, schools, community centers, universities—undermining their need for the proposed classrooms, the larger chapel,

107 Various offers for bid requests in Box LIK 10, Kahn Collection. For example: letter, Bornstein and Son Inc. (September 10, 1968) and letter, C. Raymond Davis and Sons, Inc. (October 4, 1968).

108 Meeting notes, November 12, 1968, Box LIK 10, Kahn Collection.

109 Meeting minutes of the general councilors and building committee with Mother Mary Bernadette, March 10, 1969, Archive of the Dominican Motherhouse, Elkins Park, PA.

110 For texts on Vatican II (1962–65), see the Vatican Archive, Documents of the II Vatican Council, http://www.vatican.va/archive/hist_councils/ii_vatican_council/ (accessed April 2006).

111 Interview, author with Sisters Mary Irene Lolli, O.P., and Eileen Patricia Primrose, O.P., Dominican Motherhouse, Elkins Park, PA, April 15, 2006.

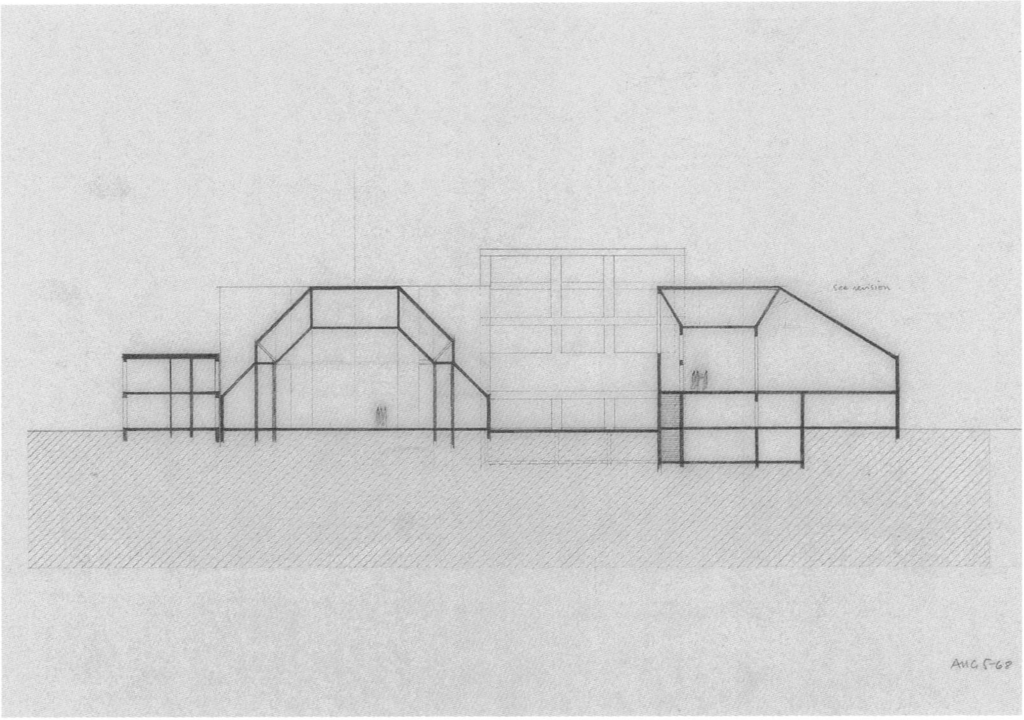
See revision
AUG 5-68

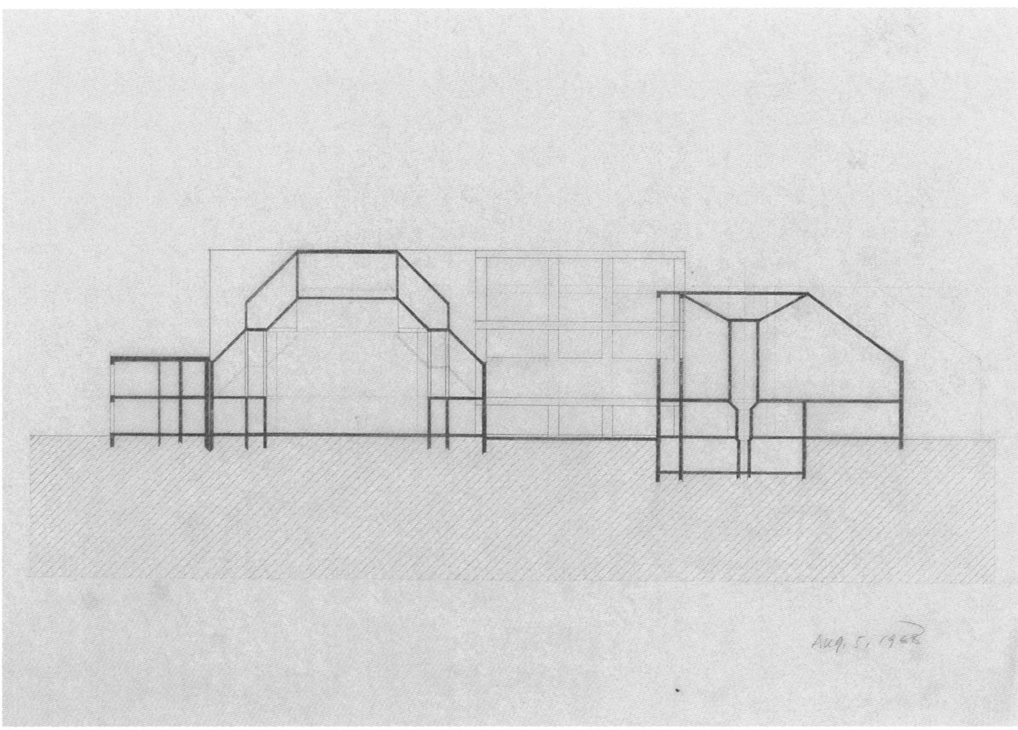
Aug. 5, 1968

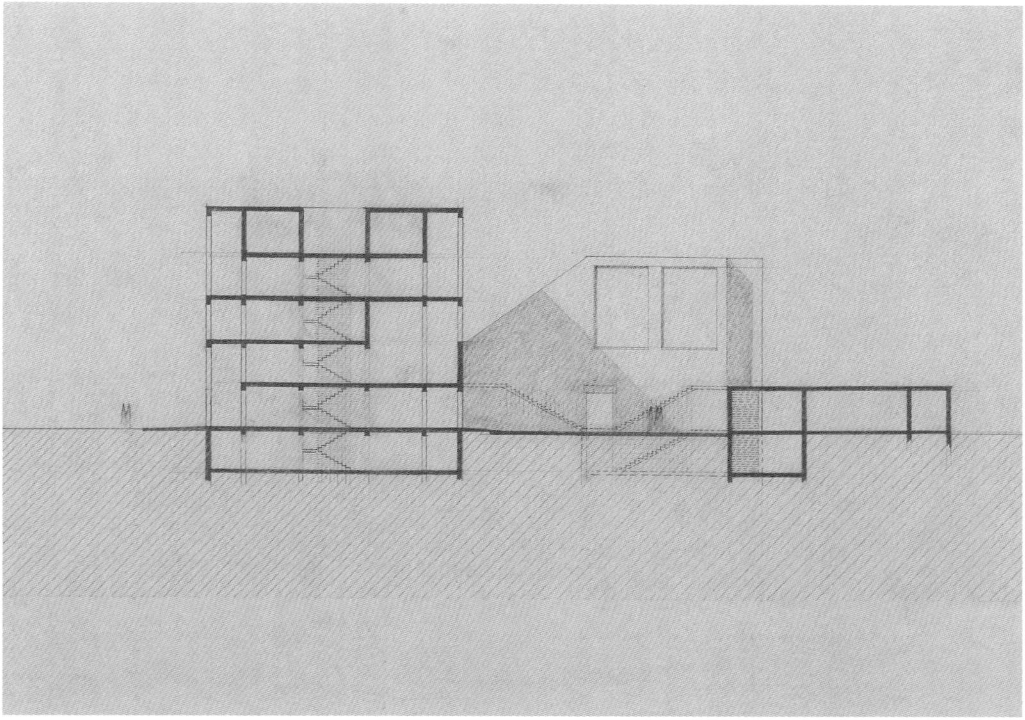

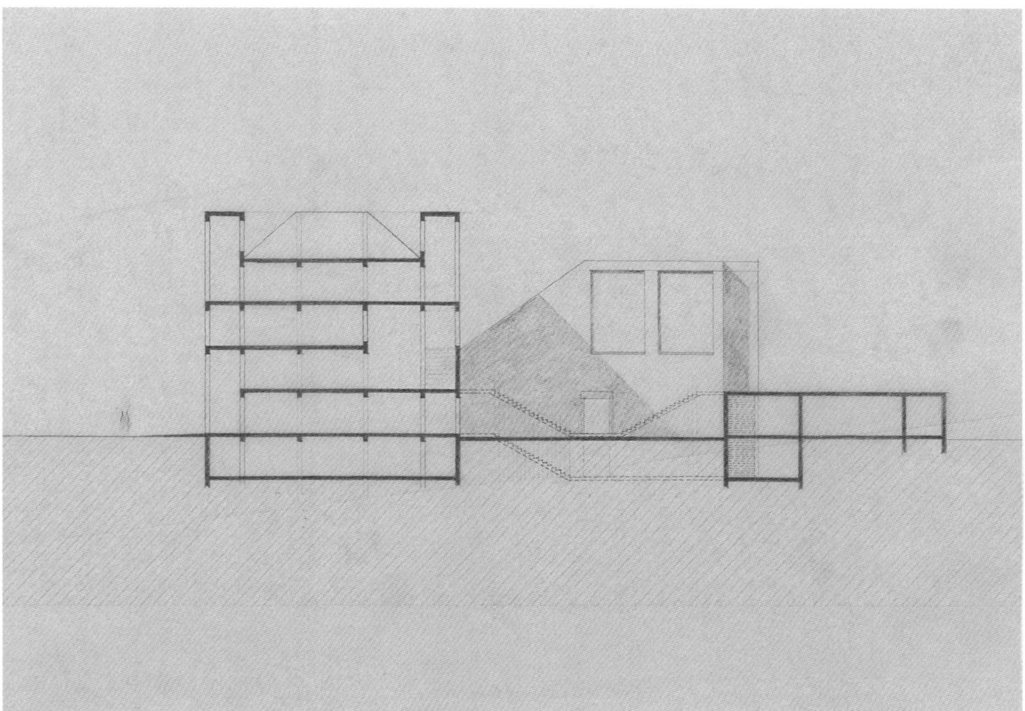

**100** East elevation, August 5, 1968

EAST ELEVATION
AUG 5-68

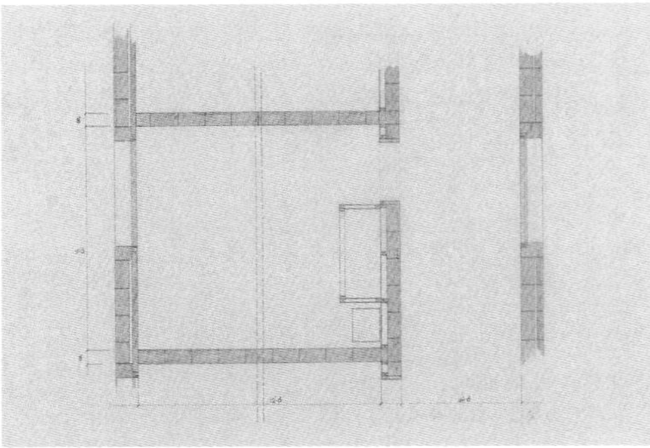

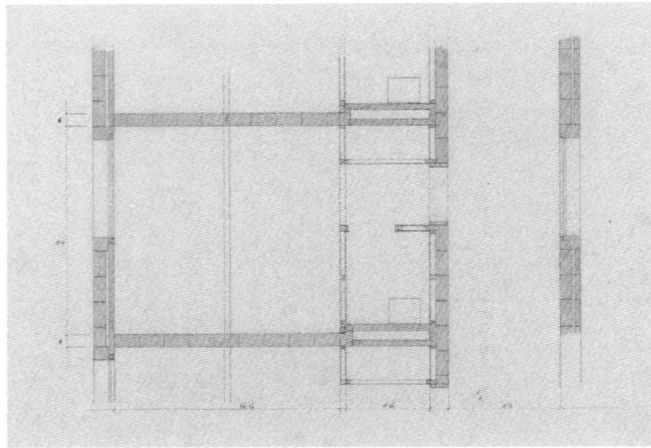

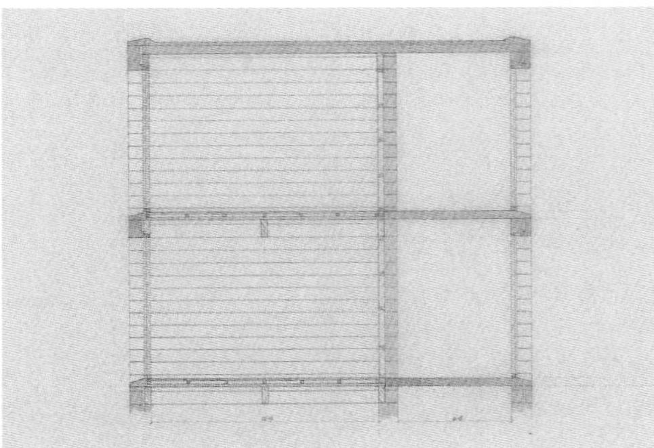

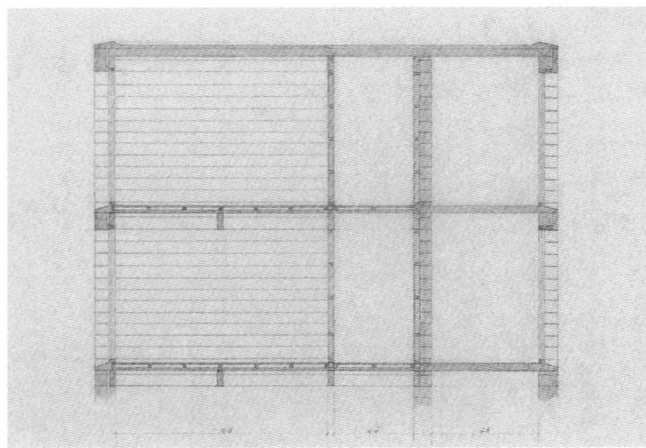

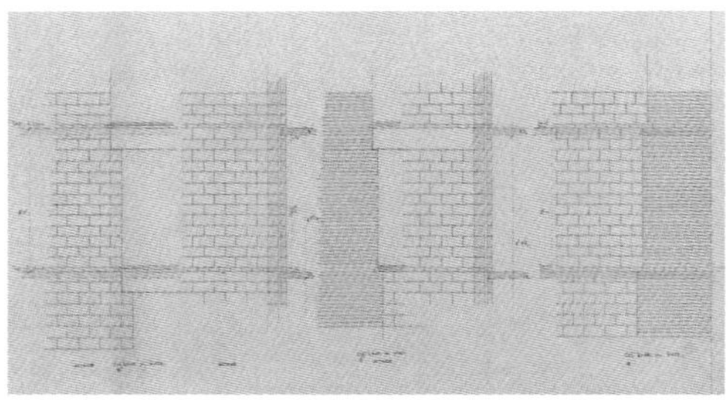

**101** Small cell: plan, October 23, 1968
**102** Large cell: plan, October 23, 1968
**103** Small cell: section, October 23, 1968
**104** Large cell: section, October 23, 1968
**105** Cells: partial elevation, Summer 1968
**106** Core buildings: wall details, Summer/Fall 1968
**107** Cells: horizontal sections, Summer/Fall 1968

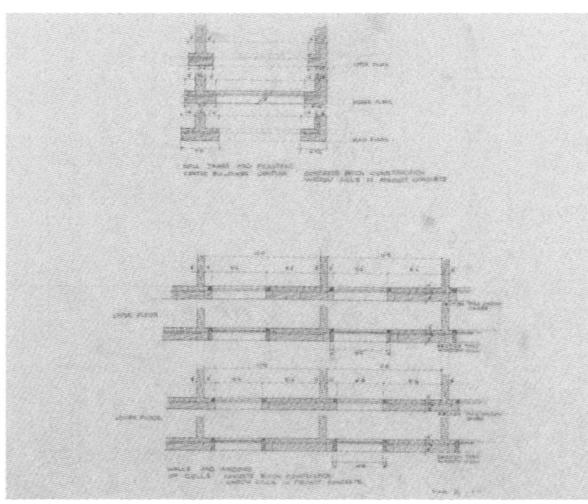

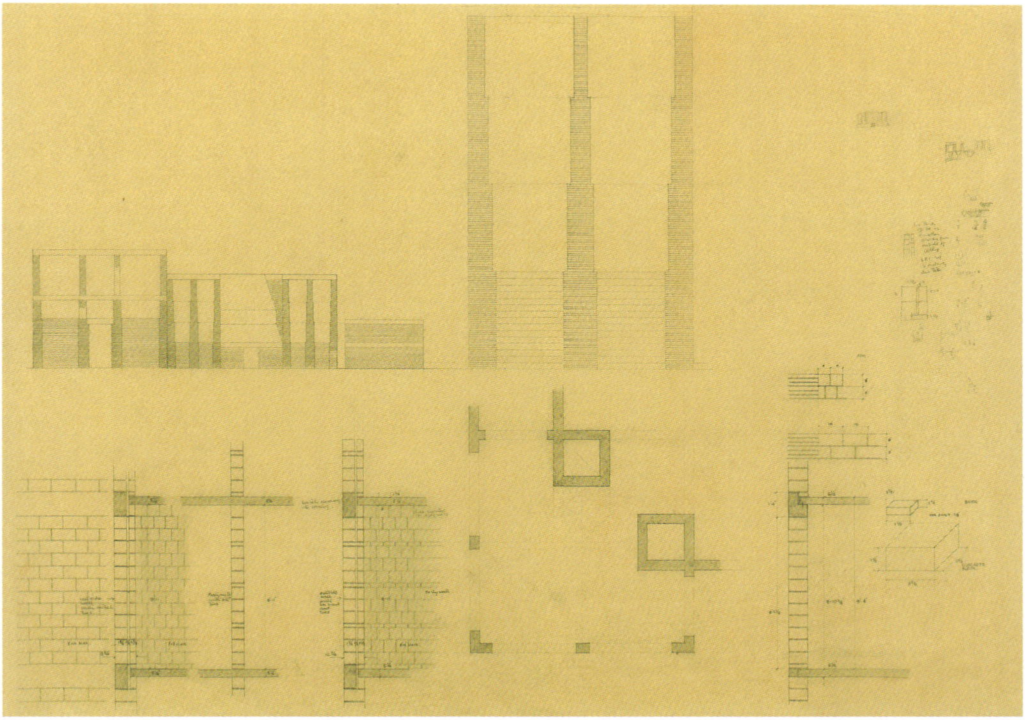

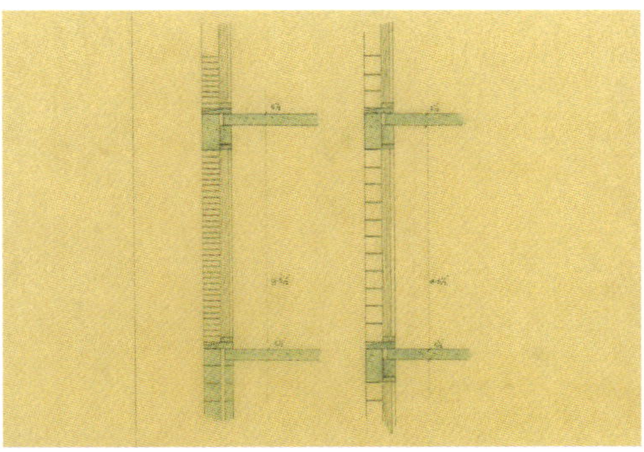

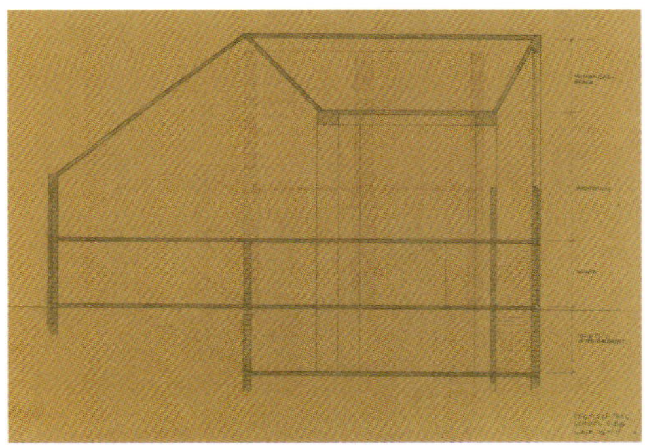

**108** Core buildings: wall details, Summer/Fall 1968
**109** Wall sections, Summer/Fall 1968
**110** School/auditorium: section, Summer/Fall 1968

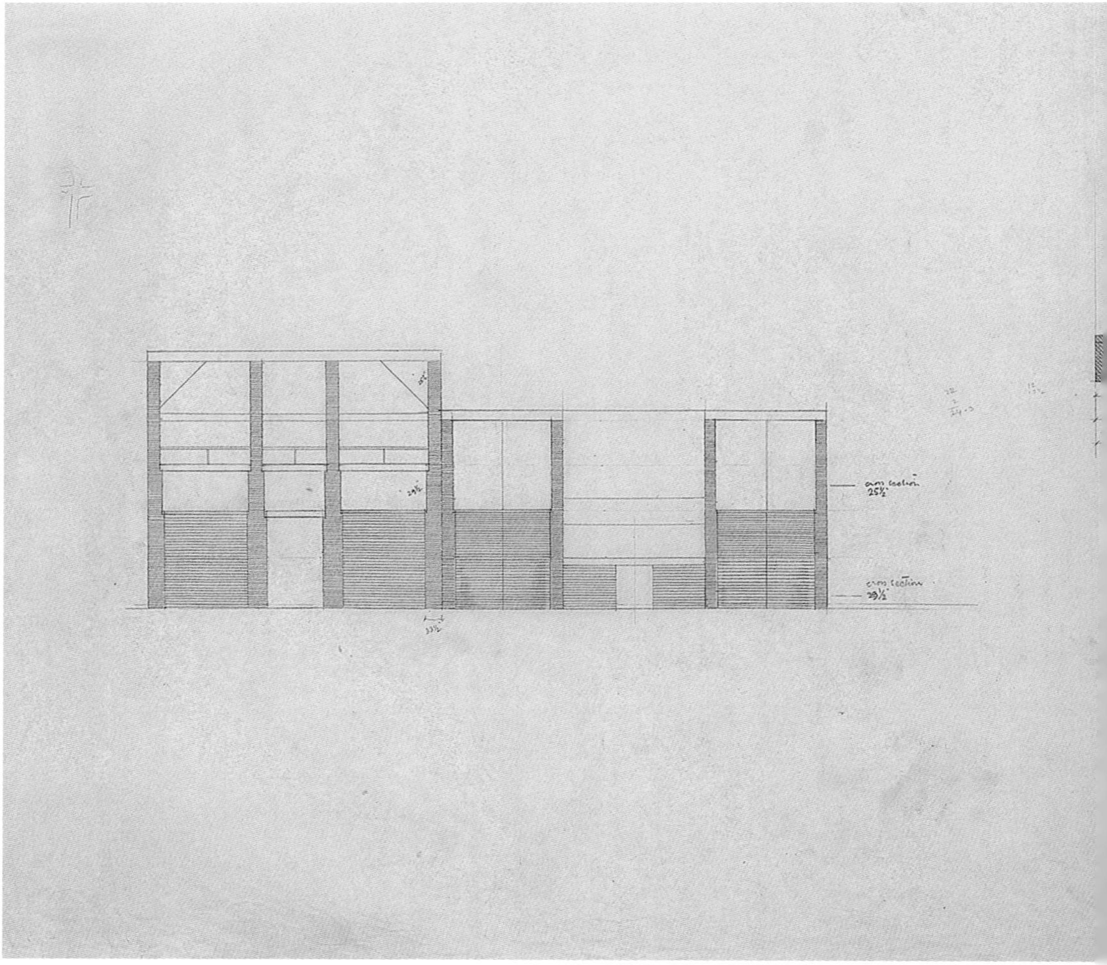

**111** Core buildings: wall details, Summer/Fall 1968

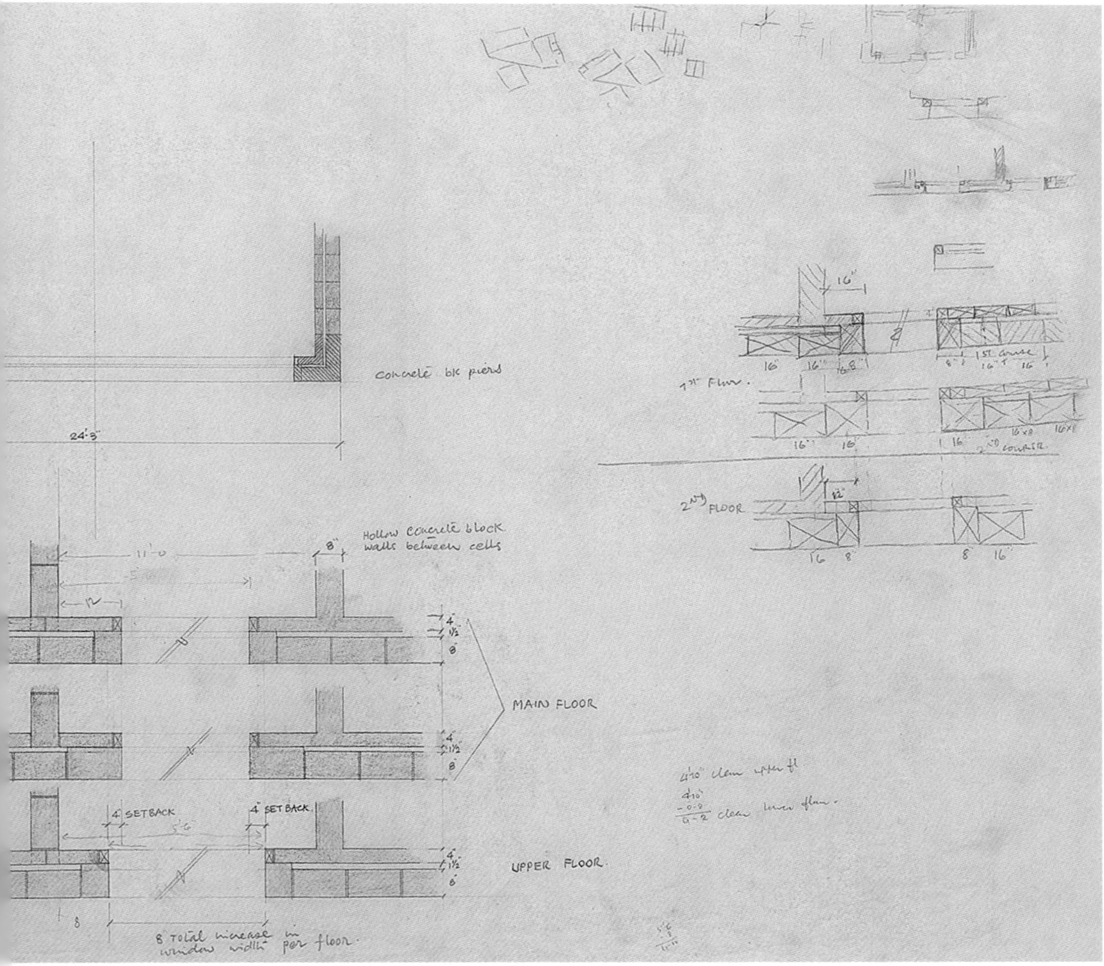
concrete blk piers
24'-3"
Hollow concrete block
walls between cells
MAIN FLOOR
4" SETBACK
4" SETBACK
UPPER FLOOR
8 total increase in
window width per floor.
1st Floor.
2nd FLOOR
1st course
2nd course

**112** Chapel: section, Summer/ Fall 1968

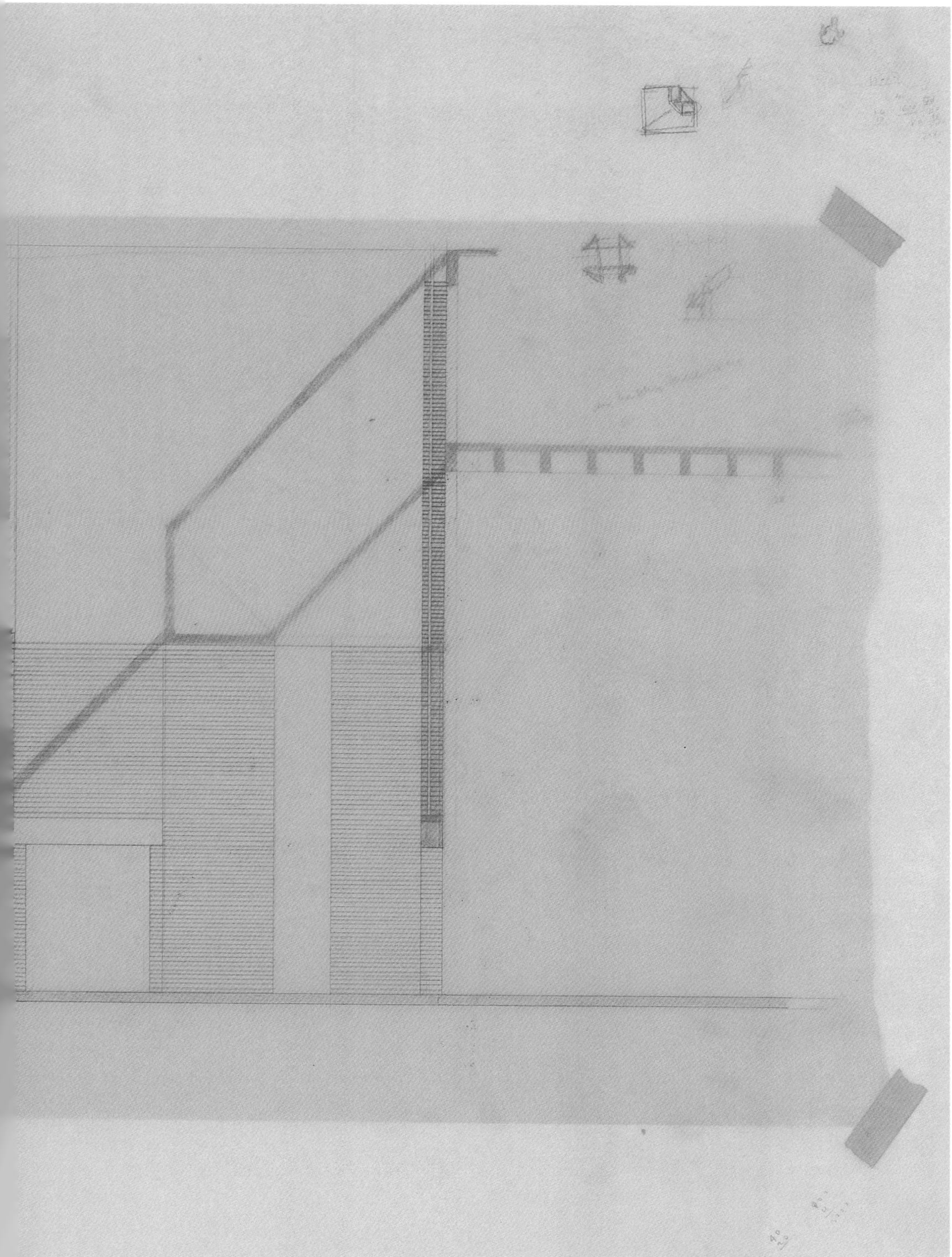

and thus the refectory and extra bedrooms. The vision of monastic life which had lead the sisters to seek out Kahn in 1965, had by 1969 slowly but surely lost its consensus within the congregation. On March 10, 1969, the congregation's general councilors and building committee, faced with the decision of proceeding to build the final scheme, voted unanimously to stop all work on the project, giving their main reasons as "cost and the constant flux of our way of life at this particular time."[112] These were the late sixties, that volatile and expansive time in which, as Kahn himself had often repeated, "All of our institutions are on trial." This meant the religious institutions as well. He could not have been anything but extremely disappointed, though, when he received the following letter, dated March 18, 1969, from Mother Emmanuel's successor as Prioress General, Mother Mary Bernadette:[113]

*Dear Mr. Kahn,*

*It is my unpleasant duty to advise you that after much soul-searching and discussion we have decided to discontinue the plans for a new Motherhouse. The reasons are many and forceful. Aside from the money, which is, of course, a very real factor, we face at the moment constantly changing attitudes toward the manner and setting of religious life which opens up distinct forms this life is taking and will continue to take in the future.*

*In these days of re-evaluation, re-newal and re-study, we feel that the complex of buildings we originally envisioned would dictate decisions on our form of life rather than permit us to vary our life to fulfill our vocation amid the needs of today. We are in unanimous agreement that we cannot proceed with the original plans at this time.*

*For the present we have decided to provide for our aging Sisters at one of our other Convents. At Media we shall make some renovations to meet immediate needs.*

*I do not wish to imply that we are merely delaying our project for a year or two. For your sake as well as our own we feel it best to conclude our mutual agreement now. Will you please have sent to us a statement of fees we still owe? At the same time we would appreciate having whatever models or plans are available.*

*It has been an enriching experience and great pleasure to have been associated with you and your staff in this venture. We have all enjoyed and profited from it. Our sincere appreciation for your understanding, patience, and wisdom.*

*Sincerely,*
*Mother Mary Bernadette, O.P.*
*Prioress General*

Sadly, this would be the last project communiqué between the convent and Kahn. Sister Mary Irene Lolli, secretary of the building committee, and Sister Eileen Patricia Primrose, member of the congregation's general councilors, vividly recalled years later how much the sisters regretted having to end their inspiring and friendly relationship with Kahn.[114]

Aside from a minor remodeling of the existing house and the addition of a small chapel in order to adapt it to their own use, the sisters would never build at Media, and the hillock they called Daffodil Hill would remain untouched over the next decades. The older sisters moved shortly after the termination of the Motherhouse project to the newly remodeled St. Catherine's Hall, a former utility building at the Elkins Park retreat, to be followed by the rest of the congregation in 1989, at which time the house and property at Media were sold for use as a private residence.[115] In the turn-of-the-century real estate boom, both the hill and the rest of the property at Media were sold again, this time to be subdivided for high-end speculative houses, unceremoniously occupying the site and closing the door on a plan which had been the source of so many rich thoughts and hopes.

### A Tenuous Resolution, Open Ends

*For all its beauty, a distinct concept always means a shrinkage of meaning, cutting off loose ends. While the loose ends are what matter most in the phenomenal world, for they interweave.* Joseph Brodsky, "Less Than One," 1986

If Kahn has led us over the past months on the long way from gesture to plan, through dissonance to resolution, it is a tenuous resolution he has found, spring-tight and seemingly waiting to further unfold. In spite of the "finished" and detailed plans, it is impossible to say how the Dominican Motherhouse would have finally appeared and found its place in the lives of the sisters had it been built. Not everything had been decided; certainly there would have been late changes during the planning, there always were, sometimes decisive and indeed often welcomed by Kahn: "When you have all the answers to a building before you start building it, your answers are not true. The building gives you answers as it grows and becomes itself."[116] If the project remains one

112 Meeting minutes of the general councilors and building committee with Mother Mary Bernadette, March 10, 1969, project folder, Archive of the Dominican Motherhouse.

113 Letter, Mother Mary Bernadette to Louis Kahn, March 18, 1969, Box LIK 10, Kahn Collection.

114 Interview with Sisters Mary Irene Lolli, O.P., and Eileen Patricia Primrose, O.P., April 15, 2006.

115 Sales information, Dominican Motherhouse archive, Elkins Park, PA, site visit by author, April 16, 2006.

116 Kahn, quoted in Johnson, *Light is the Theme,* p. 53. Among the more important "answers" which Kahn's buildings gave him during their construction include: the final state of the famous plaza at the Salk Institute, the last minute substitution of travertine for slate in that project, and the construction of the central roof of the National Assembly at Dhaka.

of Kahn's most enigmatic and compelling "uncompleted things," it is not only for its exemplary illustration of principle, but due to its combination of precise intention and "loose ends" which have been left to intertwine in our imaginations with different threads of the phenomenal world.

## SECTION II
## ON THE NATURE OF SPACE, 1940–1974

### PRELUDE TO A PARADIGM
### KAHN, THE ROOM, AND THE BEGINNING OF ARCHITECTURE

*If architecture can be understood as the construction of boundaries in space, this space must be understood as commonsense space, a space that possesses meanings and speaks to us long before the architect goes to work. The architect can, to be sure, build in a way that does not heed these meanings, indeed that self-consciously denies them. He or she can also be open to them, re-presenting and thus revealing them.* Karsten Harries, *The Ethical Function of Architecture*, 1997

*The room is the beginning of architecture. It is the place of the mind. You in the room with its dimensions, its structure, its light respond to its character, its spiritual aura, recognizing that whatever the human proposes and makes becomes a life.* Louis Kahn, "The Room, the Street, and Human Agreement," 1971

Having completed the lengthy journey of Kahn's project, the foresighted reader will ask: what—beyond the impressions, insights, and points of view along the way—might be the further relevance of this excursion? If an implicit promise of such a narrative is that the small will shed light on the large, what larger themes might be illuminated here? A work as multifaceted as the Dominican Motherhouse lights many paths; the following section is dedicated to the exploration of one which, considering the foregoing text, the existing literature on Kahn, and the current architectural context, I hold to be the most promising.

**Design as methodical accumulation**

After following the architects' acts of ordering and arranging in scores of pensive and self-forgotten drawings, one may begin to feel strangely intimate with their thoughts, and thus qualified (or at least uninhibited enough) to assert that their work has been first and foremost concerned with two basic actions: (1) the delimiting of discrete spaces, and (2) the positioning of those spaces in relation to each other and to a greater natural space of which they are a part. With evidence gleaned from Kahn's texts, one may additionally and with a certain confidence submit that the primary goal of the Dominican

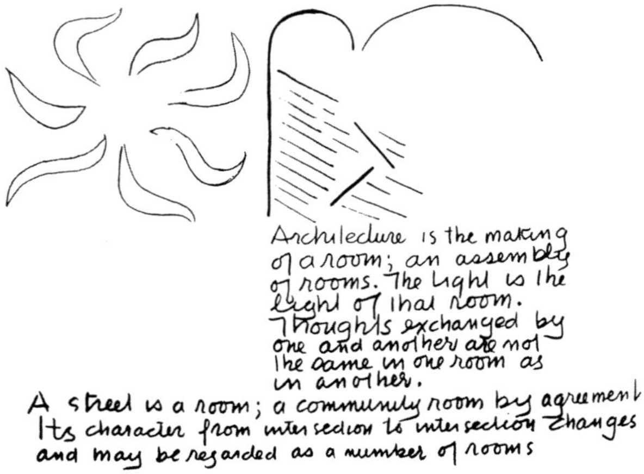


**113** Drawing from the series "Silence and Light," 1970, Louis Kahn

Motherhouse had been the creation of *dwelling* in a very primary sense of the word; that is, in the situating of its inhabitants in an ordered and comprehensible spatial continuum—ordered, that is, in respect to the natural and social worlds of which they are parts.

These conclusions may seem rather banal (doesn't, after all, all architecture do this?), and of course in moving forward the architects have always spun multiple threads of reality simultaneously, accomplishing more than "just" this delimiting and ordering. But as the drawings have amply shown, themes such as technology and methods of construction have played only supporting roles in their work, as has any overt maneuvering in the realms of semiotics, symbolism, or historicism. The willful primitivism of the architects' method seems to deny any great claims to modernism's rationalist methodologies, whether in their materialist or behaviorist forms. The project has come to life less through any sweeping expressionist gesture or illustration of "big theory," and more through its purposefully limited and elementary architectural means of accumulating a linked multitude of sensations and meanings. What is compelling is the contrast between the simplicity of the project's means and the richness of its spaces—a whole has grown which is much greater than the sum of its parts. This "accumulative essentialism" has directed our attention over the length of the project toward those fundamental architectural acts of enclosing, opening, finding distance; in short, to architecture as an *art of delimiting and configuring spaces.* For here—and not elsewhere—I would propose is where *this* project draws its greatest power.[117]

117 Once again, perhaps a banal conclusion: a quick survey reveals how rare are those projects that place the implications of the configurative act so fundamentally at their center.

It would be difficult to defend the Dominican Motherhouse as one of Kahn's "greatest" works: in terms of elegance, this is probably the Kimbell Art Museum; in terms of representing the most comprehensive embodiment of ideas—social, technological, constructive, contextual—perhaps the Salk Institute; in terms of architecture as a humanist endeavor, Sher-e-Bangla Nagar, the capital of Bangladesh. What the Dominican Motherhouse *does* embody is a fundamental expression of *intent* and *method;* among Kahn's projects it is arguably the most literal and provocative consequence of his (deceptively) simple claim that "Architecture begins with the making of a room,"[118] a claim which, when explored in all the consequences Kahn intended, leads decidedly away from conventional modernist conceptions of space and toward those "Beginnings" where fundamental sources of spatial meaning are made available through originary acts of making. Having followed this essentialism at work over the previous chapter, we may use that which we have seen as a lens to review Kahn's mature oeuvre, and that oeuvre in turn as a mirror for the modern and contemporary discourse. This, I suggest, is one of the strongest "gravitational forces" drawing us toward the Dominican Motherhouse.

### Kahn in the 1950s: Setting a Spatial Agenda

It would be both tedious and beyond the scope of this book to trace the rise of modern architecture's guiding paradigm of space in the nineteenth and early twentieth centuries.[119] It must suffice then, at the risk of oversimplification, to reiterate how much that "New Vision" of space (as propagated by Giedion, Moholy-Nagy, Gropius, et al.) has, in fact, been a manifestation of a paradigm informed by Newton, Descartes, and the not-entirely-new atomism of Plato: a notion of space as a neutral and absolute background for the objects which inhabit it.[120] It was—among other things—this (mis)understanding of architectural space as neutral and ethereal, rather than as charged and resonant with meaning, that began to draw heavy critique from all sides as modern architecture hit its stride in the fifties.[121] Although he was one of the most accomplished advocates of many of modernism's core tenets, it is no accident that Kahn's ascendance coincided

118 Kahn, "The Room, the Street," p. 263.

119 For a relatively compact and incomplete introduction to the evolution of modern paradigms of space in architecture, see Mallgrave and Ikonomou, *Empathy, Form, and Space;* Forty, *Words and Buildings,* pp. 254–75; van de Ven, *Space in Architecture;* and Ockman, *Architecture Culture.*

120 On Plato's concept of space and Newton's concept of space, see "Space Perception," *Encyclopaedia Britannica Online,* http://www.britannica.com/EBchecked/topic/557415/space-perception (accessed May 19, 2010).

121 The critique came from, among other sources, philosophy (Heidegger, Merleau-Ponty), political theory (Hannah Arendt), economics/urbanism (Jane Jacobs), landscape studies (John Brinckerhoff Jackson), and even architecture itself (Aldo van Eyck).

with modernism's great crisis, representing, as his work increasingly did, those qualities of space that mainstream modernism had so assiduously purged from its program.

Kahn, by no means a facile designer, needed to verbally come to terms with the "what" of architecture before the "how" of his mature work was to unfold. After two decades as a journeyman modernist, he began in the fifties to formulate his first original statements on architecture: defining and refining, among other things, a "spatial agenda"; attempting to talk his way out of modernism's dead ends while steering clear of its already worn jargon. His texts (a large part culled from lectures and interviews) are often the thinking aloud of a man searching: his ruminative, repetitive, self-invented language ranged from rather sensible down-to-earth dictums to rhapsodic drifts into the esoteric stratosphere. Kahn's prose has long posed a problem for his interpreters. Though timely in its reintroduction of long-neglected themes and refreshingly welcome in its reopening of the gates of wonder to a profession-gone-stale on pragmatism and opportunism, Kahn's late-life tendency to drift into obtuse and self-indulgent metaphysics can try even the staunchest of his followers.[122] While many would prefer to dismiss Kahn's pronouncements and quickly proceed to concentrate on the built work, the serious student is advised to bear with him, for a confrontation with Kahn's verbal oeuvre is essential to understanding how his best architecture came to be. Indeed, a longer look reveals Kahn to be a case study in how verbal insight might precede architectural resolution.[123]

### Nature of Space, Form, Type: Representational and Non-Representational Meaning

**"Nature of Space," "Order," "Design"**

Kahn's first verbal installation of space at the center of his agenda seems to have occurred in the early fifties. In 1953, dissatisfied with the manner by which his students would move precipitously from a shallow analysis of the program (and perhaps of some mildly historical precedents) to the design phase, Kahn proposed a threefold process of creation that began not with an analysis of "function," construction, or precedents, but rather with a reflection on what he provisionally called the "nature of space."[124] After having conjectured a viable

122 On the one hand, it may seem nitpicking to find fault with a man who reinstalled "wonder," "joy," "rapport," "desire," "discovery," "commonality," "in-touchness," and "inspiration" into the arid postwar form-follows-function vocabulary; on the other hand, koans such as "What is the shadow of white light?" do tend, for most of us, to be simply too much incense. Whether by leading to rejection or to that strange cultism reserved for gurus, Kahn's utterances do indeed often stand between us and his actual work.

123 See Kohane's "Louis I. Kahn's Search for Form" for an extended study of how word preceded deed in Kahn's architecture.

124 Tyng, *Louis I. Kahn to Anne Tyng*, pp. 79, 211–12.

"nature of space" for a given institution, the student proceeded with the search for a principle of "order," and tested these against the circumstances of "design." This "nature of space" would later become "Form" in Kahn's "Form-Design" dyad.

In asking his students to begin their work by questioning the "nature of space" or "Form" of an institution, Kahn was asking them to visualize the fundamental spatial quality (or configuration) which best represented that institution. Kahn's "Form" was, then, akin to Quatremère de Quincy's 1825 definition of "type": the search neither for a one-to-one fit with "program," nor for a specific "model" as the spatial basis of architectural form, but rather for something fundamental and irreducible, a germ or starting point which is at once powerful enough to drive the design and to invest it with cultural meaning, and at the same time something "vague and uncertain" enough to invite invention and change.[125]

Like Quatremère's type, an important part of Kahn's quest for "Form" is the search for an iconic or "message" value as the basis for the design, one that transcends mere function or material necessity:

"What was true of primitive man in all the ramifications of his practical and emotional life—namely, the need to represent the phenomenal world in a way that it becomes a coherent and logical system—persists in our own organizations and more particularly in our attitudes toward the man-made objects of the environment. An example of the way this applies to contemporary man is in the creation of what are called socio-spatial schemata. Our senses of place and relationship in, say, an urban environment or a building, are not dependent on any objective fact that is measurable; they are phenomenal. The purpose of the aesthetic organization of our environment is to capitalize on this subjective schematization and make it socially available. The resulting organization does not correspond in a one-to-one relationship with the objective facts but is an artificial construct which *represents* these facts in a socially recognizable way. It follows that the representational systems which are developed are, in a real sense, independent of the quantifiable facts of the environment, and this is particularly true if the environment is changing very rapidly. However, no system of representation, no metalanguage, is totally independent of the facts which constitute the objective world."[126]

125 De Quincy, *Dictionnaire Historique de l'Architecture.*

126 Colquhoun, "Typology and Design Method," pp. 43–50.

While in pre-modern vernacular and classical traditions, consensual answers to the questions of reproducing socio-spatial schemata tended to be "at hand," the moderns chose or were driven by circumstance to replace the subject of representation with the less resonant themes of technology, scientific metaphor, or "function." Kahn, like many others in the decades after World War II, began to question this move. Where Kahn's analysis of space goes further than both his "functionalist" predecessors (Meyer, Gropius, etc.) and his "typologist" successors (Rossi, Aymonino, Venturi, etc.), is in its attempt to both represent and to transcend representation; in its recognition that whatever great power representation may hold, architecture is not only a substitute for something which is not there, but a non-representational embodiment of a present tense which itself creates—a staging for life, action, and change. Kahn's budding holism, by starting with a metaphorical search for what he called "Beginnings" or "Volume Zero," sought to tap into the phenomenal/ontological/spiritual bases of architectural space before addressing its more circumstantial foundations. Much as Heidegger argued that modernism's fragmentation of knowledge was undertaken at the cost of understanding the wholeness of Being, Kahn argued that an architecture which limited its sources to its particular and immediate circumstances could never address the general reasons for its own existence.[127]

### Questions of Space

Kahn continued to refine his spatial agenda from the early fifties onward. Instructively, he used the word "space" rather sparsely in his texts, and when he did, most often in its concrete form: "a space," or "a room." But if he avoided that term in the abstract, his texts were often most concretely about space and spatiality. The crux of his critique of modernist space is couched in his well-known aphorisms, a number of them addressing specific elementary "questions of space"—perceptual, morphological, social, etc. When, for example, Kahn began to repeat the simple claim, "Architecture begins with the making of a room," he was explicitly contradicting the universal space of the modernist *plan libre* while reintroducing the ideas of embodied perception and empathy as fundamental measures of architectural space: "Nothing must intrude to blur the statement of how a space is made."[128] Or: "I could no more place one column in one space and another in a separate space than I could sleep with my head

127 While it is possible to view Kahn's work without his metaphysics, in the end this would be, to quote Dan Kiley, like viewing Giotto's without his religion: only half the story.

128 Kahn, "Architecture is the Thoughtful Making of Spaces," p. 271.

in one space and my body in another." [129] At the same time, the paradigm of architecture beginning with the construction of a discrete space sets up the preconditions for redefining the inside-outside morphological play as understood by the modern: "The window wants to be a little room." [130] Or: "Reflect on the great event in architecture as the walls parted and columns became," [131] or: "The plan does not begin nor end with the space which (the architect) has enclosed." [132] Thirdly, a "topological" play results from the corollary idea that a house is "a society of rooms" that "talk with each other and make up their minds where their positions are." [133] Kahn's "society of rooms" plans highlight the social dimensions of space, as did his antidote for the modernist analogy of "circulation": an "architecture of connection." Finally, the making of a discrete space implies the making of border or *temenos,* one that may begin to establish specific *places* and not just "space."

While Kahn's early essays such as "Monumentality" (1944) reveal an enthusiasm for the constructive/material basis of architecture, and in the mid-fifties his attempts to define "order" were mainly in terms of construction, geometry, and spatial hierarchy, by the late fifties "space" in Kahn's texts—and more importantly in his architecture—increasingly addressed phenomenal, social, and emotional or spiritual dimensions: "One quality of space is measured by its temperature by its light by its ring." [134] "A room is a place. A small room is a place where, if you are with one other person, you can be generative. You can say what you never said before. The walls seem to talk with you and give you a sense of what you want to say. The vectors of two meet.... The room is a marvelously sensitive thing." [135]

In brief, the student of architecture who makes the effort to sort out and unravel Kahn's texts, idiosyncratic and unsystematic though they may be, will be rewarded to find that they—when read in light of the work that followed—in fact add up to what is one of the twentieth century's most penetrating analyses of architectural space: profound hypotheses on the origins of its meanings, on how it may be conceived, how it is perceived, and how it may become part of collective experience.

129 Kahn, quoted in Tyng, *Beginnings: Louis I. Kahn's Philosophy of Architecture,* p. 174.

130 Kahn, "The Room, the Street, and Human Agreement," p. 265.

131 Kahn, "Architecture is the Thoughtful Making of Spaces," p. 271.

132 Kahn, "Monumentality," p. 25.

133 Kahn, "I Love Beginnings," p. 155.

134 Kahn, "Architecture is the Thoughtful Making of Spaces," p. 272.

135 Kahn, "I Love Beginnings," p. 157.

The three chapters in this section have taken as their starting points those elementary acts of enclosing, opening, and finding distance which have become so apparent in the Dominican Motherhouse, using them as advances toward Kahn's mature understanding of architectural space and toward an understanding of Kahn's work as a continuous *recherche architecturale.* The first chapter projects outward from the monastery's internal paths to explore the social dimensions of space in Kahn's "architecture of connection"; in the following chapter, the twin phenomena of outside and inside/architectural and natural space—so evident in the monastery's porous plan—are regarded in Kahn's work under the heading of "reciprocity"; while the final chapter explores the relationship between Kahn's discrete spaces and their contexts, or how a general "space" increasingly became a specific "place" in his late work. In exploring these spaces of Kahn's architecture, I have attempted to make explicit pertinent qualities of the work that have tended to remain implicit or to be overshadowed by other themes. In doing so, I hope to have opened some less-trodden inroads into Kahn's thought and work, and, by so doing, to the vital implications of a deceptively simple paradigm of architecture's beginning.

## CONFIGURATION, MOVEMENT, AND SPACE
## FROM "CIRCULATION" TO AN "ARCHITECTURE OF CONNECTION"

*Space is more than a neutral framework for social and cultural forms. It is built into those very forms. Human behavior does not simply happen in space. It has its own spatial forms. Encountering, congregating, avoiding, interacting, dwelling, teaching, eating, conferring are not just activities that happen in space. In themselves they constitute spatial patterns.... One thing is clear, [these activities] are not attributes of individuals, but patterns, or configurations, formed by groups or collections of people. They depend on engineered patterns of co-presence, and indeed co-absence. Very few of the purposes for which we build buildings and environments are not "people configurations" in this sense. We should therefore in principle expect that the relation between people and space, if there is one, will be found at the level of the configuration of space rather than the individual space.* Bill Hillier, *Space is the Machine,* 1996

*"Circulation" has without question been a successful metaphor—indeed, one might say, far too successful. What started as an innocent analogy is now perceived as a fixed category.... So deeply ingrained has this essentially modernist category become that for most of us it requires a positive mental effort to think of architecture without "circulation." When we ask to what we may attribute the success of this particular metaphor, it is clear that it is not due to any exactness of correspondence between the flow of substances around bodies and around buildings. Instead, I suggest, its success is due to two more structural reasons: firstly, it made architecture amenable to scientific method, and secondly it satisfies a wish to see buildings as enclosed, self-contained systems against all evidence to the contrary. It allows people to talk about what is untrue as if it were true....* Adrian Forty, "Spatial Mechanics—Scientific Metaphors," 2000

I begin this chapter with two rather lengthy quotations in reference to that modern paradigm of architectural space sketched out in the introduction to this section. At this paradigm's core has been a culturally dominant, Newtonian-Cartesian understanding of space as a neutral

**114** National Assembly Building, Dhaka, 1962–84: ambulatory

and absolute background against which the properties of objects are defined. To continue Bill Hillier's critique: "This view of space seems to most of us quite natural, no more than an extrapolation of the commonsense. Unfortunately, once we see space in this way, we are doomed not to understand how it plays a role in human affairs. Culturally and socially, space is never simply the inert background of our material existence. It is a key aspect of how societies and cultures are constituted in the real world, and, through this constitution, structured for us as "objective" realities."[136] Building upon the arguments broached in these quotations, and expanding upon the narrative, in the following I will attempt to make an inroad into Kahn's architectural spaces based on the fundamental schism between the modernist idea of "circulation" and Kahn's notion of an "architecture of connection."

**"Circulation"**

Corollary to the modernist notion of buildings as self-contained systems operating in neutral space has been the spread of the biological metaphor of "circulation." According to Adrian Forty, this analogy, relating the movement of people in buildings to fluids in the human body, seems to have gained acceptance from the mid-nineteenth century onward, gradually replacing other, alternative terms for the configuration of buildings in regard to movement such as "distribution," "communication," or "dégagements."[137] In accordance with the positivist spirit of the times, by the early twentieth century this analogy had become such an integral part of the architectural mindset that it had become virtually impossible to separate metaphor and fact. While by the end of the nineteenth century the Ecole des Beaux-Arts had, for example, adopted the term "circulation," it still supplemented this way of regarding human movement with other, non-quantifiable aspects such as cadence, ritual, and decorum.[138] (Charles Garnier's Opéra de Paris—simultaneously a circulation-and-decorum machine—remains the apotheosis of this method.) Soon, though, more literal interpretations of the biological-mechanical analogy began to inform planning at virtually all scales of the built environment: Schütte-Lihotzky's Taylorized kitchens, Alexander Klein's comparative movement analyses of apartment plans, Le Corbusier's "straight path of the modern man," Richard Neutra's "Rush City Reformed"; for much of the twentieth century, the ideal that human movement was something to be streamlined, channeled, and optimized became the norm, overshadowing those other multifarious

136 Hillier, *Space is the Machine;* see also Hillier and Hanson, *The Social Logic of Space.*

137 Forty, "Spatial Mechanics," pp. 86–101. It is important to note that—similar to the term "space"—before the nineteenth century the theme of movement was only rarely addressed in architectural theory, and virtually never as a separate "system."

138 Van Zanten, "Architectural Composition at the Ecole des Beaux-Arts," pp. 111–324.

layers of reality revealed through spatial disposition and the spatiality of movement, be they perceptual, social, aesthetic, or symbolic. The general poverty—as an influential case in point—of Walter Gropius' plans as kinesthetic moments or as "people configurations" may be directly traced to their tendency to rationalize human movement down to its most rudimentary form: the connecting lines of a bubble diagram. (A method canonized and spread in countless manuals and floor-plan atlases, and which—not incidentally—has found favor with building owners and investors, as it tends to keep—non-rentable—circulation space to a minimum.) If architecture was to be made of "circulation," then for many modern architects it was through its expression as a discrete building "system," analogous in both form and function to mechanical systems of pipes and ductwork.[139]

### Defining an "Architecture of Connection"

**A new term, new types**

In what was surely an attempt to free himself from the fetters of that analogy, in the fifties Kahn purged "circulation" from his vocabulary, replacing it with his own, at once more cumbersome and more evocative term: *architecture of connection.*[140] By now he had come to see the architect's first duty being to the institutions he served, and the development of an appropriate means of configuration and movement was integral to his search for "democratic" or "society of rooms" plans for public programs, and to his desire to see cities, streets, and buildings as synergetic, multi-use "forums of availabilities." For Kahn, "It is precisely this architecture of connection which gives the man on the street a sense of the institution."[141] The models most readily at hand—and which he had alternately employed in previous stages of his career—no longer fulfilled his needs: Neo-classicist and Beaux-Arts systems, while perhaps holistically conceived, were in the end "closed works," too rigid in their hierarchies for Kahn's progressive ideals; functionalist systems—based on the metaphor of "circulation"—were too deterministic, too linear to foreground the desired element

139 I speak here, of course, of a general tendency, additionally fueled by a mix of science envy, misunderstood *Sachlichkeit,* and economic necessity. To be sure, there *were* many great exceptions to this rule: among them Le Corbusier is perhaps the most provocative, with his intriguingly "bipolar" models based on a mechanistic *and* aesthetic/experiential view of movement: the *promenade architectural* of Maison La Roche, the double-helix served/servant stair of the Maison Baizeau, the people-moving-and-sorting ramp architecture of the Palace of the Soviets, the snaking viaduct/apartment megastructure of the Plan Orbus for Algiers, etc.... Both functional metaphor and aesthetic experience are driven to their respective extremes so that it is often impossible to judge which of the two is privileged in the equation. Otherwise, among the moderns the members of the "organicist" wing—Wright, Häring, Aalto, Scharoun—were most likely to see beyond an entirely rationalized approach to movement and connection. Especially in Scharoun's works, we sense a flowing between use-spaces that has nothing to do with "circulation" and everything to do with a view of human life that is gregarious, intertwining, and constantly unfolding in its various aspects.

140 Although I have not been able to establish the first date when Kahn used this term in a text, it was firmly installed as a part of his vocabulary by the late fifties.

141 Kahn, "Order Is," p. 58.

of personal choice; and structuralist systems tended to be too diffuse to generate the possibilities for hierarchy and identification for which he was searching. From the late fifties onward, Kahn developed a number of configurational types which come as welcome exceptions in twentieth-century architecture, often transforming or hybridizing existing models, balancing their inherent qualities in dynamic equilibriums between open and closed, provisional and stable, etc. In his attempt to transcend modernist types, Kahn began to reconsider certain elementary pre-modern configurations: the court, the agora, the ambulatory, the hall, the Palladian matrix of rooms; all reappear—compellingly transformed—in his late work.

**Resisting subjugation to program**

What, beyond its name, distinguishes this "architecture of connection" from modernist "circulation"? To begin with, if—in accordance with the credo "form follows function"—orthodox modernists sought to bring spaces together in unambiguous, cause-and-effect relationships, Kahn's new typologies of connection—which tellingly appear in his designs only after his change of vocabulary—are marked by their multivalence and their foregrounding of personal choice, by their loose fit to program.[142] While modernist doctrine tended to rationalize "circulation" space down to a tightly-tailored (even Taylorized) minimum, thus binding it tightly to its program, Kahn began to see "circulation" as worthy of as much consideration as the programmed spaces themselves: a virtually separate and equal "architecture of connection," which, in its independence, resisted complete subjugation to program. Concretely, this meant a preference for "open" means of distribution; for redundancy rather than tight fit; and for courts, loops, rings, and matrices in plan: all in contrast to the linear and branched systems preferred by the moderns.[143]

**Generosity**

Corollary to the loose fit of Kahn's "architecture of connection" is often a generosity toward an unspecified end, a sense, as in nature, old towns, or vernacular building types, that the number of possibilities for use will exceed those demanded by the inhabitants.[144] Seemingly serendipitous "found spaces" abound in Kahn's movement architecture, as if generated offhand by the space-defining structure: the great porches at the Kimbell Art Museum, the human-scaled loggias of the Salk Institute, the matrix of in-betweens at the Indian

142 What is meant here is a certain form-function independence: the "robust" capacity of buildings to exist in time, regardless of its demands on them. Aldo Rossi's description of Padua's Palazzo della Ragione in his *L'architettura della citta* of 1963 is a famous case in point, another being the *Berliner Wohnung* ("Berlin Flat"), with its neutral rooms and multiple points of access allowing for most various lifestyles and uses over the generations of their habitation.

143 For a well-known critique of this metaphor of "circulation" on an urban scale, see Alexander, "A City is Not a Tree," pp. 379–88.

144 See Benedikt's "On Adding to the Salk," or his *For an Architecture of Reality,* for an eloquent reading of Kahn's "emptiness with intention."

Institute of Management, or the oversized "playground stair" of the Korman House. These spaces serve no particular need, as need is defined by the program; they seem to exist, rather, to express the fulfillment of some undefined potential, some as yet unspoken desire. Said Kahn about the Kimbell Museum, "You know what's so wonderful about those porches? They're so unnecessary."[145] Or, on the generosity of a school: "In school as a realm of spaces where it is good to learn, the lobby measured by the institute as so many square feet per student would become a generous Pantheon-like space where it is good to enter. The corridors would be transferred into classrooms belonging to the students themselves by making them much wider and provided with alcoves overlooking the gardens. They would become places where boy meets girl, where the student discusses the work of a professor with his fellow student. By allowing classroom time to these spaces instead of passage time from class to class, it would become a meeting connection and not merely a corridor, which means a place of possibilities in self-learning."[146]

And indeed, it is often difficult to tell where the emphases of Kahn's buildings actually lie: in the programmed spaces awaiting their users, or in those unprogrammed spaces users discover on the way to those facilities. Non-programmed Flow-space and programmed Use-space become form and counterform engaged in fluctuating figure-ground ambivalence. It is the very non-programmed, non-instrumental character of these spaces—in contrast to the necessarily specific, programmed ones—which reveals their potential as true "spaces of appearance," in the sense of Hannah Arendt.[147]

While the terms "loose fit" and "generosity" tend to evoke images of inflated schemes, with Kahn design was not simply a case of "bigger is better," and it is hard to find anything flabby or uncontrolled in his best plans. To his oeuvre belong both those projects in which budget, site, and program called for or allowed ample and wide-ranging "architectures of connection" (the Salk Institute, the National Assembly at Dhaka, the Indian Institute of Management, etc.), as well as those with dense and economical plans (the Dominican Motherhouse, Erdman Hall, the Phillips Exeter Library, etc.). We ourselves have watched the Dominican Motherhouse cover the entire spectrum between the ultra-generous and the compact, and ultimately realize its unique character in the process.

145 Kahn, quoted in Johnson, *Light is the Theme,* p. 28.

146 Kahn, "Form and Design," p. 114.

147 "Action requires a space of appearance.... It is the space of appearance in the widest sense of the word, namely, the space where I appear to others as they appear to me, where men exist not merely like other living or inanimate things but make their appearance explicitly." See Arendt, *The Human Condition,* p. 199.

"Spacing" and Gestalt, proximity and distance

Beyond issues of absolute size and economy, it's important to understand that for Kahn, together with the imperative of choice, the most important measure of configuration was in the *meted spacing* between uses. He observed: "The spaces speak to each other and make up their minds where they want to be."[148] And furthermore: "Buildings (rooms) must be like a good position on the chessboard. For its symbolic value no building (room) must be in the wrong place."[149] Akin to the duration between musical notes, the in-between "duration" of the spaces connecting various uses is as relevant as the shapes of the discrete programmed spaces themselves.

It is this relative positioning of uses within the plan which Kahn employs as a primary means for interpreting the institution in question. On the one hand, this positioning establishes a spatial structure for interhuman relationships Hillier has called "engineered patterns of co-presence and co-absence."[150] On the other hand, as important as these factual/possible relationships established between people through spaces, are the *felt* synergies, *implied* magnetisms, the *suggested* powers of attraction or repulsion; the knowledge that each seemingly discrete space is in reality a *partial* space, first realizing its fullness through its relationships with others. In this sense, Christian Devillers' hypothesis, "For Kahn, space equals spacing,"[151] is an insightful one.

### Developing an "Architecture of Connection": 1949–1974

Kahn's path from "circulation" to an "architecture of connection" was more evolutionary than revolutionary in nature: for decades he worked his way through both modernist and Beaux-Arts models before finally finding a mature expression. The Y-plan Philadelphia Psychiatric Hospital (1948–54) **Fig. 115**, for example, with its single and double-loaded corridors, is still a conventional modernist trope; the final project for the Trenton Jewish Community Center (1954–59) **Fig. 116** revives quite literally the Beaux-Arts tartan grid, with Guadet's differentiation between *surfaces utiles* and *circulations;* while the Richards Medical Laboratories (1957–64) **Fig. 117** delves into then-fashionable structuralist linkage. This probing continued at all scales of the built environment. At the scale of the house, the Weiss Residence (1947–50) **Fig. 118**, still a zoned, Breueresque modern type, was succeeded ten years later by the Fleischer House's flirtation with a "Palladian" room matrix and the Goldenberg House's almost antique ambulatory. **Figs. 139, 119**

148 Kahn, quoted in Wurman, *What Will Be Has Always Been,* p. 133.

149 Kahn, Telegram to K. Ahmad, January 22, 1961, Box LIK 117, Kahn Collection.

150 Hillier, *Space is the Machine,* p. 44.

151 Devillers, "Louis Kahn's Indian Institute of Management," pp. 36–63.

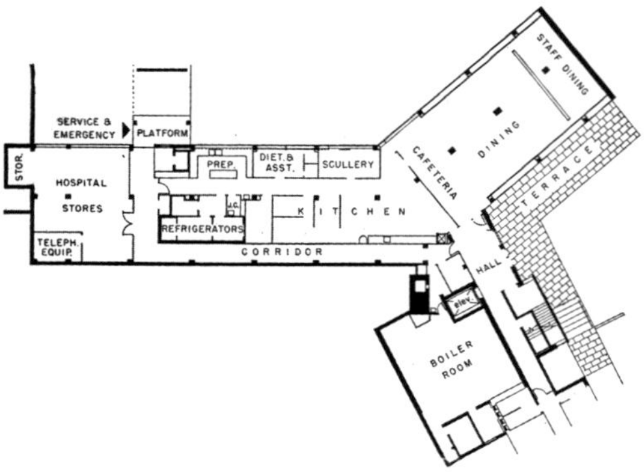


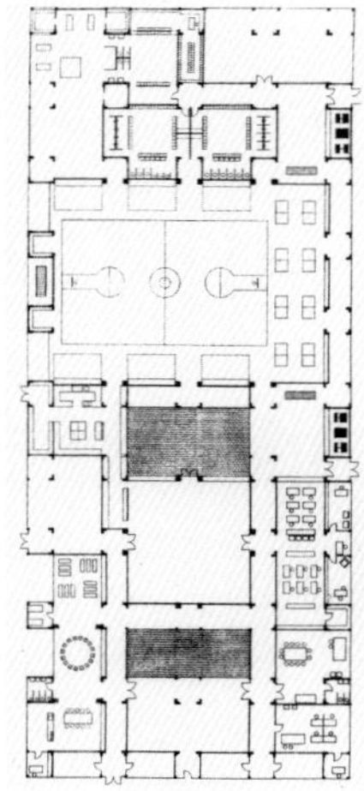

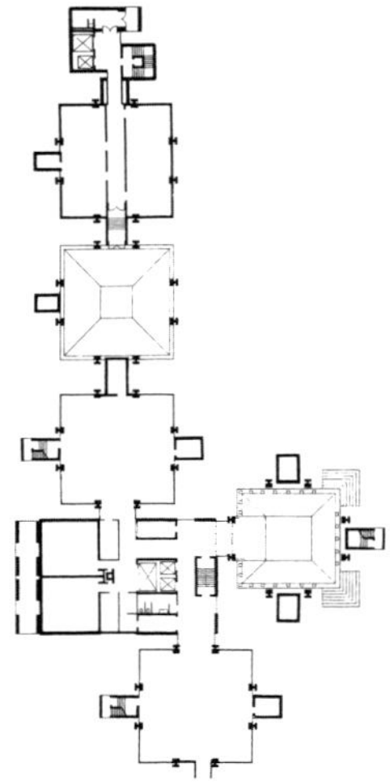

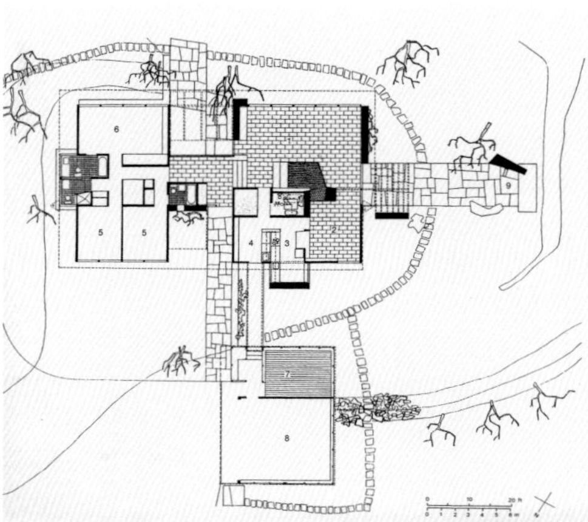

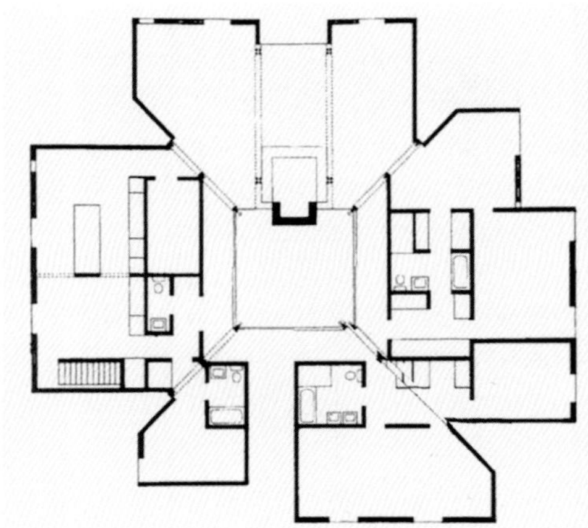

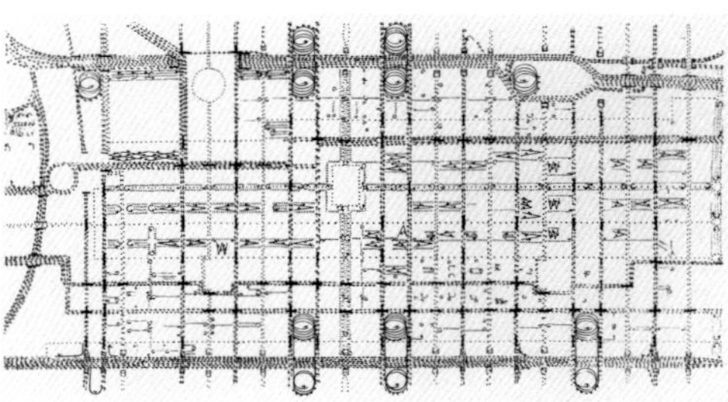

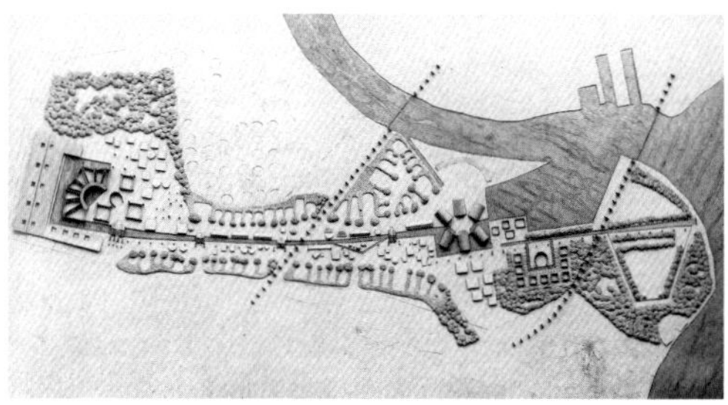

**115** Philadelphia Psychiatric Hospital, 1948–54
**116** Trenton Jewish Community Center, 1954–59
**117** Richards Medical Research Laboratories, 1957–64
**118** Weiss House, 1947–50
**119** Goldenberg House, 1959
**120** Philadelphia Traffic Study, 1953
**121** Philadelphia Bicentennial Plan, 1971

While at the scale of the city, Kahn's traffic studies and public housing projects for Philadelphia of 1948–53 **Fig. 120** still relied heavily on the modernist "circulation" metaphor, with branched and cul-de-sac plans, analogies with "rivers," "docks," "harbors," etc. By his later career he was apt to emphasize neutrality and choice over subdivision and hierarchy in urban plans such as the gridded scheme for Abbas-Abad in Iran (1973–74) or the "forum of availabilities" for the Bicentennial Exposition in Philadelphia (1973). **Fig. 121**

In order to begin to understand the spaces of Kahn's "architecture of connection," a selected group of projects are briefly outlined below.

**The Salk Institute**

The Salk Institute for Biological Studies (1959–65) **Figs. 122–125** was Kahn's first mature expression of an "architecture of connection" in a large public building. The building's parti projects a strong image of how Kahn saw the institution: a community of individual researchers dedicated toward a common goal—biological research in the service of mankind (and in the spirit of the Institute's founder, Jonas Salk, the developer of the first vaccine for polio). The closed, excluding, and enclosing exterior façades; the open, porous, and human-scaled interior façades; the scientists' small private studies craning toward the ocean and the larger research groups' laboratories behind them; the great central plaza shared by all; the series of concentric layers, of surfaces open and closed, the linked chains of proximities and distances: all these phenomena are skillfully orchestrated to contribute to and imply a finely-tuned yet open dialogue between individual and community, public and private—a dialogue which finds expression at virtually all scales. The project's consistent development of this expression has led Sarah Williams Goldhagen to see in the Salk Institute Kahn's desire to create a socially transformative architecture a monumental proposal for "a society in which people's pursuit of personal satisfaction did not overwhelm their capacity to participate in their community."[152]

The connective architecture of this porous environment consists of a total of twenty staircases and fourteen elevators, linked by balconies and loggia and arranged around a plaza, which is thus navigable in countless combinations. In contrast to the modernist practice of efficiency, here *redundancy* is seen as a virtue. The plan, which might superficially suggest a centralized baroque or classical scheme, is purposefully left open at both ends, linking ocean and land while refusing to define a single main entry or a branched hierarchy of movement.[153] Arriving by car (this is California), the visitor is left alone to find the

152 Williams Goldhagen, *Louis Kahn's Situated Modernism*, p. 4.

153 The addition to the Salk Institute by Anshen and Allen in 1995, having "completed" the eastern end of the central axis, thus creating a neo-baroque parti, has severely altered the spatial intention of Kahn's purposefully open-ended fragment. For a critique of the addition, see Venturi and Scott Brown, "Genius Betrayed," p. 43.

**122–24** Salk Institute for Biological Studies, 1959–65: site plan, floor plan, section
**125** Salk Institute Meeting House, 1959–65: floor plan

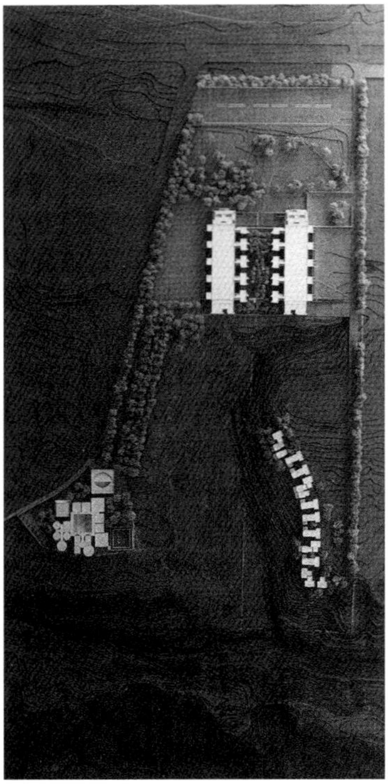

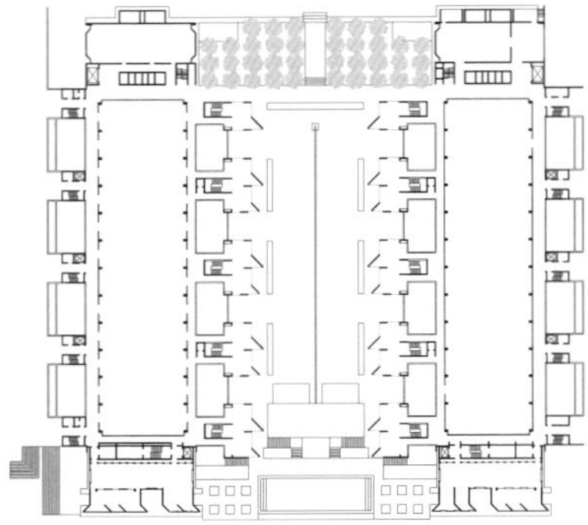

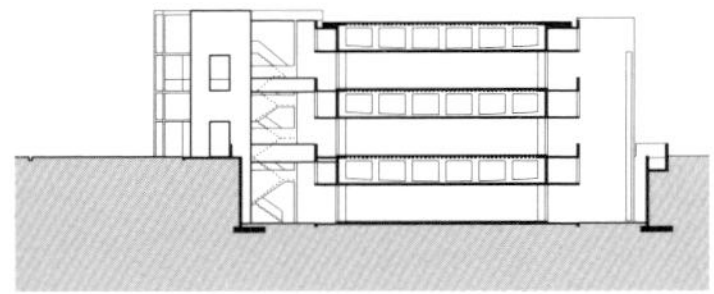

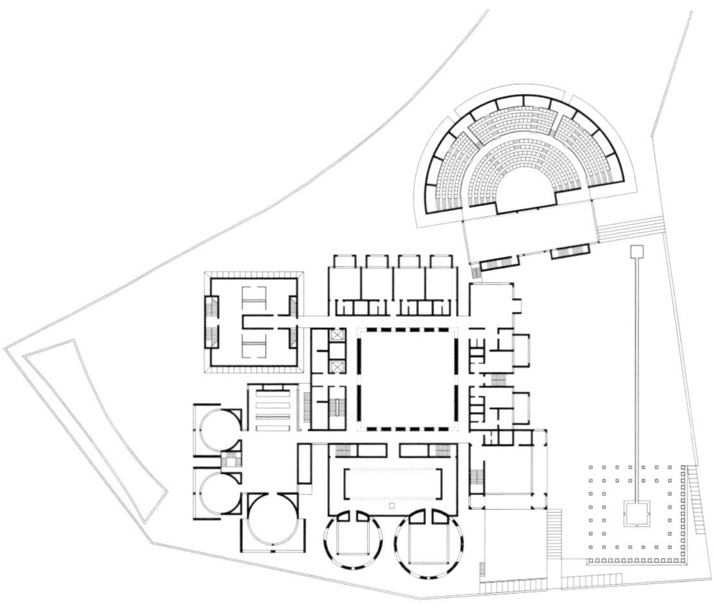

"correct" approach to the central plaza. That famous plaza—linking land, sky, and sea together in one of the twentieth century's most sublime architectural spaces—prohibits any movement along its central axis; instead, due to the placement of the stairs, it sets up a pattern of perpendicular and diagonal crisscrossing which is profoundly nonclassical. In terms of use, the plaza is both a void devoted to "Silence" and a pure "Space of Appearance," its form denying any kind of specific instrumental use while at the same time—through its numerous bordering surfaces, niches, ledges, and loggias—suggesting a multitude of possibilities for meeting, lingering, conversing, eating, etc.

The plaza is the largest in a series of generous "spacings," both horizontal and vertical, which are used to interpret the institution. These spacings are best understood when seen in the intended—yet never completed—general plan for the Salk, with its unrealized meeting house and scientists' residential village. **Fig. 122** The three complementary parts of the institution are positioned to take maximum advantage of the distances offered by the site around the ravine, and a meted chain of distances establishes the relationships between the respective parts and to their context: the primary setback of the building groups from the street behind a eucalyptus grove, the large spacings between the Institute's major elements, etc.

This linked chain of spacings was to be continued within each of the three major elements. In the unbuilt meeting house **Fig. 125**, the plaza of the laboratory tract is echoed on a smaller scale by another unprogrammed central space. This plan pushes the scheme of the First Unitarian Church a step further toward the looser, more explicitly "juxtapositional" plans such as that for the Dominican Motherhouse. Smaller peripheral spaces gravitate gently around sub-centers that in turn bunch around a large interior meeting court. The combination of three different distributive typologies—court, ambulatory, and room matrix—generates a deep and labyrinthine plan that seems to be as much rooted in antiquity as in the present.[154] Kahn and Salk had hoped with the Institute to create an environment in which scientific discourse intertwined with those of the arts and humanities: "Essentially it is a laboratory building, but you must not forget that the place of meeting is of utmost importance."[155]

In the completed laboratory tract, proximities and distances are most finely tuned in the spatial fugue that links the studies, the loggias, the stairs, and the laboratories. Kahn felt the need to articulate

154 Kahn's assistant Tim Vreeland told of tracing a portion of Hadrian's Villa as a generator for the Salk's Meeting Place (later denied by Kahn in an interview with Vincent Scully). See Friedman, "Salk Institute for Biological Studies," p. 443.

155 Kahn, "On Form and Design," p. 108.

between the differently scaled structures provided for each use. The thirty-six private studies (the "rug and oak table area" [156]) are individually articulated and given pride of place on the edge of the plaza (in reference to the primacy of conception, of formulation of the hypothesis in the creative act), while the laboratories in which these hypotheses are tested ("a clean air and stainless steel area" [157]) are set back by the width of the stair and the walkway. **Fig. 124** An additional spacing is established in section: staggering the studies on every second floor, adjacent to the Vierendeel/mechanical levels, a vertical half-step between the studies and the laboratories has been created in answer to Kahn's rhetorical question: "How near is too near and how far is too far?" **Fig. 126** Looking like beneficial leftovers, human-scaled loggias are generated below the studies and adjacent to the labs, supplementing the movement-space with regular "offerings" to chance meeting and serendipitous communication. The building's structure, at first glance straightforwardly concerned with carrying the building's weight, knits an order that simultaneously intertwines movement and use; weaving, in fact, the tectonic, the symbolic, the functional, the technical, the experiential, and the social so densely as to make their separate discussion virtually impossible: a magical—because at once so seemingly offhanded and so comprehensive—fit.

**Erdman Hall**

A women's dormitory, Erdman Hall at Bryn Mawr College (1960–65) **Fig. 128**, though at first glance only remotely related to the Dominican Motherhouse, is in terms of distribution and plan configuration an important predecessor. In spite of its dissimilar outward shape, in Erdman Hall the underlying "Form" diagram or parti is similar to that of the Motherhouse, laying out a clear yet dynamic interplay between individual and collective. As at Media, Kahn found bringing this "Form" to work in a real plan was anything but an easy task, resulting in a long and messy struggle. As at Media, in early versions of Erdman Hall the communal and private components—in this case, the students' private rooms and the larger communal spaces—had been clearly separated in plan. **Fig. 127** The sketches from this phase show an uneasy balance between a structuralist linkage of the small rooms and a more classical ordering of the larger rooms.[158] In the final version both orders coalesce in a hybrid, which is alternatively legible as three "classically" linked pavilions or as a segment of an unfinished structuralist chain. (The actual experience of the building in situ—with its

156 Kahn, quoted in Ronner and Jhaveri, *Louis I. Kahn*, p. 158.

157 Ibid.

158 The evolution of the bi-polar "Form" of the Dominican Motherhouse and Erdman Hall has interesting parallels to Kahn's description of reinstatement of the First Unitarian Church's "Form" after a client-induced, bi-polar intermezzo.

**126** Salk Institute, 1959–1965: view across the plaza with studies and loggias

**127** Erdman Hall, Bryn Mawr College, 1960–65: intermediate scheme
**128** Erdman Hall: floor plan
**129** Erdman Hall: "architecture of connection"
**130** Dominican Motherhouse, 1966–68: "architecture of connection" (draft)

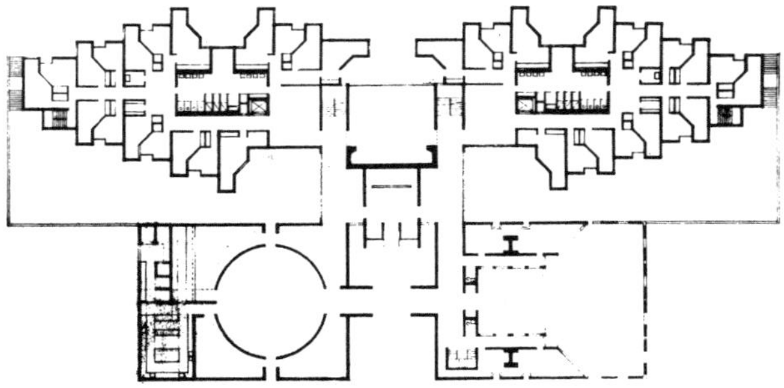

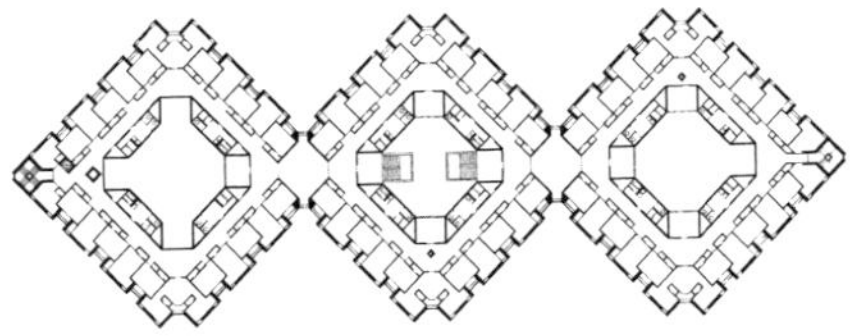

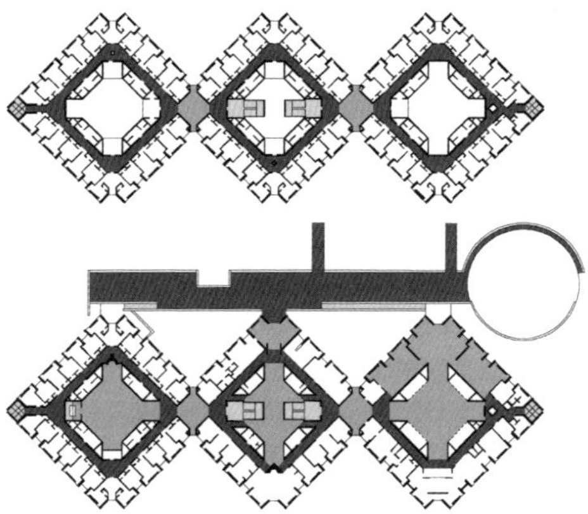

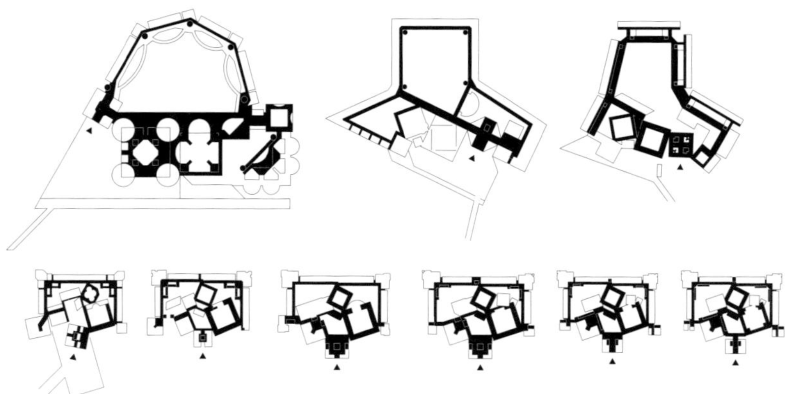

irregular silhouette, its superimposed diagonal and orthogonal orders, and its folded peripheries—being much more complex than either of these two-dimensional readings would suggest.[159]) The final scheme offers its inhabitants choices between ambulatory and linear patterns of movement. The three great communal rooms, being at once usable space and "circulation," are unconventionally skewered together over the entire length of the building by a great diagonal enfilade. The corner-as-connecter is Kahn's provocative answer to the problem of the otherwise "dead" corner of the square in plan: "I discovered at Bryn Mawr that you can connect a room over its corner."[160] Partially buffered from the communal spaces by the thickened walls of "servant" spaces, the ambulatories provide access to the dormitory rooms. The linear and ambulatory systems, in combination with a series of both extroverted and hidden stairs, give the students the choice of both exposed and hidden routes through the building, the choice between "remote or direct association" with cohabitants and with those communal "availabilities" the house has to offer.

**The Dominican Motherhouse**

The Dominican Motherhouse represents a special, and especially dense, manifestation of a "society of rooms" plan. We have already studied in the narrative the earliest bipolar scheme, with its hermetic cells and its communal "Forum of Availabilities," the great ambulatory and courts being the means of both spacing and connecting the individual spaces. By the development of the fourth and final version, the original theme had evolved into something decidedly less conventional; instead of being presented with a choice of access to various rooms from the vantage point of a generous and unprogrammed "space of appearance" (as at Fort Wayne, Ahmedabad, et al.), we are now, from our position *within* a single discrete room, presented with the choice of movement in any one of at least three directions. Something like an "ordered labyrinth" is the result. **Fig. 130** An inversion has taken place: the matrix has replaced the counterform and virtually the entire complex has become an "architecture of connection." While the Kahnian imperative of free choice has remained, that of "indirect association" has collapsed. Robin Evans' description of Raphael's Villa Madama reverberates:

"Once inside it is necessary to pass through one room to the next, then to the next, to traverse the building. Where passages and stairways

159 This ambivalence results in part from the way the spatial structure tends to give equal emphasis to the three centers and the two linking in-betweens, to orthogonal *and* diagonal geometries. The long and difficult genesis of Erdman Hall—a process somewhere between a cooperative effort and an internal competition between Kahn and Anne Tyng (as unwillingly moderated by David Polk)—illustrates the configurational crossroads—between an ebbing paradigm of structuralist "growth" and a dawning one of "composition"—at which Kahn stood. See Lewis's account in "The Dominican Motherhouse," or Anne Tyng in *Louis Kahn to Anne Tyng*, pp. 203–6.

160 Kahn, quoted in Wurman, *What Will Be Has Always Been*, p. 142.

are used, as inevitably they are, they nearly always connect just one space to another and never serve as general distributors of movement. Thus, despite the precise architectural containment offered by the addition of room upon room, the villa was, in terms of occupation, an open plan relatively permeable to the numerous members of the household, all of whom—men, women, children, servants and visitors—were obliged to pass through a matrix of connecting rooms where the day-to-day business of life was carried on. It was inevitable that paths would intersect during the course of the day, and that every activity was liable to intercession unless very different measures were taken in order to avoid it. As with the multiplying of doors, there was nothing unusual about this; it was the rule in Italian palaces, villas and farms—a customary way of joining rooms that hardly affected the style of architecture (which could equally well be gothic or vernacular), but certainly affected the style of life.... The matrix of connected rooms is appropriate to a type of society ... which recognizes the body as the person, and in which gregariousness is habitual. The features of this kind of life can be discerned in Rafael's architecture and painting. Such was the typical arrangement of household space in Europe until it was challenged in the seventeenth century and finally displaced in the nineteenth century by the corridor plan, which is appropriate to a society ... which sees the body as a vessel of mind and spirit, and in which privacy is habitual.... There is surely another type of architecture that would seek to give full play to the things that have been so carefully masked by its anti-type; an architecture arising out of the deep fascination that draws people towards others; an architecture that recognizes carnality and sociality. The matrix of connected rooms might well be an integral feature for such buildings." [161]

This sense of gregarious inhabitance—expected in a sixteenth-century Italian villa, exceptional in a modern monastery—may in the end be that which gives the Motherhouse less the character of an institutional building than that of a very large house, a quality it shares with its predecessor, Erdman Hall (for all that building's castle-like ambience). With a certain warpage of scale, it's not difficult to imagine cells as bedrooms, the refectory as dining room, the school as study, the chapel as common room, etc. The monastery plan becomes, perhaps, a Roman villa.[162] This said, not only sociality is to be served by the

161 Evans, "Figures, Doors and Passages," pp. 64–65, 88–90. (The reader may wish to qualify Evans' statement when used in regard to a monastery by omitting the word "carnality.")

162 At any rate, we may safely maintain that a monastery in which one of the sisters might be tempted to take a shortcut through the chapel while *en route* to a midnight snack in the kitchen (or vice versa) has a fundamentally more domestic character than one in which this option did not exist.

plan, but the celebration of sacred ritual as well. The layered ambulatory of the chapel (and, to a lesser degree, of the refectory) is intended to create both proximity *and* separation, Kahn's "wink at the chapel" without going in: "First you have a sanctuary, and the sanctuary is for those who want to kneel. Around this sanctuary is an ambulatory for those who are not sure but want to be near. Outside is a court for those who want to feel the presence of the chapel. And the court has a wall. Those who pass the wall can just wink at it."[163] And so, Kahn gives us another way of looking at the plan: if we divide the spaces into those which are linked together in a continuous distribution circuit and those in which activities are private or come to rest, the floor plan begins to read like a small Nolli plan, a miniature urban scheme with streets, widenings, squares, and buildings. **Fig. 131** Considering the plan in this manner, it becomes apparent that the act of entrance does not cease at the front door in the tower, but that the entire building forms a "continuous threshold." As in Evans' description of Villa Madama, an apparent paradox emerges: Kahn's at-first-glance static volumes are used to generate a dynamic sense of movement and simultaneousness, qualities typically associated with the modern free plan.

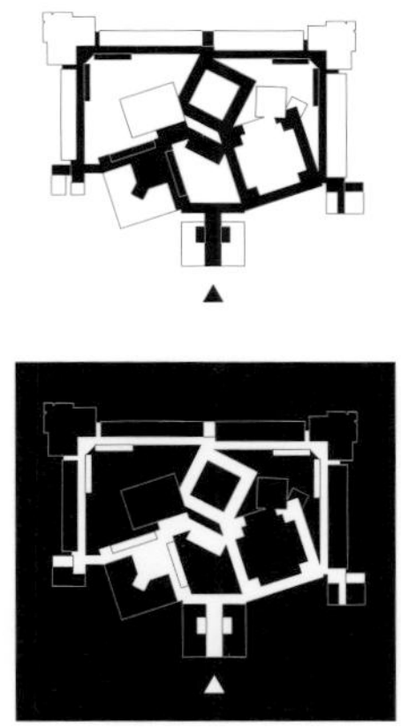

**131** Dominican Motherhouse, 1966–68: "architecture of connection" (final)

**The matrix of rooms as social condenser**

Regardless if we see it as a big house, a miniature urban plan, or both, the Dominican Motherhouse is undoubtedly one of Kahn's most provocative creations in terms of its "architecture of connection": refusing to treat "circulation" as a separate building system, at once applying and transcending the conventions of both classicist and free plans in an additive conglomeration of discrete rooms as a "social condenser." Aptly named with prepositions—the room next to, behind, above, tangent to—each space enjoys varied synergies with its different neighbors. Even more than its skewed geometry, it is likely that it is these bold juxtapositions which have caused both the plan's critics and its advocates to linger—the latter finding promise in the plan's hypothesis, the former meeting it with skepticism—for there are few institutional models on this scale which we can use to help imagine its inhabitation. How *would* it have been to live in the monastery/house/urban plan? We can only imagine the plan's spaces unfolding before us: the crisscrossing, the multiple alternative routes, the chance encounters both agreeable and disagreeable—all these qualities generating, in movement and experience, a tension which is at least equal to the formal tension of the plan's geometry. In the end, it is difficult not to sense something more than a little demonstrative or didactic about the plan, as if Kahn were teasing the limits of this particular mode of bringing spaces (and thus people) together. Unbuilt and so

163 Kahn, "Form and Design," p. 116.

untested, the plan seems to beg the question of its model character. While a similar matrix of rooms is easily imaginable in the case of a museum or a villa, the intertwined public/private interface of the monastery begins to stretch—in both positive and negative senses—the imagination. How might one apply this intertwining in other institutional buildings or urban configurations, and what would be the gains? Kahn's answer is an optimistic one: a faith that draws humans together is in the end stronger than their wish to withdraw.

I hope to have shown two things here. First, that the Dominican Motherhouse, while stretching the limits of Kahn's "architecture of connection," is in no way an exception to its basic premises; second, for all its collage-like dynamism, the Motherhouse, like Kahn's other related juxtapositional plans, was not merely an exercise in formal composition. In decided contrast to common modernist practice, which aimed at tightly binding use and movement together in unambiguous "cause and effect" relationships, Kahn directed his efforts to identifying the varied forces which brought the elements of a program together in a "society of rooms," and subsequently let those forces work as vectors in an equation that included the complementary vectors of geometry, structure, and the conditions of site. We have already traced some of the considerable work required to identify those forces and to configure those spaces, work which in retrospect was directed toward a plan that might awaken the potentials of sociality while at the same time guaranteeing the greatest freedom of its inhabitants, applying the smallest element of force.

### An Architecture of Connection: Experience, Agency, and the Search for Commonality

Like few architects of his time or of the present, Kahn directed his energies toward recognizing and making manifest those aspects of spatiality which so much of modernist culture had reduced to mere "circulation." (And which so much of contemporary capitalist culture either abandons or instrumentalizes as a commodity.) By redirecting our attention to the oft-neglected in-betweens of architectural connection and to the spatial nature of human behavior, Kahn, without claiming a patent recipe for achieving it, pointed toward a *participatory* architecture of "human agreement." Choice, "remote" contact, multivalence, generosity, resistance of subjugation to program: all are qualities of his "architecture of connection."

References to these aspects of spatiality were among the most lucid and human moments in Kahn's texts, most evocative, perhaps, in his 1971 acceptance speech for the AIA Gold Medal, "The Room, the Street, and Human Agreement." In that speech, beginning at the scale of a stair and working up to that of a city street, he conjured up an ideal picture of social space. The room, the court, the street, the city: all these architectural spaces are human "institutions," and thus based on the establishment of "human agreement." For a generation of architects raised on rationalist cant, bubble diagrams, and the scientific analogy of "circulation," his words might have seemed homespun and romantic… or like a breath of fresh air:

"The society of rooms is knit together with the elements of connection which have their own characteristics. The stair is the same for the child, the adult and the old. It is thought of as precise in its measures, particularly for the young boy who aspires to do the floors in no time flat, both up and down. It is good also to consider the stair landing as a place to sit near a window with possibly a shelf for a few books. The old man ascending with the young boy can stop here, showing his interest in a certain book, and avoid the explanations of infirmity.... The street is a room of agreement. The street is dedicated by each house owner to the city in exchange for common services. Dead-end streets in cities today still retain this room character. Through-streets, since the advent of the automobile, have entirely lost their room quality. I believe that city planning can start with realization of this loss by directing the drive to reinstate the street where people live, learn, shop and work as the room of commonality.... One realizes the deadliness of uninterested movement through our streets which erases all delicacy of character and blots out its sensitive nature given to it of human agreement. Human agreement is a sense of rapport, of commonness, of all bells ringing in unison—not needing to be understood by example but felt as an undeniable inner demand for a presence. It is an inspiration with the promise of the possible." [164]

While his efforts were among the most remarkable of his time, Kahn was of course not alone in his rediscovery of the spatiality of human action and the forgotten dimensions of connective architecture. By the mid-fifties, a number of architects and theoreticians—some of them in Kahn's circle—were engaged in a revision of modernism's paradigm of "circulation." At the same time that Kahn coined his term "architecture of connection," the architect Aldo van Eyck began, in a related fashion, to speak of "thresholding"—changing noun into verb—and of architecture as mediation become manifest: *das Gestalt gewordene Zwischen* (the concretization of the in-between). His famous orphanage in Amsterdam (1955–60)—a revelation for Kahn—was for him

164 Kahn, "The Room, the Street, and Human Agreement," p. 265.

**132** Kimbell Art Museum, 1966–72: entry loggia

a portrayal of the "medicine of reciprocity" at work through its connective, mediating spaces"[165] Alison and Peter Smithson, at the first CIAM congress to be organized by Team X in 1956, presented a challenge to the modernist idea of the functionally subdivided community in the form of the concept of "clusters" related according to movement between "scales of association."[166] Kevin Lynch attempted, first in *The Image of the City* (1960) and later in *The View From the Road* (1966),[167] to codify the means by which the city is perceived and mentally processed by its moving inhabitants; while in a contemporaneous effort, Jane Jacobs directed architects' attention toward the disappearing social life of the urban street (*The Death and Life of the Great American Cities,* 1961).

### An Architecture of Connection: The Sentient Body Moving in Space

While the emphasis of this—by no means exhaustive—chapter has been on Kahn's environments as "people configurations," it is important to remember that buildings were strongly but not *only* social configurations for Kahn. Intertwined with the social logic of the plan are countless other realities—programmatic, symbolic, atmospheric, kinesthetic, poetic, formal—which are equally integral to his "architecture of connection." Kahn often saved his best and most expressive moments for his connective architecture. Here is where his buildings shine and where the user often experiences a heightened corporeal awareness while becoming engaged as an active participant in the work: navigating between periphery and center, unraveling its formal structure, unearthing its themes, prying into its ambiguities, enjoying its sensual pleasures. There are many rich examples, more than enough for a detailed study: the Exeter Library, planned around a reader's movement with book from darkness into light; the Kimbell Art Museum and the Roosevelt Memorial, where the visitors' paths are like threads which weave architecture and site; Dhaka's National Assembly, where movement within the great Piranesian halls generates a near-sublime "rhythm of light, no light, light, no light"; or the Yale Center for British Art, where the friction of the visitor's diagonal movement animates the building's orthogonal structure.

The moving and sentient body is a privileged means of access to a preverbal world of understanding, a means of experiencing the richness of the world by re-establishing access to its "origins." These origins may be corporeal or psychic, social or material; for Kahn they were always wonderful.

165 Ligtelijn, *Aldo van Eyck: Werke,* pp. 88–109.

166 Alison and Peter Smithson, *The Charged Void: Architecture.*

167 At Lynch's request, Kahn had in 1955 reviewed his master's thesis, which would later become *The Image of the City.* See Williams Goldhagen, *Louis Kahn's Situated Modernism,* p. 120.

## THE TWIN PHENOMENA OF INSIDE AND OUTSIDE "DICHOTOMOUS THINGS" OR THE THEME OF RECIPROCITY

*We must build something that satisfies this, and (something that) satisfies the other. We must express dichotomous things. We must express them because dichotomous things inspire.* Louis Kahn, letter to landscape architect Karl Linn, May 1965

*What has right-size is at the same time both large and small few and many, near and far, simple and complex, open and closed; will furthermore always be both part and whole and embrace both unity and diversity.... Right-size will flower as soon as the mild gears of reciprocity start working—in the climate of relativity; in the landscape of twinphenomena.*
Aldo van Eyck, "Steps Towards a Configurative Discipline," 1962

*Don't play what's there. Play what's not there.* Miles Davis, 1959

**Architectural space within natural space**

The previous chapter focused on Kahn's enclosing and meted distancing of discrete spaces, and especially in this spacing's role in architecture's service as a "people configuration." Beginning with this chapter our focus shifts from architecture's engagement with the social world to its relationship with the natural world, to those aspects of enclosure and configuration which concern the delimiting and inhabiting of a built space within a greater natural space. Starting with the fundamental problem of defining relationships between that which is *inside* and that which is *outside,* we will move in the following chapter to those phenomena that begin to differentiate between *space* and *place.* It is a premise of this study that Kahn's mature work represents a concentrated attempt to reinterpret the relationship between interior and exterior, between architectural and natural space as defined by modernism. Building on the lessons of a classicist training and a modernist practice, by the mid-fifties Kahn began to rethink interior and exterior space in terms of their interrelationship and to develop means for engaging both realms in a dialogue that would eventually transcend conventional classicist or modernist modes. By the early sixties he

**133** Suhrawardthy National Hospital, 1962–74: loggia

had expanded his field, moving beyond general inside-outside schemata to engage the specific sites and the broader contexts in which he planned. The results of this research-through-designing amount to a significant enrichment of the twentieth century's culture of architectural space—a development that has yet to be comprehensively described.

**Reciprocity versus "Either-Or"**

The following chapter unfolds around a term which is used here to describe a potential relationship between architectural and natural space: *reciprocity*—"the mutual dependence, action or influence" between two things.[168] In contrast to conventional modernist hierarchies, which have tended to either privilege architectural space over that of its surroundings or have attempted to merge inside and outside into a single, undifferentiated continuum, the concept of reciprocity presumes the coexistence of two distinct, yet inseparable realms.[169] It is an understanding, then, of architectural space which regards both interior and exterior as equal partners in a linked system of relationships, its setting-in-work requiring the articulation of both partners and their subsequent coupling in a resolved and comprehensible form. Each component, while apparently whole, inflects toward its complement, and is thus simultaneously complete and incomplete. What to binary logic sounds paradoxical is to the complementary thinker as commonsensical as day and night. While this interrelationship has experienced innumerous manifestations in history—belonging, indeed, to much of architecture's vernacular and classical traditions—it has tended to disappear to the extent that binary or exclusivist thinking becomes dominant in (architectural) culture.[170]

With Kahn, complementary thinking returns with an unexpected richness within the "either-or" context of mid-twentieth-century mainstream architectural culture. The reciprocity between built space and unbuilt space was corollary to Kahn's general tendency to articulate and differentiate between things while at the same time establishing their interdependence; be it at the scale of a joint between bearing and non-bearing building materials, between "servant" and "served" spaces, or at the scale of a building's complementary uses, such as in the functional rings in the Exeter Library or in the "dichotomous space" of the Salk Institutes' laboratories, where "Kahn realized that a research laboratory was 'really two buildings' a 'fireplace and a study' kind of building (the offices) and a 'microbe and test tube' kind of

168 *The Penguin New English Dictionary,* Hammondsworth, 2000, p. 1147.

169 For a wide-angled view of reciprocity in architecture, see van Eyck's "The Medicine of Reciprocity Tentatively Illustrated" and "Steps Towards a Configurative Discipline"; for a more close-up view, see Berrizbeitia and Pollak, *Inside Outside: Between Architecture and Landscape,* pp. 14–42.

170 Whether in some form of Platonic atomism, Newtonian-Cartesian dualism or pragmatic reductionism, etc.

building (the laboratories). He decided that these differences should be exaggerated rather than elided ... later he realized that from this parti a general principle could be derived."[171]

*Coincidentia oppositorum*

One need not listen to him for long to realize that this "general principle" of codependent complements was for Kahn ultimately more than a method to be applied to the making of buildings, but rather was part and parcel of a non-dualist metaphysics populated by "twin phenomena," be they named "Silence and Light," "Form and Design," "the Measurable and the Unmeasurable," etc. A universe made not of mutually exclusive but of cogenerative things. In this, Kahn—philosophically aspiring without being particularly philosophically versed—echoes the non-dualism of Taoism, Buddhism, or that strain of Western thought exemplified by Aristotle's Holism or Nicholas of Cusa's *coincidentia oppositorum*. It was Nicholas of Cusa who saw that the highest truth is neither to be found in the choice between two opposites nor in their resolution in a third term (as later proposed by Hegel), but in the recognition of their coincidence. Indeed, as Kahn would have been pleased to read, it is only through the existence of contradictions that the meaning of "unity" may be understood at all.[172]

**Four steps toward reciprocity**

Rather than following Kahn out on a metaphysical limb, the following chapter will attempt to remain close to those physical and spatial consequences of his *coincidentia oppositorum*, particularly with how this applies to the relationship between built and unbuilt, between architectural and natural space. Beginning with the description of basic morphological aspects of space as represented by the complements of figure and ground, mass and void, the text then questions the role of the wall or border-space in establishing inside-outside reciprocity. In a next step, the "dyad" figure-ground scheme will be expanded to consider the role of a "third space" in relativizing interior and exterior. Finally, the question is posed how this theme may be experienced on other levels.

## Seeing Space as Mass and Void: Reciprocity and Figure-Ground Ambivalence

The Gestalt notion of the "figure-ground phenomenon" refers to the characteristic organization of perception into a figure that "stands out" against a neutral background. What is at any one moment figural depends on patterns of sensory perception and on the momentary interests of the perceiver.[173] While our "default mode" seems to focus on that which is built rather than the space it forms, as architects we are per se obliged to learn to reverse these ingrained figure-ground seeing habits. Giambattista Nolli's seminal plan of Rome from 1748 **Fig. 134**

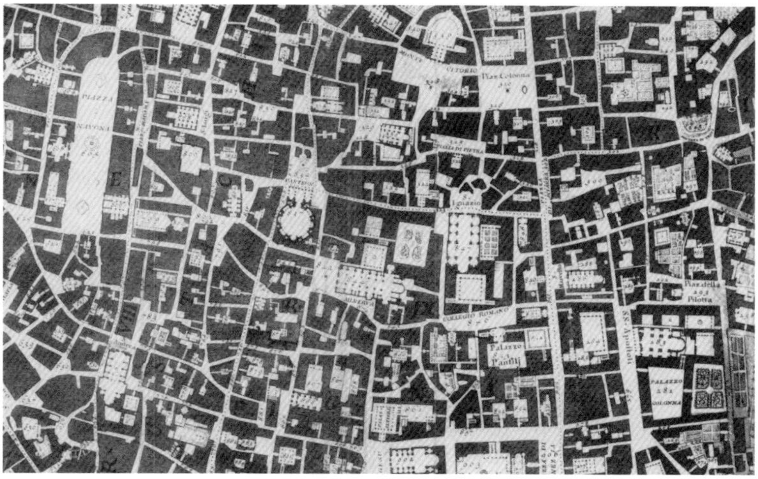

**134** Plan of Rome, 1748, Giambattista Nolli
**135** Rubin Vase, from Colin Rowe and Fred Koetter, *Collage City,* 1984

is a reminder that the figure-ground scheme has served as a means for thinking architectural space long before its twentieth-century codification in Gestalt psychology's theory of perception.[174] **Fig. 135** Used as an analytic and generative tool to varying degrees in history, the figure-ground scheme has been an indispensable part of recent architectural culture at the latest since its inclusion in the pedagogy of the University of Texas at Austin in the fifties and sixties, and its subsequent dispersal by those influential *cognoscenti* of the modern such as Colin Rowe, Robert Slutzky, John Hejduk, Werner Seligmann, and Bernhard Hoesli.[175] (The canonical late-twentieth-century text on figure-ground phenomena undoubtedly being Rowe and Koetter's *Collage City* of 1978.[176]) In spite of the timeliness of its reintroduction,

171 Williams Goldhagen, *Louis Kahn's Situated Modernism,* p. 193.

172 Nicholas of Cusa (Cusanus), *De coniecturis,* vol. II, 1:2. According to Cusanus, the only, highest truth that resolves all opposites is to be found in God. See Flasch, "Nikolaus von Kues: Die Idee der Koinzidenz," pp. 221–61. Of course, Kahn was not alone in the profession at this time in his attempt to break out of the mold of dualist thinking. The greatest of the moderns—Wright, Le Corbusier, Aalto—had refused to see reductionism as the highest virtue; in the late fifties Aldo van Eyck began to call for relativism, "twin phenomena," and architecture as an attempt to portray "the medicine of reciprocity" at work; with Venturi's "gentle manifesto" for complexity and contradiction soon following in 1966. In a more heady manner, the architect O. M. Ungers first described the Cusanian *coincidentia* as an architectural principle in his 1982 *Architettura come tema/Architecture as Theme.*

173 *The Fontana Dictionary of Modern Thought,* New York, 1977.

174 Although Max Wertheimer is credited as the founder of the Gestalt psychology movement (with Rudolf Arnheim his most influential disciple for the world of architecture), the concept seems to have been first introduced to modern philosophy and psychology by Christian von Ehrenfels in the nineteenth century. The idea of Gestalt has its roots in the theories of Goethe and Kant. See Bruce et al., *Visual Perception,* p. 110.

175 See Caragonne's *The Texas Rangers* on the teaching method at Austin in the 1960s and its subsequent spread and worldwide influence. The figure-ground scheme could take on different intonations in its various interpretations: Rowe and Koetter's *Collage City* tended to stress basic morphological aspects of space and mass, while Hoesli and Hofers' "Dialogische Stadt" stressed the role of the surface in mediating between figure and ground. O. M. Ungers' later *Die dialektische Stadt* (1999) tended to explore the "topological" aspects of thinking with the figure-ground scheme.

176 Rowe and Koetter, *Collage City.*

in spite of its necessity as a conceptual tool, the scheme's capacity to make comprehensive statements regarding space has often been overestimated by planners and architects, if only due to the fact that that which so clearly appears as "figure" or as "ground" to the omniscient reader of a two-dimensional plan is seldom as legible for a person moving through the complexities of the space represented by that plan. In spite of its limitations, though, the figure-ground scheme has been an essential means for thinking architectural space in terms of mass and void, positive and negative, convex and concave, foreground and background, object and texture, etc.

As the figure-ground scheme remains one the most basic means for discussing and designing architectural space, and as its black-or-white nature is so quintessentially *contrary,* it is appropriate to begin our discussion here. For Kahn, the planning method of the nineteenth-century Ecole des Beaux-Arts—his first touchstone as a student and young professional—provides a natural starting point.

**The Ecole des Beaux-Arts as touchstone**

While the compositional system of the Ecole des Beaux-Arts was criticized by its successors as a tired repetition of worn-out formulae out of touch with the needs of a modern world, the great success of that system was at least in part due to its quality as a teachable, operative means of resolving spatial relationships. Alan Colquhoun recognized that while perhaps justified in their critique of its academic formalism, the Ecole's modern successors were for the most part unable to see that "inherent in that method was a way of regarding space as a total field which is ordered and totally humanized ... a codified survival of a system of spatial organization which symbolized a certain relation of man to the world."[177] In Beaux-Arts methodology, this "certain relation" was not only made manifest in the architect's first act of establishing a comprehensible figurative layout in a diagram or parti sketch,[178] it was systematically set into work at different scales by drawing upon a repertoire of planning plays and "readymade" elements for ordering mass and space: the use of *poché,* of major and minor axes, of greater or lesser *salles,* of colonnades, galleries, courts, etc., represented a repertoire that—regardless of its inherent academism—provided the initiated architect with means of establishing hierarchies, negotiating spatial boundaries and differences in scale, for balancing centers and peripheries, programmed and unprogrammed areas, figure and ground; in short: *for situating its inhabitants in an ordered and comprehensible spatial continuum.* As Colquhoun described,

177 Colquhoun, "The Beaux-Arts Plan," pp. 161–68.

178 In the Ecole's method, the establishment of a parti (or today, "concept diagram") was to be the first act of the architect.

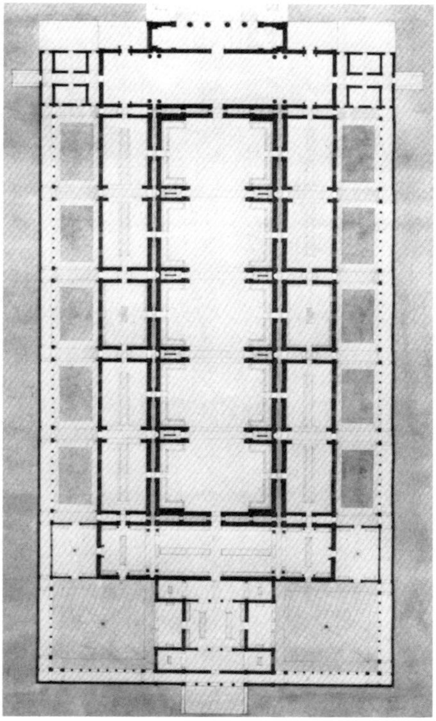

136 Design for a library, Ecole des Beaux-Arts
137 Design for a hospice, Ecole des Beaux-Arts

the all-important space-modulating floor plan/site plan was to be developed as a sort of Gestalt pattern in which the black of the built mass and the white of the unbuilt voids were treated as two inseparable and cogenerative parts of a whole. Figs. 136–137 In this respect, at least, the Ecole may be seen as fostering something approaching a holistic view of architectural and natural space. Kahn, through his education under Paul Philippe Cret at the University of Pennsylvania, was a late heir to this simultaneously scripted and comprehensive method, which, even during his studies, was being succeeded by the modernist paradigm of autonomous *objets-types* set in a boundless and abstract space.[179]

### The Development of the Figure-Ground Scheme in Kahn's Work

While he was at home in the Beaux-Arts system, Kahn's work of the thirties and forties may be seen as an attempt to jettison what he had come to regard as the conservative influence of his academic training and to develop buildings in a "progressive" modernist interpretation of form—and space. The early houses and housing projects (ca. 1939–50), the Philadelphia Psychiatric Hospital (1948–53),

179 Colquhoun, "The Beaux-Arts Plan," p. 43.

**138** Adler House, 1954–55
**139** Fleisher House, 1959

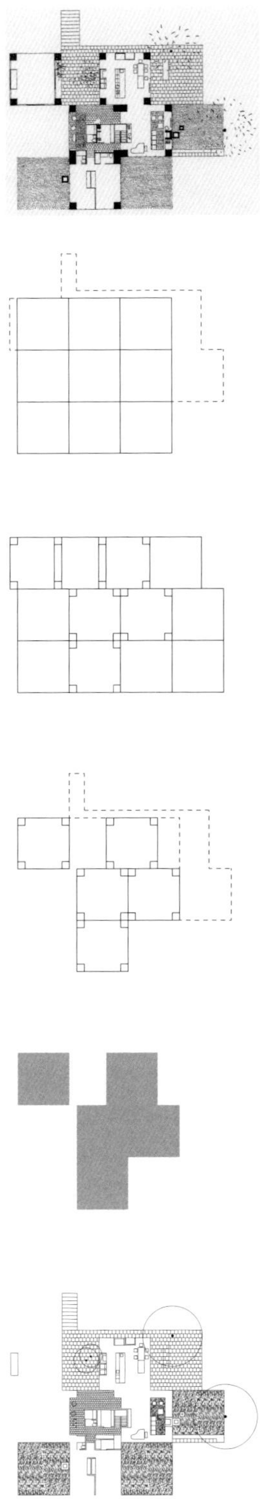

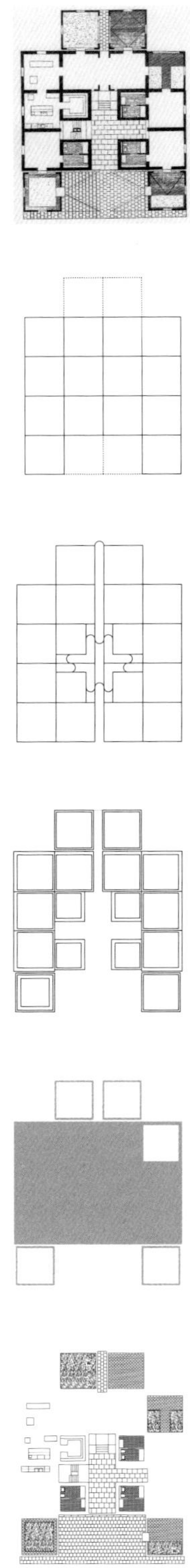

the Yale University Art Gallery (1951–53): in these works "site" tends to equal little more than "setting" for relatively autonomous architectural objects. Beginning in the mid-fifties, though, concurrent with his unfolding thoughts on the nature of institutions, monumentality, and hierarchic space, he began to reconsider the Beaux-Arts notion of the site as a comprehensively ordered field of equally weighted exterior and interior spaces. In the following, we will trace his explorations of this theme from the fifties onward in a group of related projects.

**DeVore and Adler Houses**

With the DeVore and Adler House projects—both designed in 1954–55—Kahn begins with an elementary cell seeking appropriate "spacings" to its neighbors. In these two projects structural-space and use-space begin to coincide in an early denial of the modernist free plan and are a premonition of Kahn's later, more complex "society of rooms" compositions. Part of Kahn's self-imposed program for these houses was to regard the *configuration* of spaces as intensively as their individual shaping: "In searching for the nature of the spaces of a house, might they not be separated theoretically before they are to be brought together? A predetermined total form might inhibit what the individual spaces want to be."[180] While this statement may initially evoke the functionalist credo of developing a building "from the inside out," with only secondary regard for how exterior space is to be shaped by the resulting object, the drawings for the DeVore—and especially for the Adler House—show that this apparently purely functionalist thought was indeed to provide a method for ordering a larger spatial field.

For the Adler House, a segment of a chessboard grid provides a frame of reference for the spaces to be ordered. **Fig. 138** This segment—its generic form resembling a nine-square plan—is allowed to slip and is subsequently occupied by pavilions roughly sized to house the program's needs, or by the equally figural "captured air" which forms the intervals between those pavilions.[181] As suggested by the floor plan's graphics—which are essential to Kahn's intent—"figural" space is not only defined by the enclosures of the pavilions themselves, but also *implied* by a second layer of a more ephemeral "texture" representing both human and natural life occupying the neutral structure. In spite of Kahn's claim about "what the spaces want to be," there is a purposeful looseness of fit between structural space and

180 Kahn, quoted in Ronner and Jhaveri, *Louis I. Kahn: Complete Work,* p. 70.

181 The fitting term "captured air" was coined by Alison and Peter Smithson in reference to the Adler House: "We tend to think of our architectural mentors quite often. Last week, thinking of Kahn, we wrote, 'The most mysterious, the most charged of all architectural Forms are those which capture the empty air.'" In Wurman, *What Will Be Has Always Been,* p. 298. Originally published in *The Architect's Yearbook,* 1960.

texture which allows interior and exterior to intermingle: "nature" occupies the grid in the form of three square grass carpets, while two paved areas project the life of the house into natural space. The entire composition spirals loosely around the paved square of the entry foyer: the former center of the nine-square grid and the only field in which an "exterior" texture has infiltrated an interior space. The "empty" pavilion of the carport makes this loose fit explicit while at the same time announcing the structural principle in *Reinkultur,* in early anticipation of the Kimbell Art Museum's porches or the Salk Institute's loggias. Kahn's intent did not go unrecognized by his clients; as Mrs. Adler remarked, "I share so many of your ideas, Lou—the texture of a surface-live-space."[182]

The incompletely filled-in grid, the "captured air" of the voids, the layered and interlocking textures, the plan's irregular contours: all suggest the house is a segment of a mass-and-void mosaic, a fragment of a larger ordered spatial field. While the spiraling composition inflects outward, we have been given no information as to how the rest of the site might be filled; merely a retaining wall and a set of steps hint at its presence. The plan fragment has been left to float on the white of the page in a gesture of reciprocity, which promises more than it reveals. While suggesting a new take on the modernist inside-outside problem as it had been established by the free plan, the Adler House project still remains mute as to how this new take might be worked out on a greater scale.

**The Fleisher House**

The mass-and-void play of the DeVore and Adler Houses is taken up again in the 1959 project for the Fleisher House. **Fig. 139** Here the grid is left strongly manifest as the pavilions of the earlier houses coalesce into discrete cells in a nearly "Palladian" plan; the Adler House's grass and paved "carpets" evolved into something approaching "gardens wrapped in ruins." Space is much denser, the "captured air" of the gardens almost palpable. Although structure-space and use correspond much more closely than in the DeVore and Adler Houses, again a certain loose fit between structure and texture has been sought, as gardens and paved areas are allowed to invade the Palladian grid. Instructively, the Fleisher House does not seem to beg the question of a specific site to the same degree as the Adler House. The formal geometry and regular periphery of the house make a more robust statement of the mass-void scheme, imaginable in a variety of situations, whether urban or suburban.

182 Letter, Mrs. Adler to Louis Kahn, June 17, 1954, Box LIK 32, Kahn Collection. That Kahn explicitly sought this texture-structure ambivalence is also evidenced by the fact that he let columns and texture be illustrated separately in a first 1955 publication of the house in *Perspecta:* "Two Houses," pp. 60–61.

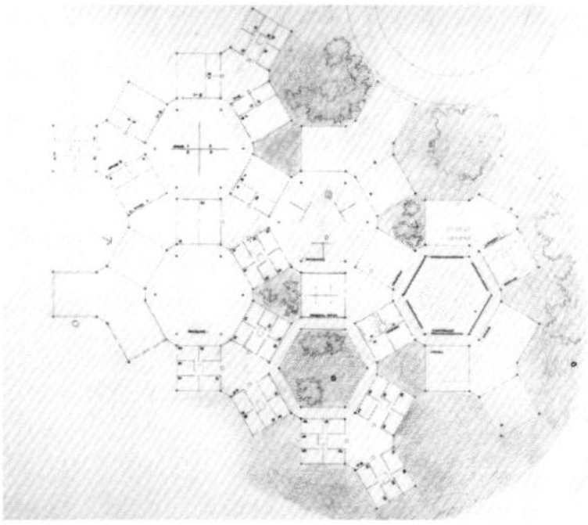

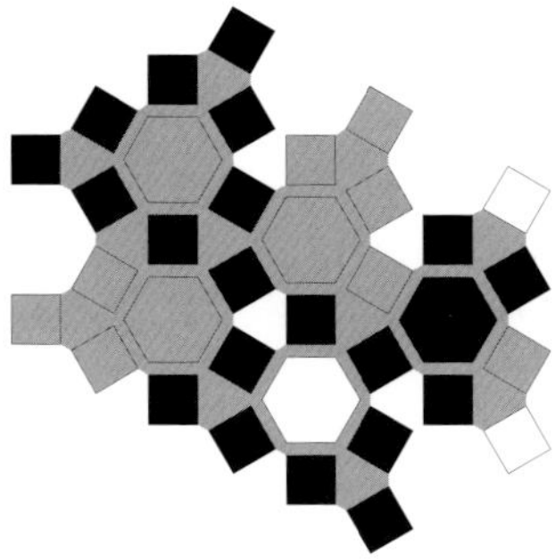

**140–41** Research Institute for Advanced Studies, 1956–58

**The Research Institute for Advanced Studies**

The 1956–58 project for the Research Institute for Advanced Studies near Baltimore is a remarkable example from a series of mid-fifties projects in which a basic structural unit is repeated in an additive, non-orthogonal matrix or "structuralist" plan. Figs. 140–141 Square pavilions housing laboratories and offices rotate and interlock like gears' teeth around hexagonal courts, an auditorium, and exhibition spaces, with interstitial triangles becoming either foyers or courtyards. The ornamental character of the plan is used as a means to interlock built and unbuilt space while establishing a sort of parity or ambivalence between the courtyards and the larger interior spaces. Although Kahn would slowly abandon such literal interpretations of "structuralist" plans—unsatisfied, no doubt, with their inability to reveal hierarchy and figural space and realizing their limits in urban situations—he would try to retain certain of their qualities for his later plans, such as their diagonal movement and their interlocking, ornamental parity of indoor and outdoor space.

**The Trenton Jewish Community Center**

Contemporary to these projects, Kahn was presented with an assignment which allowed him to shape figure and ground on a scale worthy of a Beaux-Arts public work: the Trenton Jewish Community Center of 1954–59. In early versions of that design, Kahn's (in retrospect still rather mechanical) insight into the servant-served hierarchy of spaces merged with the geometric-constructive paradigm of his associate Anne Tyng to generate an octagon-and-square mat that translated into a complex polyhedron-and-cube structure. While other architects might have extended the mat over the site to govern exterior spaces as well as interior (a weaving of architectural and natural space similar to Wright's hexagonal-grid projects such as the 1939 Hanna House comes to mind), Kahn ended the grid at the ribbed edge of the building, strengthening its object character and isolating it on its site. The resulting site plan is a curious collage, uneasily balancing its antagonistic geometries of hexagonal architecture and circular landscaping elements. Fig. 142

**142** Trenton Jewish Community Center, 1954–59: scheme 2
**143** Trenton Jewish Community Center, 1954–59: scheme 3
**144** Trenton Bath House, 1957: floor plan

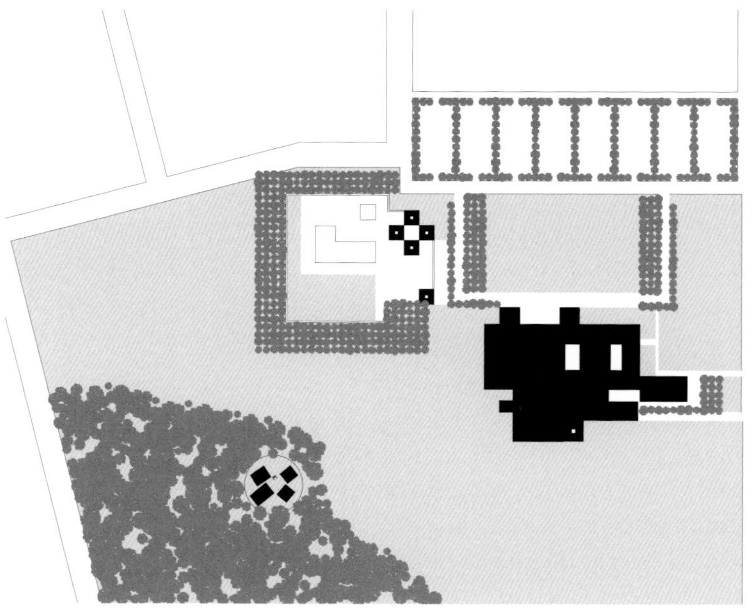

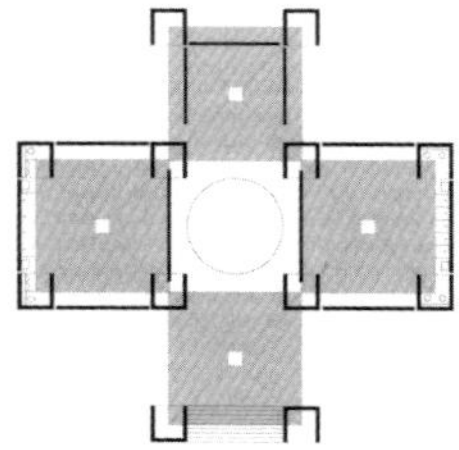

The more conventional third version from 1957 not only reinstalls Beaux-Arts axiality and its tartan grid, but the site is—albeit tentatively—now treated as a comprehensive spatial whole, with architecture, newly-planted groves of trees, and voids coalescing into a unified Gestalt. **Fig. 143** The site plan is tightly knit to the North, with both trees and architecture (a grove and the day-camp pavilions) loosening their order to the South. The site may begin to be read as a series of linked "insides" shaped by arboreal and architectural mass. Although through these means Kahn succeeded for the first time in structuring a large and rather characterless suburban site, the spatial linkage of the multipurpose building is, when seen next to the Research Institute for Advanced Studies for example, comparatively weak. It is the little bathhouse—with its fluctuating pattern of (implied) mass and void, of servant and served, covered and open spaces—which sets figure and ground oscillating in the most adroit manner. **Fig. 144** For more than this reason a breakthrough, Kahn later remarked, "If the world discovered me after I designed the Richards Medical Research Building, I discovered myself after designing that little concrete block bathhouse in Trenton."[183]

**Fort Wayne Fine Arts Center**

With the Fort Wayne Fine Arts Center of 1961–73, Kahn thematized figure-ground parity for the first time in an urban context. **Figs. 145–147** Situated on the edge of the city's grid against a railroad embankment, the new Fine Arts Center was to be a cultural "town in town" with philharmonic hall, theater, historical museum, art gallery, and art school. Kahn broke the program into building blocks scaled to match those of the city, and then drew these carefully together until, in the final version, the blocks are alternately legible as individual objects in a field or as segments of a continuous urban texture. Kahn's early charcoal studies **Fig. 145** show that this kind of figure-ground/object-texture ambiguity was his goal from the start. As the project progressed, the voids gradually lost their initial "left-over" character, with interior and exterior evolving toward equality in size and quality. Keyhole-like "negative bay windows" and punched-out courts interlock mass and void like pieces of a jigsaw puzzle. The treatment of the façades as Möbius-like surfaces that "fold" into the concave mass of the built spaces strengthens this sense of "all-over," of positive-negative, figure-ground ambiguity. In order to complete the block-filling scheme, small groves of trees have—as at Trenton—been treated as "architectural" mass. The interior-exterior ambivalence of the site plan is restated at the scale of the theater (the only part to be realized): the auditorium—"the violin in its case"—a house-in-house with overtly "exterior" foyer and distribution spaces.

183 Kahn, quoted in Brady, "The Architectural Metaphysics of Louis Kahn," p. 58.

**145–47** Fort Wayne Fine Arts Center, 1961–73: sketches, site plan, morphological plan
**148** De Menil Foundation, 1972: site plan

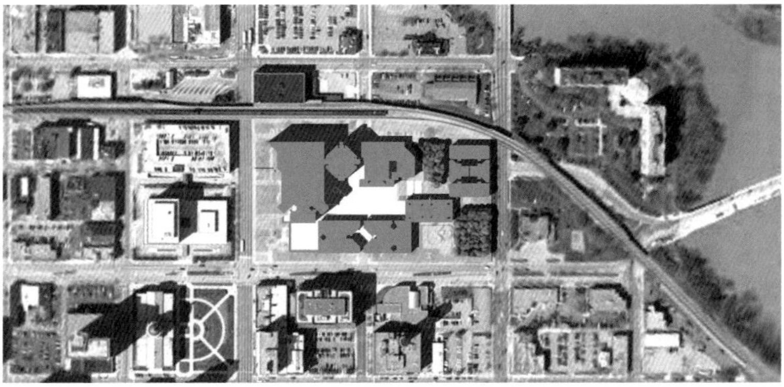

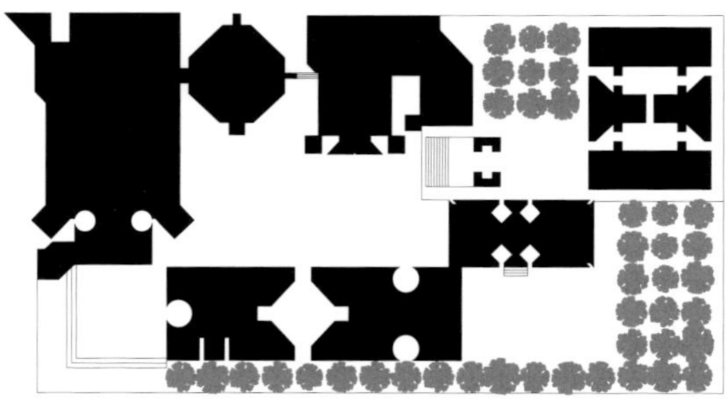

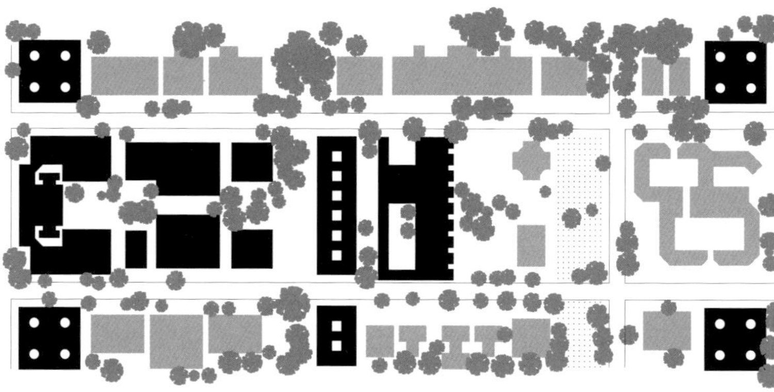

The diagrams for the Fine Arts Center and the Dominican Motherhouse illuminate a corollary source of ambiguity in Kahn's late work: the general tension between the additive and the subtractive, between the assembled and the grown. If the Dominican Motherhouse reads as an interrupted *fusion* of individual parts, the Fine Arts Center tends to give the impression that it has been developed from the opposite direction, as if through *subtraction* from a great rectangular block. Morphologically, much of Kahn's work straddles this border between the—classical/functionalist/additive—idea of linked pavilions and the—baroque/organicist/plastic—tendency toward "grown" organisms.[184]

**Figure-ground: further ensembles**

The Fort Wayne project was paralleled by other unrealized urban ensembles in which Kahn expanded upon Fort Wayne's vocabulary for defining "figural" urban space with free-standing architectural objects: the Philadelphia College of Fine Arts (1964–66), the Broadway Church-Apartment Tower (1966–67), the Inner Harbor Development for Baltimore (1970–73), and the De Menil Foundation in Fort Worth (1973–74). The projects in Philadelphia and New York not only expand upon Fort Wayne's scale, they illustrate the potential of mass-void play in section.[185] The project in Baltimore extends Fort Wayne's vocabulary by using a modernist structural frame—an inherently additive system—to generate through an origami-like folding of its envelope a plastic ensemble which once again begins to oscillate between the additive and the subtractive. The project for the De Menil Collection in Fort Worth is exemplary for the way in which a series of volumes is superimposed over a suburban block in order to stake out a small cultural district, concurrently creating institutional presence while preserving the neighborhood's residential scale. **Fig. 148**

In contrast to then-emerging postmodernist strategies, which often called for the insertion of traditional "textural" and European models into the modern American city, Kahn's attempts at creating urban "forums of availability"—being at once loose-fitting and dense, expanding upon yet never fully discarding the free-standing architectural object as the primary building block and the grid as the organizing matrix—seem in retrospect uniquely appropriate suggestions for the American morphology of the object-filled grid.[186] In light of the paucity of attractive alternative urban and suburban planning models in

184 See Bottero, "Organic and Rational Morphology in the Work of Louis Kahn."

185 David Polk, who in addition to the monastery projects worked with Kahn on the Broadway Tower project, recalled that as that project was being developed, "Lou came into the office with a book on the ancient Indian rock-cut temples: those which have been hewn directly out of the cliffs. 'How do you make architecture out of that?' he wanted to know. He was really interested in *poché* architecture and how to achieve something analogous with modern means." Interview, author with David Polk, October 20, 2004.

186 For more on the grid as American Vernacular, see Scully, *Architecture: The Natural and the Manmade,* ch. 11; Riley, "The Landscapes of Frank Lloyd Wright: A Pattern of Work"; or, particularly in respect to Kahn, Venturi, "Genius Betrayed," p. 43.

**149** Dominican Motherhouse: figure-ground, June 1966
**150** Dominican Motherhouse: built and grown, August 1968

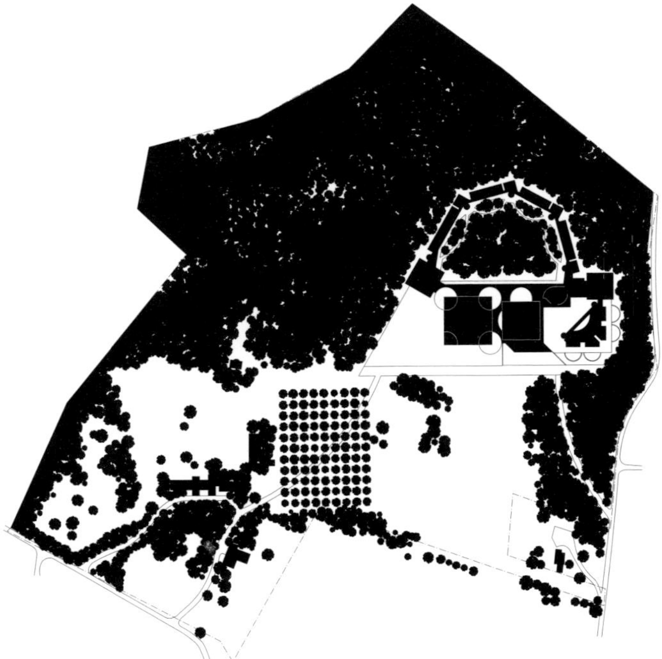

the United States in recent decades, their unbuilt status seems even more regrettable.

The Dominican Motherhouse

While the projects above unfold their figure-ground characters on relatively generic sites, the Dominican Motherhouse "figure-grounds" itself into a specific situation. We have seen how architectural mass, arboreal mass, and interstitial spaces were manipulated to underscore the project's evolving "Form." By the final scheme, the forest, the irregular spaces of the clearing, the monastery's volumes, and the spaces between them have all been assigned equal status in terms of figure and ground, effectively conjoining architecture and landscape. **Figs. 149–150** While the figure-ground scheme has provided an indispensible tool for seeing and describing this phenomenon, the narrative has shown that the subtle reciprocities between the two spatial realms are based on more than figure-ground phenomena, and include a multi-layered and intertwined system of relationships including inflection, linkage of scales, the perception of the body in space, symbolic imaging, etc.

### Further Steps Toward Reciprocity: From Membrane to Border-Space, From Dyad to Triad, From Figure-Ground to Threefold Spatial Demarcation

The basic figure-ground scheme (and by "basic" I mean the scheme as conventionally used, with buildings solid black and all else white) provides a first as yet incomplete tool for describing—or designing—reciprocity between architectural and natural space. While this basic scheme offers a means for seeing and manipulating plan-space in terms of mass and void, positive and negative, convex and concave, etc., it remains limited in regard to the projection of our experience into those spaces. One simple reason for this is because within the "dyad" scheme we tend to picture ourselves *either* within the black *or,* more likely, the white; or, as it has been observed, while we are able to recognize *both* the two faces *and* the vase in Rubin's familiar figure-ground diagram, we seem to be able to experience them only *sequentially,* rather than *simultaneously.*

Relativity of inside and outside space

What is missing, then, in the simple twofold figure-ground diagram (and in buildings conceived in this manner) is an additional dimension to help us experience both realms simultaneously; or more exactly, to experience ourselves in regard to both of these realms. In short: *a means for experiencing that inside and outside are never absolute, always relative to each other; that each architectural space is a partial space: a portion of a greater space from which it has been separated.* With plan notation as our means of representing spatial reality, we tend to experience this relativity while reading older *poché* plans—such as Nolli's and the best of the Ecole des Beaux-Arts—more than we do reading modernist figure-ground plans. In those older plans, there are at least two phenomena which we miss in modernist plans and which we have missed so far in the description of the "basic" figure-ground schemes. First, the thick walls of the *poché* plans which create the intervals necessary to perceive inside and outside as *independent* spaces (the first prerequisite in establishing reciprocity), a thickness which in some Beaux-Arts plans is considerable enough to achieve parity with void spaces. Second, there is the porous, ornamental, Gestalt character of these plans, which not only generates spaces that are purely "inside" and purely "outside," but a third type of mediating space between these two.[187]

At this point we might continue to explore the remaining "rules of seeing" laid out by Gestalt principles, for the figure-ground scheme is based on only one of these: the principle called "multistability." Gestalt principles offer additional means of seeing "wholes through parts," principles which, taken together, provide a more comprehensive set of answers than any single one alone.[188] While it would undoubtedly be fruitful to view Kahn's spaces under these aspects, I have chosen another—because architecturally immanent—theory as an aid in the exploration of reciprocity.

**Hans van der Laan: Architectonic Space**

The two "missing" phenomena described above—first, a means of dividing space which has the property of a *body* rather than of a *membrane;* second, a "third space" from which the relativity of inside and outside become apparent—are two cornerstones of a modern theory of architectural space which finds compelling parallels in Kahn's mature work. This is the theory developed by the remarkable Dutch architect-scholar-monk Dom Hans van der Laan (1904–1991) in his magnum opus, *De architectonische ruimte* of 1977 (*Architectonic Space,* 1983). In what is undoubtedly the twentieth century's most ambitiously fundamental theory of architectural space, van der Laan attempted nothing less than a synthetic description of space, which is grounded in the existential need of bodily shelter, moves over an empirical/perceptual analysis of how we experience form, and finally proceeds to develop a perception-based rational system for proportioning mass and space. The three levels of this theory are evident in van der Laan's claim: "The space of nature has three aspects which leave us at a loss: it is unlimited, without form and without measure....

187 David van Zanten has described this phenomenon in a comparison between the compositional/drawing methods of Sullivan, Wright, and Kahn. On Sullivan's drawings: "I would propose that not only were the switches in scale from ornament to building space a fact but also the whole point—and that these switches embraced many scales, especially the cartographic." On Kahn's drawings: "And what is the scale of these images? That of a building plan? Or merely a pattern? Or doesn't that matter: might not the whole point be that the largest relationships mirror the smallest to bind the design at all scales to achieve a kind of flicker in scale?" Van Zanten, "Kahn and Architectural Composition," unpublished manuscript.

188 Others being "emergence," "reification," "invariance," "prägnanz." For a thorough description of the Gestalt principles mentioned above, see Metzler, *Gesetze des Sehens.*

Architecture is nothing else but that which must be added to natural space to make it habitable, that is, delimited in relation to our bodies, visible to our senses and measurable to our intellect."[189] While a summary of van der Laan's theory is well beyond the scope of this study, a brief outline of that theory in respect to the spatial phenomena mentioned above will begin to provide us with a means with which to bring Kahn's work further into focus.

### From Membrane to Border-Space

*The Graeco-Roman decides to separate himself from the fields, from "Nature," from the geo-botanic cosmos. How is this possible? How can man withdraw himself from the fields? Where will he go, since the earth is one huge unbounded field? Quite simple; he will mark off a portion of this field by means of walls, which set up an enclosed, finite space over against amorphous, limitless space.*

José Ortega y Gasset, *The Revolt of the Masses*, 1930

**Enclosure and opening**

For Hans van der Laan, architecture begins with man's separation of a piece of space from the larger whole of natural space. The vertical wall is responsible for this task. While Ortega y Gasset ends his description of human habitation with enclosure, for van der Laan enclosure is only a first step; once separated, a built space must be brought back into relation with the space of nature in order to create a usable human dwelling place. Architecture's—the wall's—primary function is not division, but *mediation.* Van der Laan argues that only a space that has first arisen between walls can engage in a genuine relationship with natural space. After developing this hypothesis, his theory extends to work out a means for establishing empirically derived, perception-based proportional relationships between enclosed spaces and the depth and openings of their enclosing walls.[190] (Means which will not be worked out in respect to Kahn's work here.)

**Paradox of the membrane-wall**

As van der Laan was developing his theory—and Kahn was building his mature work—modern technology had worked to maximize roof spans and minimize wall thickness. As walls were reduced to bubble-like enclosing membranes, the enclosed space began to take on a self-contained quality, which was for van der Laan no different in principle from that of a cave. In contradiction to the modernist assumption that, with the help of technology, "Only now can we articulate space, open it up and connect it to the landscape" (Mies van der Rohe),[191] van der Laan recognized the paradox that if a room's

189 Dom Hans van der Laan, lecture to architecture students, 1985, quoted in Padovan, *Hans van der Laan*, p. 30.

190 Van der Laan, *Architectonic Space*, chs. 7–12.

191 Van der Rohe, "Was wäre Beton, was Stahl ohne Spiegelglas?" p. 378.

walls are completely of glass, that space is perceived as divorced from the space outside.[192] Van der Laan's premises find echo in Kahn's insistence on enclosure as the first act, on the "making of the room" as the primary act of inhabitation. Only after this enclosure was established could "the walls part and architecture begin."[193]

Recovering the wall

If Kahn's early work in the modernist genre in the thirties and forties is not completely convincing, this is in no small part due to his reluctance to completely dissolve the wall. Compared to the self-assured transparency of contemporary works of van der Rohe, Neutra, or Breuer, for example, his own works seem rather tentative and ungainly. By the fifties, though, he had begun to question such literal transparency as the sine qua non of a modern architecture and to sense the loss of the wall as a bearer of meaning and a necessary "third term" between enclosed and natural space. Writing home from Rome during his 1951 fellowship at the American Academy, he waxed envious on ancient Roman architecture: "All of our stuff looks tinny compared to it."[194] Although the real mass of the pre-twentieth-century wall was not an option for him, he began in the mid-fifties, at first tentatively (Adler House, Trenton Bath House), then with a conscious fervor (the First Unitarian Church, the Esherick House, the Salk Institute, the Indian Institute of Management, etc.), to redefine the modernist membrane as a shaper of a *spatial layer*—folding it, capsizing it, doubling it, "wrapping ruins around buildings," and gradually devising a uniquely modern mediating architectural space. He had in fact rediscovered what untold generations of arcade-, gallery- and cloister-builders had already known: that depth could be virtual, "captured air" instead of mass. Indeed, if anything, the separating effect of the layered or house-in-house scheme was even stronger than that of a massive wall of the same depth, giving both inside space and outside space emphatically separate "façades." **Figs. 151–152**

Both the *means* for establishing depth and the *uses* assigned to that depth were varied in Kahn's late work according to circumstance: functioning as *brise soleil* (the American Consulate at Luanda, Salk Meeting House, National Assembly at Dhaka), as gallery or loggia (Salk Institute, Kimbell Art Museum), as "servant space" (Richards Medical Laboratories, Salk Institute), as "hollow columns" (Mikveh Israel and Hurva Synagogues), and/or as human-scaled habitable space (First Unitarian Church, Exeter Library, Dominican Motherhouse). Robert Venturi recognized in his *Complexity and Contradiction*

192 Dom Hans van der Laan, letter to Jos Naalden on the Naalden House (1978–82), September 7, 1985, quoted in Padovan, *Hans van der Laan,* p. 124.

193 Kahn, "Architecture is the Thoughtful Making of Spaces," p. 271.

194 Letter, Kahn to Office, December 6, 1950, quoted in Johnson and Lewis, *Drawn From the Source,* p. 72.

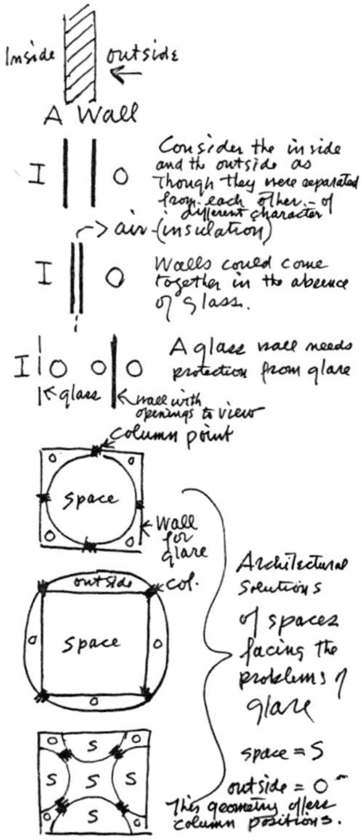


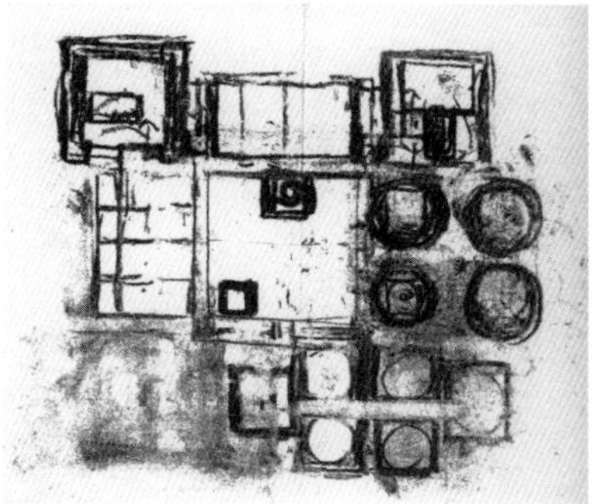

**151–52** Salk Institute Meeting House, 1959–65: from membrane to border-space

"Because a wall has an interior which is different from an exterior ... we have come to the point where this realization now can separate an exterior wall from an interior wall ... and create space between them that you could walk between, that which you couldn't do with a stone wall." Louis Kahn, 1973

*in Architecture* that Kahn's thickened wall-zones simultaneously violated two modernist dogma: in their redundancy, they broke with the modernist rule of efficiency; while in their double-active quality, they broke the rule of functionalist cause-and-effect clarity.[195] But by the mid-fifties both Kahn and Venturi had realized that the wall was the locus of architecture's appearance, and one of modernism's greatest mistakes was to reduce it to the smallest necessary climatic barrier. According to Venturi: "I would say that architecture occurs at the meeting of particular interior forces of use and space, and particular and general forces of environment. Architecture as the wall between inside and outside becomes the spatial record of this reconciliation and its drama."[196] Kahn's morphology of the wall-as-border-space would provide more than enough stuff for a separate, extensive study: its tectonics, its habitability, its reintroduction of the window, its evocation of antecedents, its spatial nuances, etc. For the purposes of this study, though, this description and the accompanying illustrations must suffice to establish its existence as a tangible, Janus-faced, and multivalent border-space between inside and outside.

This necessity of depth, of a "border-space" for defining inside and outside, applied not only to the vertical plane of the wall, but to the horizontal plane of the roof as well. Accordingly, there are never conventional "greenhouse" skylights in Kahn's work: top-lit spaces are illuminated by reflecting natural light around a corner or obliquely through an intermediate space. This horizontal "border-space" is at least as palpable as its vertical partner and establishes the interior-exterior relationship in a similar way.

### From Twofold Figure-Ground to Threefold Demarcation

**Workspace, walking-space, visual field**

According to van der Laan's theory, the wall as a "border space" fulfills the first prerequisite for establishing reciprocity between architectural and natural space. Corresponding to the aforementioned "third space" in the Gestalt diagrams and *poché* plans is the next precondition for reciprocity in his theory.

Van der Laan named man's image of that segment of natural space involved in his own existence his "experience-space." He then proposed that this experience-space might be further described according to man's vital activity in the world. A threefold superposition of progressively larger spaces is the result of this corporeal activity: the immediate "workspace," the larger "walking-space," and the still larger "visual field": a hierarchy in which the smaller space always lies at

195 Venturi, *Complexity and Contradiction in Architecture,* p. 107.

196 Venturi, "Ideas of Reconciliation in Architectural Composition," unpublished proposal sent to John Entenza of the Graham Foundation, February 15, 1962, p. 10.

the center of the larger. After defining these three spatial zones, van der Laan proceeded to map out their architectural consequences:

"The threefold nature of our experience-space has its architectonic consequences. We have already seen that the functional role of the house lies in the fitting of the architectonic space that comes into being between the walls to the space of our experience. We have presented this fitting together as a fusion of two space-images. On one hand we have the space of nature, within and from which a limited space is set free between vertical walls; on the other a limited piece of space in the midst of nature which we, as its core, involve in our presence. We have seen the combination of images result in the dyad inside-outside: habitable human dwelling inside, natural space made habitable outside.

"If we experienced space in one way only, a single boundary would be enough to separate the totally inner from the totally outer. It appears, however, that our experience-space has various zones; therefore several boundaries are needed, and architectonic space is necessarily composite.

"It is therefore not enough to mark out only the intimate space needed for work. We may well withdraw into this limited space for a while, but inevitably we soon feel the need of a larger space to walk in, and this too must be drawn into our existence by vertical walls. Lastly, our visual field is too much restricted even by this second boundary, and therefore needs a wider enclosure of its own. So the complete human habitat demands a threefold demarcation of space.

"Each of these spatial boundaries is wider than and contains the one before. The architectonic effectiveness of the boundaries decreases progressively as they get wider, because the wider the space, the weaker the directional force of the vertical wall. In relation to the breadth of the visual field, or even the walking-space, the height of the wall is very slight, and therefore provides a very weak basis for the space around us that we relate to ourselves.

"So although after staying some time in the intimate space we work in we seek relief in these wider spaces, it cannot be for long. Within the vast enclosure of the visual field, which divides the inside from nature, we again feel the need of a more confined demarcation that relates space more strongly to ourselves.

"Thus the human habitat is like an interplay between three demarcations that alternately call for and reject each other; we call them, in order of size, cell, court and domain.

**153–55** Dom Hans van der Laan, threefold demarcation of space, in *De architectonische ruimte,* 1977

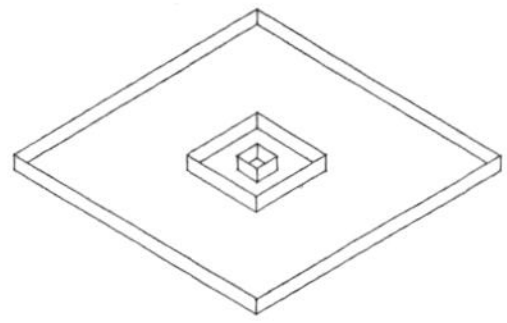

1 Central court with central cell
2 Central court with peripheral cell
3 Peripheral court with central cell
4 Peripheral court with peripheral cell

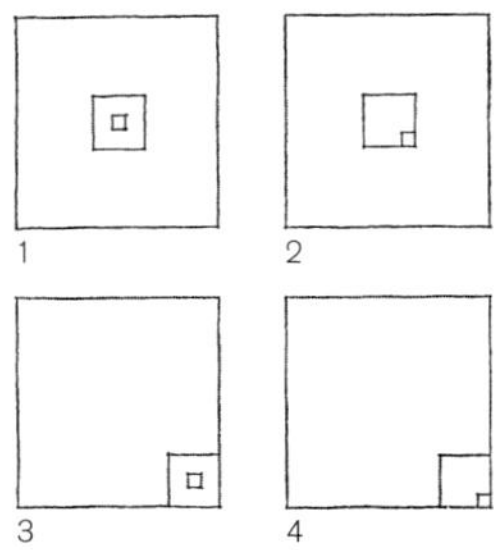


1 Central court with central cell
2 Central court with peripheral cell
3 Central court with peripheral juxtaposition of cells
4 Peripheral court with central cell
5 Peripheral court with peripheral cell
6 Peripheral court with peripheral juxtaposition of cells
7 Peripheral juxtaposition of courts with central cell
8 Peripheral juxtaposition of courts with peripheral cell
9 Peripheral juxtaposition of courts with peripheral juxtaposition of cells

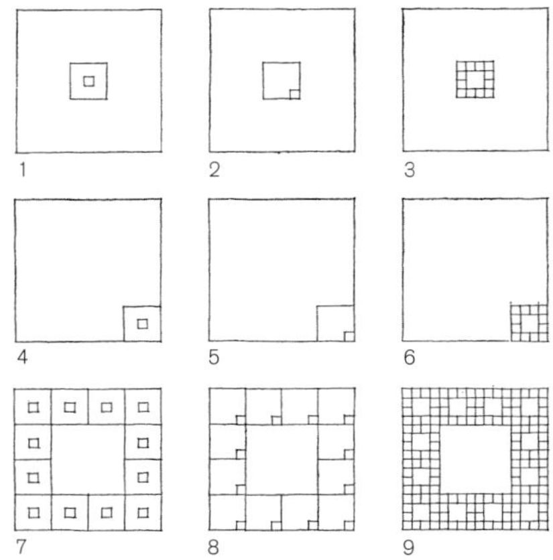


"Since the architectonic effect of the three demarcations is not equally strong, a different 'inside' arises in each case. For the intimate interior of the cell the wider walking-space of the courts counts as an outside, though compared to the large domain it counts as an inside. The threefold articulation of the absolute inside in the midst of the absolute outside of nature introduces us to two secondary relations between inside and outside—on the one hand between cell and court, and on the other between court and domain.

"Thus the same thing takes place at a secondary level within architectonic space as occurs between architectonic space and natural space. We shall meet this phenomenon again in relation to form and size. The advantage of this is that it enables us to experience and envisage in a comparable way, within the limits of the finite space its relation to the infinite space, within the limits of the formed mass its relation to formless space, and within the limits of the measured quantity its relation to measureless quantity."[197] **Figs. 153–155**

**A linked chain of insides**

If we adopt van der Laan's tenet that architectural space is composite, that a simple boundary can not adequately separate inside and outside,

197 Van der Laan, *Architectonic Space,* pp. 23–25.

and if we view his linked, threefold chain of spatial demarcation as a means of relativizing architectural space in respect to natural space, then we are equipped with richer means for seeing and thinking about space than the "twofold" figure-ground scheme he has provided us. If the figure-ground scheme directs our gaze *sequentially* toward the complements of mass and void, the threefold demarcation supplements this scheme with an extra dimension and directs our attention toward the *mediating* capacity of mass and space and the *relativity* of interior and exterior in respect to the sentient human body. Van der Laan's linked chain of spatial scales, while extant in much pre-modern and vernacular architecture, is largely absent in the modern, which in its attempts to either fetishize or dissolve the object tended to eliminate the middle spatial term. Kahn's "ornamental" or "porous" plans are compelling attempts to re-establish this rule. As his thought and architecture strongly parallels van der Laan's thought regarding the wall, so too does Kahn's work echo van der Laan's concept of linked spatial demarcation.

If we regard the works described above in terms of figure and ground—in terms of van der Laan's linked chain of scales—it is easy to find concentric layers of enclosure approximating van der Laan's "cell," "court," and "domain." What in the Trenton Community Center is a still-schematic interpretation of the middle scale of "court" or "walking-space," has, in later works, taken on much a greater richness. In open landscapes, where mediation between small scale and large is most necessary, the linked chain of spatial demarcation is most pronounced: the Salk Institute, the Indian Institute of Management, the National Assembly at Dhaka, et al. In the Salk Institute, for example, a threefold (or even fourfold) layering of space structures the entire ensemble: from the small studies over the loggias to the plaza; from the grove to the plaza to the Pacific landscape, etc. The Fort Wayne Fine Arts Center, the Dominican Motherhouse, St. Andrew's Priory, and the Indian Institute of Management may all be used to further illustrate van der Laan's theory.

**Central spaces as "Courts"**

If Kahn's familiar top-lit communal spaces are seen as the equivalent of van der Laan's "courts" (for this *is* how Kahn would like us to see them), then the sponge-like spatial diagram reveals a further dimension. The ornamental plan of the Research Institute for Advanced Studies, with its parity between its courts and its large central spaces, is a pithy case in point. The sanctuary of the First Unitarian Church, the central spaces of the Exeter Library, the Hurva Synagogue, the halls of the Yale Center for British Art: all "want" to become "courts" to their surrounding "cells" of space. Figs. 156–159 This is underscored by Kahn's treatment of these spaces with explicitly "exterior" materials and "ambivalent" roofs.

**156–59** Kahn's threefold space: Salk Meeting House, Dominican Motherhouse, St. Andrew's Priory, Fort Wayne Fine Arts Center
**160** National Assembly Building, Dhaka: diagram, Louis Kahn

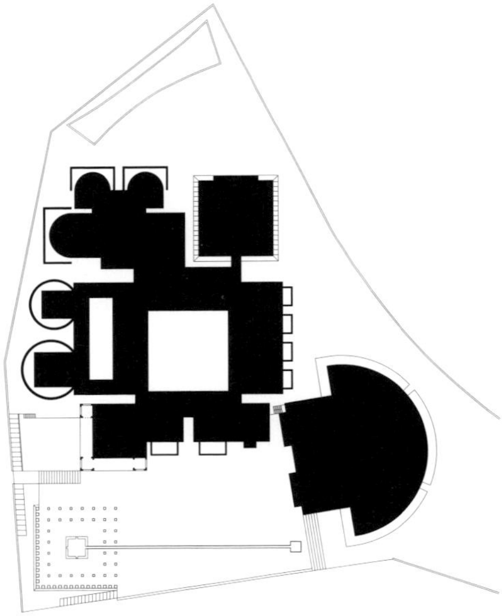

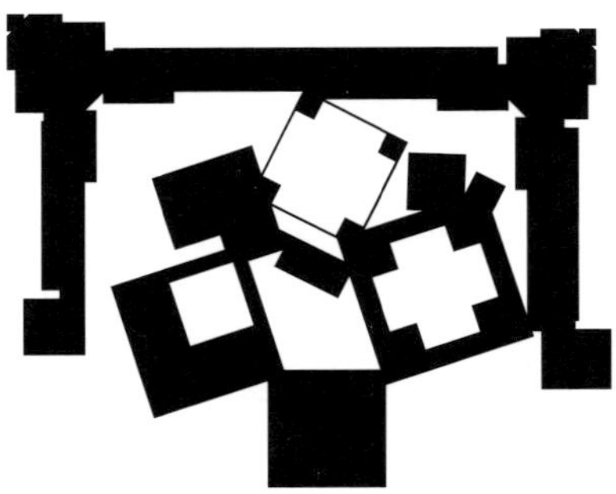

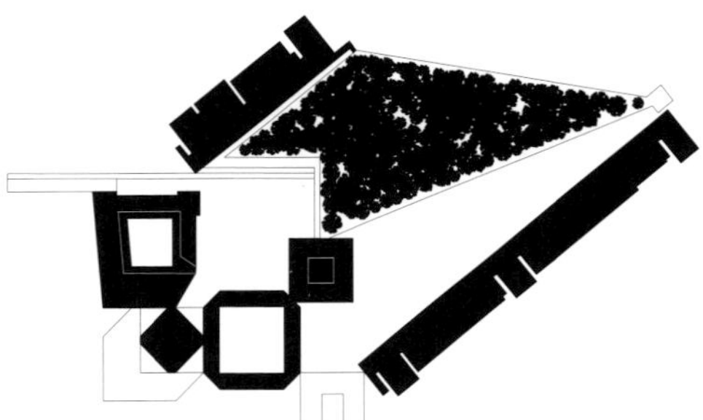

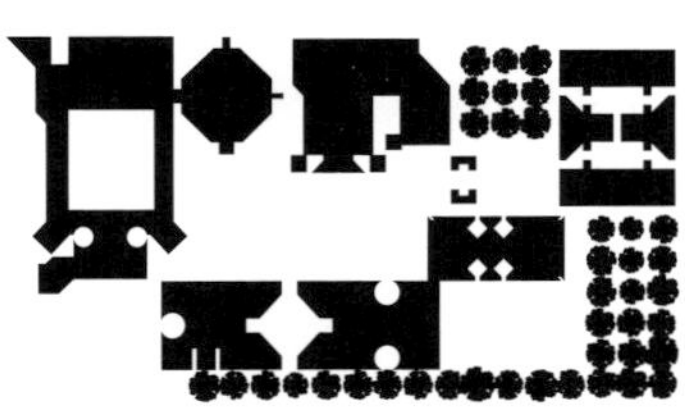

### On Twin Phenomena: Reciprocity and Inversion

This exploration of reciprocity has centered on the *physical* terms of bringing mass and void, indoor and outdoor space, into resolved, comprehensible, and multivalent relationships with each other, with van der Laan's rational theory providing one means to explore something at once commonsensical yet strangely difficult to describe. There are countless other manifestations of the term which both underscore and expand upon the phenomena outlined above. In closing, I would like to briefly sketch out two of these.

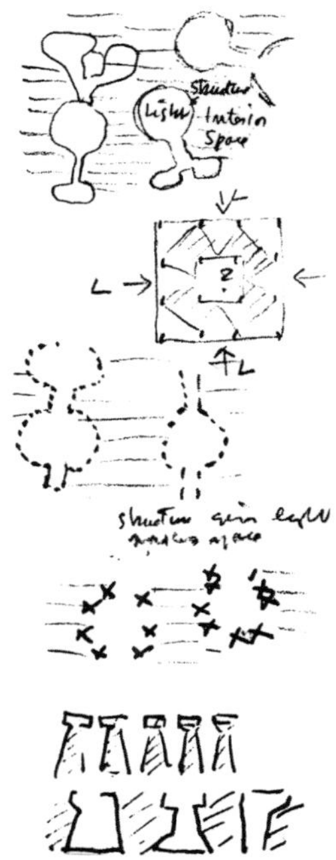

In Kahn's *coincidentia oppositorum,* a thing is often (purposefully) mistaken for its opposite. Kahn not only sought to bring mass and void, inside and outside, into *resolved balances,* he later wished them virtually *interchangeable.* In a remarkable statement on the National Assembly at Dhaka, he said:

"In the assembly I have introduced a light-giving element to the interior of the plan. If you see a series of columns you can say that the choice of columns is a choice in light. The columns as solids frame the spaces of light. Now think of it just in reverse and think that the columns are hollow and much bigger and that their walls can give light, then the voids are rooms, and the column is the maker of light and can take on complex shapes and be the supporter of spaces and give light to the spaces. I am working to develop the element to such an extent that it becomes a poetic entity which has its own beauty outside of its place in the composition. In this way it becomes analogous to the solid column I mentioned above as a giver of light." [198] **Fig. 160**

If solid and void, light and dark, are encouraged to trade places in a Kahnian world, so too are interior and exterior. Just as Kahn's tendency to treat major interior rooms as pieces of "dislodged" exterior space was essential to his spatial vision, corollary and complementary was his treatment of exterior spaces as discrete "insides." While we have observed this principle at work thus far on the architectural scale, it is a principle applicable at the scale of urban planning, as in his "viaduct" and Bicentennial plans for Philadelphia, which treat the city as a great "inside" or a "society of rooms." With Kahn there is a purposeful willingness to confuse architecture with urbanism and vice versa:

"The street: it is really the first communal space. From this outside room with the sky as a roof must have come the notion of having the first meeting place, which, because of the weather conditions

198 Kahn, June 1964 (on Dhaka), quoted in Ronner and Jhaveri, *Louis I. Kahn: Complete Work,* p. 239.

suggested that a roof make an enclosure, which you called also a meeting house, within which you put some benches and with the simplest devices transfer the street into a building. The street is really a room by agreement. I can tell you that as soon as I thought this simple thing, I could design any city in the world." [199]

**Reciprocity: built and grown**

Reciprocity becomes further manifest in Kahn's use of phenomena traditionally associated with landscape as "architecture" and his use of architecture as "garden." [200] The use of trees as arboreal/architectural mass at the Trenton Jewish Community Center and the Fort Wayne Fine Arts Center; or the modeling of the forest at Media into a *cabinet de verdure* for the Dominican Motherhouse: from the late fifties onward, Kahn increasingly grew and shaped landscape to complement architecture while shaping architecture to complement landscape or to accept her as an equal within the limits of its structure. The Dominican Motherhouse, St. Andrew's Priory, the Kimbell Art Museum, the Salk Institute, the Levy Memorial Playground, the Graduate Theological Union Library, the Presidential Estate in Islamabad, the plan for the Philadelphia Bicentennial: in these works and others architecture and landscape are conjoined as mutually dependent parts of a whole. While modernism's ideal of "the machine in the garden" tended to treat landscape architecture as a naturalistic background for its *objets-types,* and while ecological issues tended to dominate much of landscape architecture in the sixties and seventies, Kahn was almost alone at this time in his rejection of both the Corbusian *tapis vert* and naturalism in his rediscovery of this—essentially classical—view of seeing earth mass, built mass, and vegetative mass as interdependent.[201]

**Roosevelt Memorial**

One of Kahn's most compelling illustrations of built-grown reciprocity is the project for the Franklin D. Roosevelt Memorial (1973–74) on the tip of New York's Roosevelt Island in the East River between Manhattan and Brooklyn. **Fig. 161** Unhindered by a program and the necessity of creating enclosed space, and working in close cooperation with landscape architect Harriet Pattison, Kahn's first insight was a memorial as a reciprocal pair of spaces: "a room and a garden." The "room," a sixty-foot foot square enclosed on three sides by great granite megaliths, was open on its fourth side to the horizon. The

199 Kahn, interview in *Silence and Light,* documentary video, 1995, Kahn Collection.

200 Interview, author with Harriet Pattison, Architectural Archives, University of Pennsylvania, October 21, 2004. Transcript in Merrill, "Louis Kahn and the Dominican Motherhouse," pp. 175–80.

201 It is important to note that in contrast to certain current (in the end anti-urban) tendencies which conceive of buildings as "artificial landscapes," Kahn was never interested in confusing or blending that which is landscape and that which is building, but rather saw the necessity of maintaining their differences as a precondition for true reciprocity. The tendency to attempt to make buildings disappear as "landscapes" may be seen as a misunderstanding and the flip side of the object-fetishist coin.

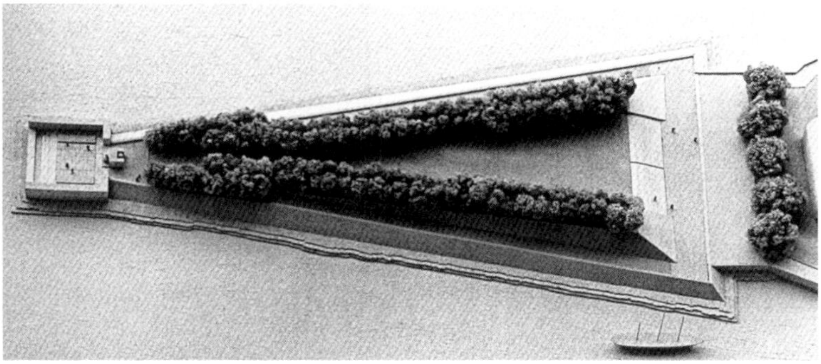

**161** Franklin D. Roosevelt Memorial, 1973–74

"garden," a triple-sloped earthen wedge planted with trees was to be the visitors' route to and from the "room" on the island. The experience of the memorial is heightened by the subtle manner in which the visitor's perception is choreographed to gradually trade wide views of the cityscape for a concentrated view of sky and horizon. Architecture and landscaping are treated as inverted equals. The architectural "room" is in fact the most exposed and "exterior" experience in the memorial: upon entering, the skyline of Manhattan slips away to be replaced by an unobstructed view toward the horizon with the sky as ceiling. In contrast, the botanical "garden" offers the visitor the most sheltered and "architectural" space, with tightly spaced tree trunks as walls and crowns as enclosing roof. There's something poignantly archetypical at work here, as if Kahn's "room" ("the beginning of architecture") were slowly emerging from (or submerging to) some pre-architectural geological state, while trees coalesce into an *Urhütte* of the sort described by Abbé Laugier.

**The Kimbell Art Museum**

The Kimbell Art Museum **Figs. 162–164** is one of Kahn's most accomplished and subtle demonstrations of grown-built reciprocity at work. (The landscape plan was a collaboration with George Patton and Harriet Pattison.) As Michael Benedikt has eloquently pointed out,[202] ambivalence is already set up in the building's plan: are we to read the symmetrical parti of the building as a "classical" solution to the problem of museum-making (and thus a type with a long-standing tradition), or are we to see the whole as an additive "modernist" rowing of identical modules (such as a warehouse or train station)? The building presents itself to us in both manners at once without indicating a preferred reading. "Classical" at first glance is also the use of trees—here the existing *allées*—as well as the disposition of fountains and paths to strengthen major and minor axes and to set up relationships between museum and park. Yet, a small, dense *bosque* of holly trees which has

202 Benedikt, *Deconstructing the Kimbell*, p. 55.

**162–64** Kimbell Art Museum, 1966–72: porch, section, site plan

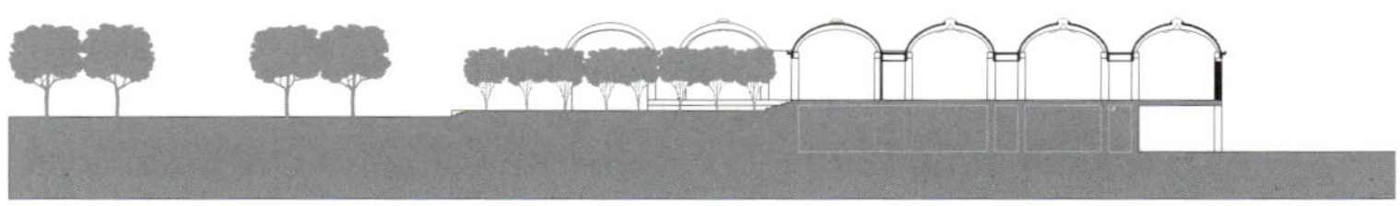

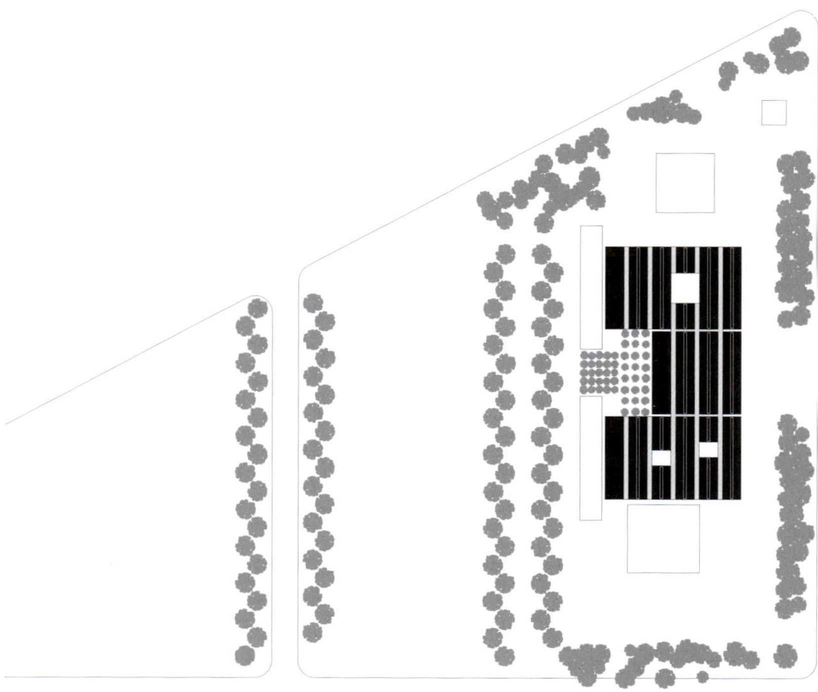

been planted directly in front of the park-side entry blocks the main axis in an exceptionally "non-classical" manner—again, an ambivalence between symmetry and asymmetry, closed and open systems. The *bosque* "grafts" the museum onto the *allée* while forming a shaded and welcoming entry area that seems to belong equally to park and museum. (Kahn thought it appropriate that the undecided visitor might be given a chance to peek into the museum before deciding whether or not to go in.)

As always in Kahn's mature work, the building's floor plan tells only half the story. Viewed both in site plan and in site section, the intended built-grown reciprocity becomes more fully apparent: here, the museum's regular gridded framework supporting its great vaults; there, the park's regularly gridded *allées* with the spaces defined beneath their crowns. The section makes it tempting to think of architecture as tree-mimetic and of an architecturalized garden plan. In any case, between enclosed spaces of the galleries and the open space of the park is a rich and ambivalent threshold zone formed by both architecture and trees. On the one hand, the gallery module has "dissolved" into the two great porches and an entry portico; on the other hand, the space defined by the park's trees has densified in the form of the *bosque*. Said Kahn of the porches, "It is the same realization behind Renaissance buildings which gave the arcade to the street, though the buildings themselves did not need the arcade for their own purposes. So the porch sits there, made as the interior is made, without any obligation of paintings on its walls, a realization of what is architecture. When you look at the building and the porch, it is an offering. You know it wasn't programmed, it is something that emerged."[203] Like their antecedents, the Kimbell's exterior vaults are "made as the interior is made." The *bosque* and hardscape features such as benches and paths, on the other hand, begin to "interiorize" outside space; Michael Benedikt has pointed out that here in the park "one is already in."[204] Approaching on the gravel surface underneath the low branches, one is given views both to the park and to the entry portico. After having ascended the steps to the portico, the view back into the park is now blocked by the crowns of the trees; one is now even more "in." Through this built-grown plan-section reciprocity, Kahn and his landscape partners have woven site and building into a dense and multivalent experience, at once transforming the character of the rather ordinary semi-urban site and giving breadth to the rather small museum.

203 Kahn, quoted in Johnson, *Light is the Theme*, p. 28.

204 Benedikt, *Deconstructing the Kimbell*. Benedikt's analysis of the Kimbell includes a more thorough description of the masterful play between building and site than is possible here; a play later diminished by Renzo Piano's addition to the museum.

**165** Library, Phillips Exeter Academy, 1965–72, the space of "twinphenomena": large-small, inside-outside, rough-smooth, etc.

#### Reciprocity: Complementary Thinking vs. Binary Thinking

This concept of reciprocity invites a richer way of thinking about human dwelling and the built environment than conventional modernist and most contemporary hierarchies have produced, whether by privileging one type of space over the other or by to attempting to eliminate the differences between the two. Through this thinking in terms of "twin phenomena" we arrive at a critique not only of our particular métier's way of thinking, but of a deep-seated cultural paradigm and of a resulting habitual either/or "default mode." In architecture, reciprocal thinking fosters an Albertian vision of a house as a collection of unique locales, as well as that of a city as a big house. Interiors may be conceived of as exteriors, and vice versa, without losing the necessary distinction between these two realms. The promise of all this, in the words of Aldo van Eyck, being an "architecture as an instrument of connection rather than separation, a more true habitation of both city and house."[205] Columns may be massive, or hollow, or may grow to the size of a room; shadow and light may trade places. We may begin to understand Kahn when he says, "The plan does not begin nor end with the space he (the architect) has enveloped, but from the adjoining delicate ground sculpture it stretches beyond to the rolling contours and vegetation of the surrounding land and continues farther out to the distant hills."[206] By further dwelling in Kahn's work and thought, we may better understand how architecture may at the same time be both open and closed, big and small, simple and complex, monist and pluralist...

205 Van Eyck, "Steps Towards a Configurative Discipline," pp. 81–94. No architect has argued as passionately and articulately for the principle of reciprocity in (architectural) thinking as Kahn's younger contemporary, Aldo van Eyck. His definition of "right-size" overlaps with and extends the descriptions of Kahn's work on the previous pages, thus making a fitting conclusion for this chapter: "I am again concerned with twinphenomena: with unity and diversity, part and whole, small and large, many and few, simplicity and complexity, change and constancy, order and chaos, individual and collective, with why they are ignobly halved and the halves hollowed out, why too they are withheld from opening the windows of the mind! As abstract antonyms the halves are rendered meaningless. As soon, however, as they are permitted to materialize in to house or city their emptiness materializes into cruelty, for in such places everything is always too large and too small, too few and too many, too far and too near, too much and too little the same, too much and too little different. There is no question of right-size (by right-size I mean the right effect of size) and hence no question of human scale. What has right-size is at the same time both large and small, few and many, near and far, simple and complex, open and closed; will furthermore always be both part and whole and embrace both unity and diversity. No, as conflicting polarities or false alternatives these abstract antonyms all carry the same luggage: loss of identity and its attribute—monotony. Monotony not only in the sense of uniform because as I have already said: If a thing is too much and too little the same, it will also be too much and too little different. Right-size will flower as soon as the mild gears of reciprocity start working—in the climate of relativity; in the landscape of twinphenomena."

206 Kahn, "Monumentality," p. 25.

## FROM SPACE TO PLACE
## FROM ESTABLISHING THE GENERAL TO REVEALING THE SPECIFIC

*The site confirms the possible and encourages agreement on the beginning in the making of man's place. A mere foothold is confident of the settlement, the first institution of man. The works of man reveal his nature.* Louis Kahn, Master's Studio, September 29, 1969

*The plan does not begin nor end with the space he [the architect] has enveloped, but from the adjoining delicate ground sculpture it stretches beyond to the rolling contours and vegetation of the surrounding land and continues farther out to the distant hills.* Louis Kahn, "Monumentality," 1944

While the previous chapter attempted to bring into focus the oscillating twin phenomena of inside and outside, of man-made and natural space, the present chapter begins an exploration of how architecture moves beyond this universal framework to engage its specific contexts, its unique landscapes and locales. It begins to explore, specifically, how Kahn's mature architecture became increasingly not only one of *space,* but of *place.* With this as the third and final inquiry of this section, I seek to intimate how the previously discussed themes are intertwined with other threads of the phenomenal world, to point toward ways in which Kahn's invention was rooted in the physical and cultural contexts from which it emerged.

**Context in presentation, reception**

There has been a long-standing tendency to neglect or underrate the roles of place and context in Kahn's architecture, themes which have only slowly begun to emerge as integral to his work. Before approaching these themes, it is worthwhile to question their comparatively minor role in Kahn literature: although forty years of criticism have given ample opportunity for the examination of a wide spectrum of topics in his architecture, and for those who have experienced Kahn's mature buildings in situ, a compelling sense of locale, of participation, of real *here-ness,* is often one of the most lingering impressions taken from the encounter. Certainly most receptions of Kahn's work have

Following page:
**166** Salk Institute for Biological Studies, 1959–65

seen it chiefly in terms *other* than its connectedness with place. Until recently, at least, the majority of interpretations have been divided between those that stress the technical, formal, and material aspects of the work, and those that explore Kahn's philosophical or social worlds. In comparison, those studies dealing specifically with Kahn's architecture and its contexts have been exceptional.[207]

The reasons for this reticence are various, and, to a degree, understandable. The first of these, I propose, is inherent in the work itself and especially in its presentation. Photos and plans in monographs and magazines are the means through which architecture—Kahn's included—is most often "experienced" by a wider public. (A public that includes those who write about buildings.) Kahn's plans, with their impeccable formal geometries, *do* initially seem aloof to conventional ideas of accommodating or drawing inspiration from the natural or contextual, their disciplined orders apparently generated by purely internal rather than site- or context-based logic. The tendency to publish those floor plans without corresponding site plans has not helped to clarify matters. The Dominican Motherhouse is a convenient case in point. Although its site-free floor plan has often been discussed in terms of its geometry and space, the full scope of these phenomena are in fact first comprehensible when seen within the context of the site, as the preceding narrative has, I hope, amply shown.

The frozen aesthetic chosen for much architectural photography tends to compound the problem, often seeming to verify that those "abstract" plans translate into "abstract" buildings. Stark and bold, the buildings' engagement with the landscape—if present—seems to be one of simple framing or contrast. The subtle porosities and spatial linkages accomplished by those very "abstract" geometries, the linked chains of scale, and the kinesthetic realities of the buildings are all rather illusive photographic subjects. The general exclusion of the structure, texture, and feel of the greater context (including its population) has been chronic in much photographic documentation of the buildings. (A problem, of course, not limited to Kahn's

207 In Kahn literature, aside from cursory mention in several cases, there exists a small body of texts which deal specifically with his work in regard to context. Christian Norberg-Schultz, in his *Genius Loci* (1979), assigns Kahn a key role in the reestablishment of "place" in modern architecture. Michael Benedikt's *Deconstructing the Kimbell* (1991) contains an astute and provocative analysis of Kahn's masterpiece and its site, an analysis briefly taken up by Anita Berrizbeitia and Linda Pollak in their book *Inside Outside: Between Architecture and Landscape* (1999). Sarah Williams Goldhagen's *Louis Kahn's Situated Modernism* (2001) discusses the role of landscape and site in its chapter on the National Assembly at Dhaka, a work which both William J. R. Curtis ("Cosmos and State: The National Assembly in Dhaka") and Kazi Ashraf (*The National Capital Complex of Bangladesh*) have described in terms of its relationship to its landscape and cultural context. Ashraf is the scholar who has most consistently addressed this theme. See for example his "Taking Place: Landscape in the Architecture of Louis Kahn," pp. 48–58. It goes without saying that at the time of this writing, "Landscape" has gained a privileged place in the discourse, and rightly so. So the time for Kahn's reappraisal in this light may simply be ripe.

work.) Landscape or context, if present, is often only generically so: as shadow-giving natural light, as a green foil to geometry.[208]

Kahn: Form first

There are additional reasons for the modest role played by context in the discussion of Kahn's work. Kahn himself stressed the realization of an institution's "Form" as the primary act in making architecture, a search for an essence transcending the variables of circumstance, including those of material, technology, budget—or place: "The realization of what is an auditorium is absolutely beyond whether it is in the Sudan, or in Rio de Janeiro."[209] While this may in fact be an accurate self-appraisal of his approach, Kahn occasionally neglects to remind us that it is precisely the disciplined addressing of contingencies such as place in the "design" phase that makes the ideal manifest in the real world. Again, with the Dominican Motherhouse we have followed how, after a site-free interpretation of the institution's "Form," that site was successively engaged in order to intertwine with and underscore the original hypothesis: driving its evolution, adding layers of depth to its meaning, making the general specific. This engagement is an intertwining of realities that intimates how human use might poetically engage and transform place, while place underscores program and use.

If the engagement of a building with a specific place was one theme on which Kahn himself remained verbally hesitant or inconsistent, most interpreters have followed suit. If "context" and "place" slowly became catchwords in the sixties, those terms were soon a favorite means of "postmodern" architects to chastise the modernists, those who, according to contemporary polemic, had virtually exorcised those realities from architecture's program. The "posts" who would have condemned Kahn to the ranks of the "moderns" (or at very best "proto-postmoderns") were apparently more interested in downplaying the environmental complexity of his architecture than in investigating it in search of its subtleties.[210] Even the historian Vincent Scully—certainly Kahn's greatest advocate in American academia—was, in the intellectual climate of those years, reluctant to see anything approaching "contextualism" in his architecture when lecturing at a Kahn symposium at Yale in 1980.[211]

The exceptional architectonic qualities of Kahn's work have lead in the last decades to a number of analytical studies addressing, among other topics, the tectonic (Kenneth Frampton's *Studies in Tectonic*

208 See Raymond Meier's photo essay, *Louis Kahn Dhaka,* for a welcome exception.

209 Kahn, "New Frontiers in Architecture," pp. 81–99.

210 Michael Graves, for example, was skeptical of Kahn's siting of his buildings. See Nakamura, "Louis I. Kahn: Conception and Meaning," pp. 217–20.

211 Scully, "Works of Louis I. Kahn and His Method," pp. 286–99.

THEODORE

*Culture*, 1995), the technological (Thomas Leslie's *Louis I. Kahn: Building Art and Building Science*, 2005), the geometrical (Klaus-Peter Gast's *Order of Ideas*, 1998), natural light (Urs Buttiker's *Louis I. Kahn: Light and Space*, 1993), and construction (Edward Ford's *The Details of Modern Architecture*, vol. 2, 1996). Although most of these studies have contributed to a deeper understanding of Kahn's work, their (unintentional) combined effect may have arguably been—through their emphasis on issues which are at play "within the walls" of a work—to further isolate Kahn's buildings as objects in their surroundings: certainly exemplary, complex, but nonetheless separate "things."[212]

**Learning Landscape: 1929–1959**

**Drawing from ground up**

It is also true that until the late fifties Kahn's work gave little occasion to expect any kind of paradigm shift regarding locale and landscape. While works such as the Oser and Weiss Houses (1940 and 1947) may, with their walls of local Pennsylvania bluestone, amiably affirm their locale, the truest sense of things to come was not to be found in Kahn's buildings, but privately welling up in his travel sketchbooks. Unlike many colleagues' travel drawings, which tend to concentrate on pleasant architectural particulars, Kahn's are apt to play down detail and play up mass and volume while dramatizing figure-ground relationships and atmosphere. While a favorite subject from Kahn's 1929 European Grand Tour were landscape-embedded Italian hill towns, the drawings from his second European tour in 1950–51 amplify the gravity, geology, sunlight, and shadow, while architecture and non-architecture, mass and void, shadow and light merge into parity on the pages. Kahn's magnificent drawings of the Athenian Acropolis or the ruins of Delphi are as much geological as architectural studies; his Egyptian temples seem as much products of desert sun and shadow as of architects' plans. In his mature drawings we sense Kahn looking with an eye primed toward "origins," for these are as much studies on the reciprocity of elemental phenomena, of architecture as a landscape event, as they are representations of any *particular* monuments.

Much (following Scully) has been made of the *gravitas* Kahn's architecture began to assume after the 1950–51 tour, and indeed whether that experience was a serendipitous trigger or a confirmation of something that had been slowly mounting: gravity and grounding increasingly became Kahn's first means for taking possession of site. Kahn, the builder, put it thusly: "I draw a building from the bottom up

212 Of the studies named, Frampton's is the most wide-reaching in terms of situating Kahn's work in a deeper cultural and physical context. As one term in his "typos-topos-tectonic" triad, the tectonic is regarded as a trait of an "ontological" rather than merely "representational" architecture. Among the studies listed, it is Gast's highly speculative geometric constructions that most strongly abstract Kahn's work and distance it from the real world.

because that's the way it is constructed. It depends on gravity. You begin with the way the weights can be distributed on the land, and then you build up. If you do that, then you draw like an architect."[213] Christian Norberg-Schulz, the historian, situated Kahn so: "In the place of the abstract shells of early modernism, Kahn placed concrete 'things,' which stand, rise, open and close in relation to the 'places' of the planet."[214] If this initially meant an increased emphasis on tectonic expression and grounding, Kahn soon exaggerated that grounding in an unbuilt series of veritable earthworks: the Levy Memorial Playground (1961–66), the Lawrence Memorial Hall of Science (1962), the President's Estate in Islamabad (1963–66), the Pocono Arts Center (1972–74), the Roosevelt Memorial (1973–74). In these projects, Euclidian architecture sinks into (or emerges from) plastic earth so that the two are virtually merged as one. The growing use of plastiline models, with both building and terrain molded of the same material, of smeared charcoal sketches, and the habit of drawing extremely large site sections are all outgrowths of Kahn's increasingly earthbound architecture, seemingly reiterating in his own designs that which he had "seen" in his sketches of ancient ruins.[215]

**Contributors to an architecture of place**

By now, a number of contributors to Kahn's professional growth have been acknowledged. It is well known, for example, that through the fifties Anne Tyng was a crucial influence on Kahn's synthesis of geometry and structure; or that Kahn's most structurally ambitious designs were dependent on his running dialogue with teaching partner Robert Le Ricolais, and especially on his collaborations with the engineer August Komendant; the mastery of detail in buildings such as the Kimbell Art Museum and the Yale University Art Gallery may be largely traced to his more technically versed associates such as Marshall Meyers; while exchanges with progressive colleagues such as Aldo van Eyck or Alison and Peter Smithson seem to have helped cement his convictions on the social role of architecture, etc.[216]

Less well documented than these creative give-and-takes have been those with landscape architects, exchanges that are likely to have lastingly shaped his ideas on landscape and building. Daniel Urban Kiley, who would go on to become one of America's foremost landscape architects, befriended Kahn in the late thirties while working with him for the U.S. Housing Authority, and later collaborated with him in the

213 Louis Kahn, conversation with Richard Wermischner, April 17, 1971, quoted in Wurman, *What Will Be Has Always Been,* p. 121.

214 Norberg-Schulz, *Architecture: Presence, Language, Space,* p. 337.

215 Ashraf describes at length Kahn's exposed and meticulously designed foundations; see "Taking Place: Landscape in the Architecture of Louis Kahn," pp. 48–58.

216 See Williams Goldhagen, *Louis Kahn's Situated Modernism,* for more on these relationships.

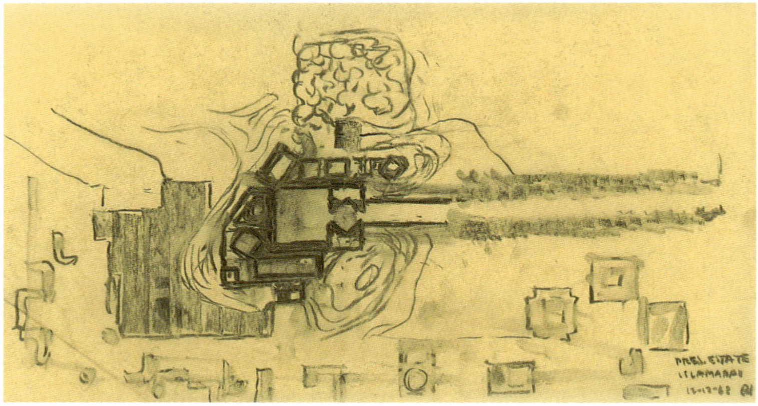

**167** Temple of Ammon at Karnak, 1951, Louis Kahn
**168** President's Estate, Islamabad, 1963–66, Louis Kahn
**169** Hurva Synagogue, Jerusalem, 1967–74, Louis Kahn

fifties (Mill Creek Housing). In 1951 Kahn was able to spend much of his watershed residence at the American Academy Rome with George E. Patton, a fellow in landscape architecture and later collaborator (Erdman Hall, Kimbell Art Museum, Exeter Library). From the beginning of his teaching career at the University of Pennsylvania in 1958, Kahn found himself in close company with some of America's most accomplished landscape architects. Among Penn's faculty during Kahn's professorship were not only Patton, but also Ian McHarg, Karl Linn, and Lawrence Halprin, each of whom would engage with Kahn in both academic discourse and professional practice. Further alliances, such as those with Luis Barragán for the plaza of the Salk Institute (1964), or with the sculptor Isamu Noguchi for the Levy Memorial Playground (1961–66), continued to provoke Kahn's thought, while new projects on the Indian subcontinent would give him deeply inspiring firsthand experience of fantastic Mughal gardens and of an intense partnership between monumental architecture and landscape.[217]

Certainly not incidental, evidence of Kahn's growing interest in landscape paralleled his romance with the landscape architect Harriet

217 See the Architectural Archives of the University of Pennsylvania for more on these collaborations: http://www.design.upenn.edu/archives/majorcollections/kahn.html.

Pattison. Pattison, Kahn's "soulmate" and mother of his son Nathaniel, met him in 1959 and remained a partner and collaborator until his death in 1974. She—either by working with Kahn on such projects as the Kimbell Art Museum, the Exeter Library, the Franklin D. Roosevelt Memorial, or the Bicentennial Exposition in Philadelphia, or by generally serving as a sounding board for his ideas—would become a steady voice of landscape in Kahn's work. Said Pattison, "I think we inspired each other. I think I helped bring a sense of nature and of the site into Lou's work."[218] Judging from transcriptions of his lectures in the early sixties, Kahn himself seems to have seen a parallel to this creative symbiosis in the relationship between the architect Edwin Lutyens and the landscape architect Gertrude Jekyll.[219]

Questions of influence are always messy ones, and rather than attempting to sort these out here, I will continue to concentrate on the work itself. In a manner similar to that of the previous two chapters, this question of space and place will be explored below by following its growing presence in Kahn's buildings and projects.

### Revealing the Qualities of Place: 1959–1974

**U.S. Consulate, Angola: revealing, intensifying**

In the project for the American Consulate in Luanda, Angola (1959–62), Kahn was confronted for the first time with a landscape and climate considerably unlike those of his native Philadelphia. Although throughout the fifties architects from the United States and Europe had become increasingly active around the globe, those many acolytes of the "International Style," which had been spawned in their own temperate middle latitudes, had been largely reluctant or unable to convincingly respond to the challenges posed by different landscapes, climates, and regional traditions. As Harriet Pattison later remarked in reference to the Luanda project and to the era's stereotypical "international" solutions, "The climate, the atmosphere at Luanda: you just couldn't neglect them in a place like that—though most architects at the time would have."[220] More than its topography or vegetation, the climate and atmosphere of southern Africa left vivid impressions on Kahn—impressions calling for response: "The glare is killing, everybody looks black against the sunlight.... I came back with multiple impressions of how clever was the man who solved the problems of sun, rain, and wind."[221] Kahn quickly established

218 Interview, author with Harriet Pattison, Architectural Archives, University of Pennsylvania, October 21, 2004.

219 For example, in a lecture at the University of Virginia in 1972; see Wurman, *What Will Be Has Always Been,* p. 137.

220 Interview with Harriet Pattison, October 21, 2004.

221 "All windows must recede to where cool air can open to the rooms. The outside of the building belongs to the sun, the inside belongs to where the people live." Wurman, *What Will Be Has Always Been,* p. 217.

that the buildings—a chancellery and an ambassador's residence—aside from embodying the dignity called for by the program, should *reveal* and *intensify* the essence of the place by addressing its climate. His solution: multi-layered houses with sun-and-glare-taming walls placed before the inhabited spaces within. **Figs. 170–172** "I thought of the beauty of ruins, the absence of frames, of things that nothing lives behind, and so I thought of wrapping ruins around buildings."[222] More than the merely picturesque "beauty of ruins," Kahn sought in those walls an expressive architectural means for preventing heat gain and glare without adding "devices" to the windows, such as the contemporary modernist grillwork of Edward Durrell Stone, which he had criticized for its "department store" prettiness. The unabashed directness of Kahn's shadow-giving wall solution was intentionally so: "The purpose was to state it in a rather primitive, unknowing, unsophisticated way."[223]

This layering continued on the horizontal plane; Kahn, having seen an indigenous double-roof solution for the heat generated by the sun on roofs, translated it into his own terms: "And it came to mind to have a sunroof purely for the sun and another roof for the rain."[224] Kahn's sunroof, a tree-like shade canopy of tightly spaced precast concrete leaves, spanned a good six feet (1.8 m) over the entire rain roof, forming a sluice for cooling breezes and an ample shadow-generating gap for a shifting light-dark patterning of the buildings over the course of the day. Again, it is important to note that of apparently equal importance to the effectiveness of his solution was, for Kahn, its expressive legibility: "I feel that in bringing the rain roof and the sun roof away from each other I was telling the man on the street his way of life. I was explaining the atmospheric conditions of wind, the conditions of light, the conditions of sun and glare to him. If I used a device—a clever kind of design device—it would only seem like a design to him—something pretty. I didn't want anything pretty, I wanted to have a clear statement of a way of life."[225]

Faced with the extreme conditions of Angola, Kahn for the first time allowed local climate and atmosphere to give substantial cues for what a building "wanted to be." (Said Pattison: "With that project Lou seemed to become more aware of the role that climate might play in the making of a building."[226]) By drawing upon and abstracting

222 Kahn, "Louis I. Kahn: A Discussion," p. 123.

223 Ibid., p. 124.

224 Ibid., p. 126.

225 Ibid.

226 Interview with Harriet Pattison, October 21, 2004.

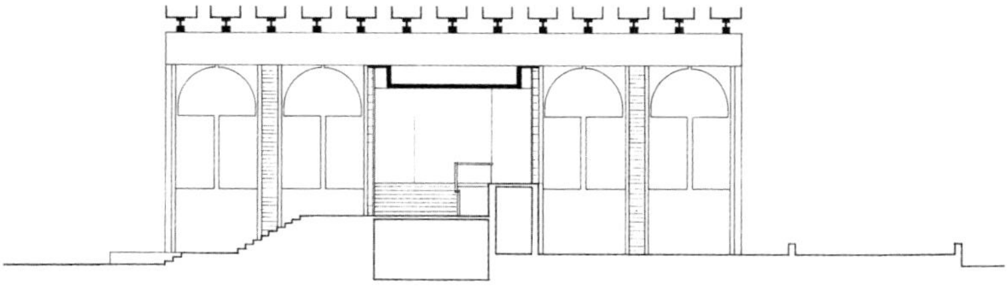

170–72 U.S. Consulate, Luanda, 1959–62: section, axonometric, perspective

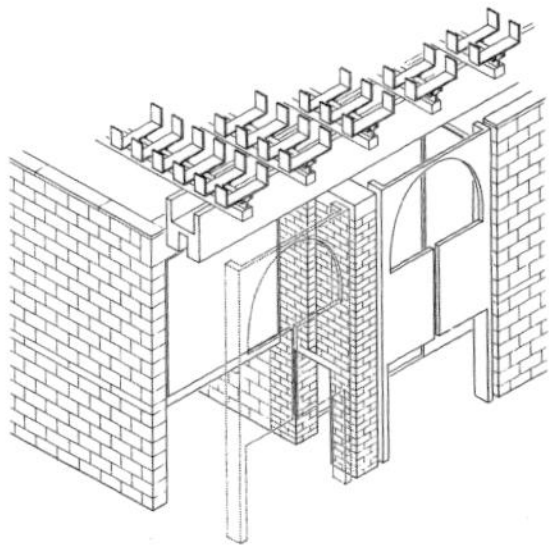

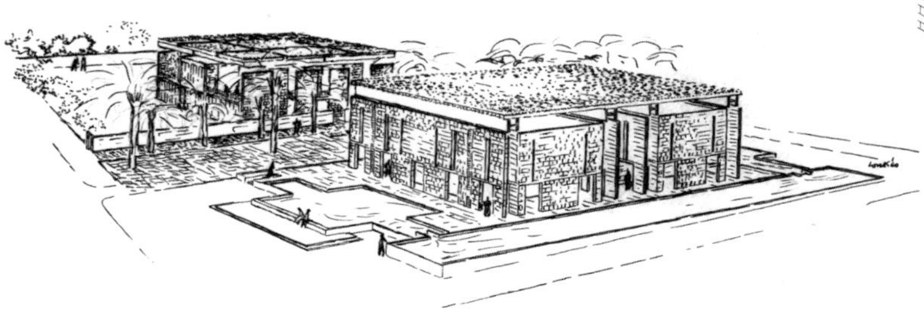

from indigenous tradition, by responding to local conditions with the invention of "wrapped ruins," Kahn made an intriguing first step toward a responsive and expressive "modern regionalism," in a manner at once uniquely his own, yet not unrelated to those in which Wright, Le Corbusier, Aalto, and Barragán had been working to transform the abstractions of the modernist idiom through the particulars of place.[227]

**The Salk Institute**

If the project in Luanda found its expression almost purely through its engagement with that locale's climate and sunlit atmosphere, the contemporary Salk Institute (1959–65) sought and found a deeper, more complex revelation of its context. Much has been said and written about the Salk and its site, making it the single greatest exception to the general rule of silence regarding place in Kahn's work. (Intriguingly, it is precisely in this case that the loquacious Kahn remained quiet.) Photos of the central space belong in the meantime to the most iconic in twentieth century architecture. Like some kind of modern-day Stonehenge, Jaipur-like celestial instrument, or James Turrell sky piece, the central plaza seems to have been expressly built to gather

227 What is disappointing is the fact that today, fifty years later, so few attempts of similar quality, originality, and appropriateness have been made in the realm of climatically responsive, regionally sensitive architecture.

and focus nature and cosmos within its space. Framed segments of sky and ocean meet at the horizon just above the sharp cut of the plaza's western edge, while ocean and a central liquid rivulet fuse landscape and plaza together in an unforgettable gesture. It is as if Kahn wished to place those scientists who tinker daily with the building blocks of Life in steady contact with the sublime. **Fig. 166**

One "gathering" gesture of the configuration—closed by the laboratory slabs on its outward flanks, open and porous where its individual studies meet on the central plaza—underscores how Kahn saw the Salk as an *institution:* a collective of individuals working in common accord. (Note how important it is for the parti that the most private spaces of the studies are present directly on the Institute's most public "space of appearance.") A second "gathering" gesture of the configuration is its intense collecting and focusing of the *landscape.* Although the central space apparently "faces" west toward the ocean, the axis has in fact been purposefully left open at both ends, with filtering orange and eucalyptus groves providing only veil-like closure to the east. This makes the central space as much an east-west threshold as a concave viewing space. The most lingering sense of participation, of *hereness,* at the Salk resides undoubtedly in this amplification of its edge condition. There are innumerous other buildings in similar situations on this frontier edge of California, yet few can compare with the Salk in the way that the east of the continent behind and the west of the horizon ahead are made to merge in a single space. Both "gathering" gestures, the institutional and the landscape/cultural, the metaphorical frontier of biological research and the physical border of the continent's edge, intertwine and resonate with each other.[228]

As at Luanda, climate and atmosphere were key cues for the making of the Salk, especially the characteristic Californian light. "You cannot forget that the light of a certain character has to do with that which distinguishes the architecture of one region from another."[229] The bleached-bone hues of the pozzolanic concrete, the tuft travertine and the left-to-weather teak are perfectly sympathetic to the native colors of Southern California's parched vegetation and its exposed sandstone undercrofts. The sharp-edged figures of the totem-like studies seem expressly made to cast sundial shadows across the travertine

228 "Our great American cities do not conform to the European urban ideal, where a whole is defined within confining borders and axial terminations, but acknowledge rather an order that is incomplete—fragmented—as it accommodates inherent expansion and progress toward eternal frontiers. Louis Kahn designed the Salk Center in La Jolla ... as an eloquent composition that is spatially and symbolically incomplete, with its two richly rhythmical buildings ... [which] define a powerful axis that is open at each end and that constitutes thereby a significant gesture within an American landscape. The composition of this common space ... is perceptually, physically, poignantly American as it frames the sea and the land where the old western frontier ends and the new eastern frontier begins." Robert Venturi, "A Protest Concerning the Extension of the Salk Center," p. 82.

229 Kahn, "Louis I. Kahn: A Discussion," p. 124.

**173** Salk Institute for Biological Studies, 1959–65, Louis Kahn

plaza, the deep cut-in galleries in front of the laboratories to generate a darkened backdrop for those studies.[230]

**Focusing the regional: Exeter and Kimbell**

Perhaps Kahn came closest to a conventional definition of regionalist or contextualist architecture with the library of the Phillips Exeter Academy in New Hampshire (1965–72) **Figs. 174–175**. In deference to its neocolonial neighbors on the school campus, Kahn chose brick as the primary material: "Brick was the most friendly material in this environment. I didn't want the library to be shockingly different in any way. I never lost my love of the old buildings."[231] With its taut volume and reined-in reticence, its strong vertical articulation, its regular window rhythm and Shaker-like woodwork, its exterior indeed passes—for all the archaic otherliness of its concrete core—as a "New England" building. While the window openings may seem to echo those of its earlier neighbors, this is more an appropriation of this puritan vernacular's brick-on-brick uprightness, of "asking the brick what it wants to be," than a direct quotation. It was of utmost importance for Kahn that brick be used not merely as a veneer, but, as in the best of its neighbors, as a means to construct a human-scaled spatial structure.[232] The building draws much of its aura from this subtle yet muscular tectonics, binding it with its place more through a sense of empathy, scale, and gravity than through historicist representation.

Contemporary to the Exeter Library, Kahn designed the Kimbell Art Museum (1966–72) for an entirely different kind of American

230 "The studies behind the Salk laboratories provide shade for the laboratories. It was necessary to have light but not sunlight." Kahn, October 10, 1973, quoted in Wurman, *What Will Be Has Always Been,* p. 216.

231 Kahn, quoted in Jordy, "The Span of Kahn," p. 330.

232 In a round of cost-cutting, Kahn was willing to reduce the building's height by a floor rather than revert to brick veneer. Kohane, "Library and Dining Hall, Phillips Exeter Academy," p. 392.

**174** Library, Phillips Exeter Academy, 1965–72
**175** Academy Building, Phillips Exeter Academy, 1914–15
**176** Kimbell Art Museum, 1966–72

landscape: the Texas plain of Fort Worth. Raking, horizontal, and generously shade-giving in the stark Texas sun, the long-vaulted Kimbell sympathizes with the extended lines of these dry flatlands. Fig. 176 Like the Salk Institute, the materials—here concrete, travertine, and lead roofing—with their subdued colors and toothy textures, were chosen for their bleached, archaic presence in the strong sun. Details are kept flush to emphasize the simple shapes in sunlight, revealing subtle tectonic relief only at closer range. It has been suggested by Lawrence Speck that the long multiple vaults are references to the bow-topped Texas livestock sheds which are so common around the Fort Worth area, while the museum's great loggias may be seen as interpretations of the vernacular domestic Texas porch.[233] Whether Kahn consciously abstracted from these antecedents remains a source of speculation, as he never spoke of the building in this way. (Although later in Texas, the project for the De Menil Collection seems to wink even more explicitly at local domestic architecture.) What *is* certain is that the Kimbell demonstrates a strong sense of its locale—a deep insight into its atmosphere, its colors, its topography, its vernacular—without the vaguest hint of the Southwestern vernacular pastiche which has become so common in this part of America. (This *ur*-sense of place would later lead the artist Donald Judd to ponder if the Kimbell was not, perhaps, the first building to be erected in Fort Worth, built by an earlier—more civilized—culture than the one now living there.[234])

**Gathering, revealing, focusing**

What these four buildings begin to intimate is that while Kahn's mature architecture is not "about" contextualism in the style-emulating and motif-seeking postmodernist sense of the word (nor "about" landscape in the contemporary, literalist, "building-as-landscape" sense of the word), it *is* indeed very much about *gathering, focusing,* and *revealing* the conditions of its context. This revealing may take place at the micro-scale of the particular site: the diagonal geometries of Erdman Hall and the Fisher House may be discussed in purely formal or in phenomenal terms. Anyone who has visited these buildings knows the undeniably physical experience of these diagonal foils on their sloping sites, how their prow-like shapes exaggerate and intensify the sense of the immediate topography. (Richard Serra's site-specific "elevations" come to mind.) This revealing may—as in Angola—have to do with atmosphere, may be experienced in the way that sun, wind,

233 Speck, "Regionalism and Invention," pp. 75–76.

234 "The Kimbell Museum looks the way a Greek temple must have looked among the huts. It looks the way the Roman temple, now a church, looks among the ordinary medieval buildings of Assisi. The temple looks like civilization. The Kimbell is civilization in the wasteland of Fort Worth and Dallas." Judd, "Lecture at Yale, September 1983," p. 178.

shadow, and shade "landscape" the buildings in hot, sunny climates such as those of the Salk Institute, the Indian Institute of Management, the Hurva Synagogue, or the National Assembly at Dhaka; or in the way that the special matte, pewter-like, stainless-steel and glass façade of the Yale Center for British Art in New Haven, Connecticut was conceived to reflect that latitude's weaker, more tranquil light: "On a grey day, it will look like a moth; on a sunny day, a butterfly."[235] Or this revealing may refer to a larger and more general, deeper and more psychic cultural sense: the "frontier" condition of the Salk Institute in California ("The way of life in California is very different from say Seattle or Hong Kong—or in a closed place like Vermont."[236]); or to a native culture strangely echoed in the National Assembly at Dhaka, which has been alternately seen to carry traces of Mughal monuments, of vernacular water-and-mound architecture, of Bengali figure-ground relationships, and Buddhist mandalas.[237] William Curtis has even seen in the building's ornamental marble veins not only an expression of the reinforced concrete's construction process, but, following a Semperian line of reasoning, a *Stoffwechsel* transformation of Bangladeshi bamboo-and-reed delta hut construction into more durable materials.[238]

### Two Monasteries, Two Archetypes: The Form of Landscape-Space

**St. Andrew's Priory**

For a last look in this chapter at how space becomes place in Kahn's architecture, it is helpful to consider the Dominican Motherhouse again, this time in light of its unequal sibling: St. Andrew's Priory in Valyermo, California (1966–67). **Figs. 177–181** Because it was developed parallel to the motherhouse, because of its almost identical size, program, and kit-of-parts/society-of-rooms paradigm, St. Andrew's Priory invites comparison on many levels, one of the most instructive being the interpretation of its place. For in contrast to Media's pastoral landscape, St. Andrew's Priory was to be built on a parched and solitary hill in the high Sonoma Desert northeast of Los Angeles. Cold in winter and exceedingly hot in summer, dramatically barren and of an existential vastness, the landscape made a vivid impression on Kahn, who felt that anything built here must in some way celebrate the site's precious water, that all decisions made must refer back to that which made a foothold possible in that arid place:

235 Kahn, quoted in Prown, *The Architecture of the Yale Center for British Art,* p. 43.

236 Kahn, untitled lecture at Princeton University, February 1960, Princeton Architectural Archive.

237 See Ashraf, *National Capital Complex of Bangladesh.*

238 Curtis, "Cosmos and State," pp. 101–3. There are additional cases for the contextual. The morphological: compare Hurva Synagogue (plan and section) and the morphology of the old town, the morphology of the neighboring ruin; the climatic: the wind-diagonals of the Indian Institute of Management; patterns of use: the mixed Yale Center for British Art and its neighbors; the typological: the Korman House as a play on the Pennsylvania country house, etc.

"Recently I was asked to do a monastery in California.... I was asked by the monks to tell them what I thought about monasteries.... And when I heard that they had found water in this very high desert, I felt that they have that upon which a monastery can really exist. Without water, one couldn't begin to build, couldn't make a plan. I realized then that water is not only necessarily in pipes. When the father asked me: 'What would be your plan for the monastery?' I said: 'The first thing I would do (and please excuse my infringing on your sense of what is important to you) but I would build a chapel where the water came from. And if you agree to do this, we can settle on the fountain. And then I think we should build the architecture of water ... the architecture of water being the cisterns and the reservoirs ... not just casually but very consciously in the shapes and dimensions which assert themselves very clearly. And then build whatever modest or strong aqueducts that may lead from these water sources to logical places using the law of gravity, and making good rules so that you don't spend a cent more than necessary ... And from this order of water you may place your chapel and the church and the cells and the workshop and the little community.' "[239]

While in the end Kahn did not literally "build a chapel where the water came from," his interpretation of the monastic type is deeply informed by climate and topography and the felt need of an "order of water." The monastery has been wrapped around the brow of the hill in order to enclose a plateau, a grove, and a water garden. Whereas in the Dominican Motherhouse, Kahn's tower or "place of arrival" was positioned at the periphery like a gatehouse of a miniature walled town, at St. Andrew's the tower is first discovered by the visitor after slipping through the monastery's sheltering walls. Occupying the geometric center of the complex and the highest point of the hill, the tower is both the tallest and most expressive building in the group.[240] Crowned by a reservoir with the all-important water, the tapered base of the tower seems to lift that water to the sky as if in some sacramental cup. Indeed, the prime architectural gesture is one of clearing and protecting a place in the desert for the water tower and its garden. Inside the *temenos* described by the buildings, the grove is a hidden treasure. Out of the necessity of irrigation has been made architecture;

239 Kahn, "Law and Rule," transcript of a lecture at Princeton University, 1961, folder, LIK Lectures 1969, Box 53, Kahn Collection. (In a literal land-architecture gesture, Kahn originally suggested adobe brick for the buildings.) The gesture of "water architecture" was proposed on an urban scale in Dhaka and in the Abbasabad project for Teheran. For a more detailed description of St. Andrew's and its development, see my dissertation, Merrill, "Louis Kahn and the Dominican Motherhouse," ch. 7.

240 One can't help think that this stepped tower worked better here than in the motherhouse. In fact, comparing the dates of the designs, this form seems to have originated with St. Andrew's.

**177–79** St. Andrew's Priory, 1966–67: section, elevation, plan
**180–81** St. Andrew's Priory: model

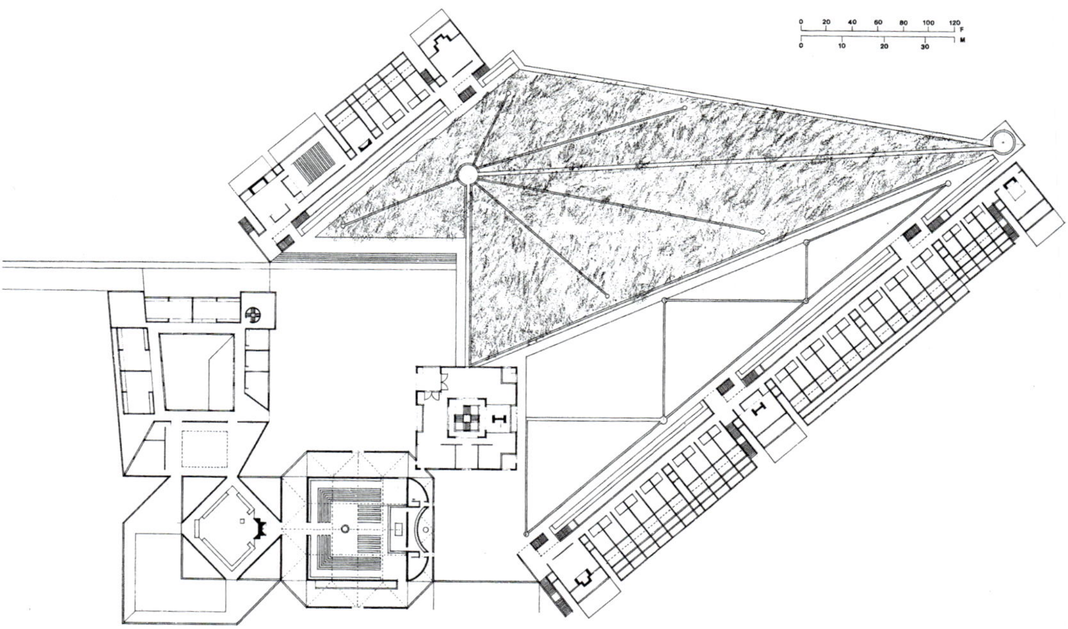

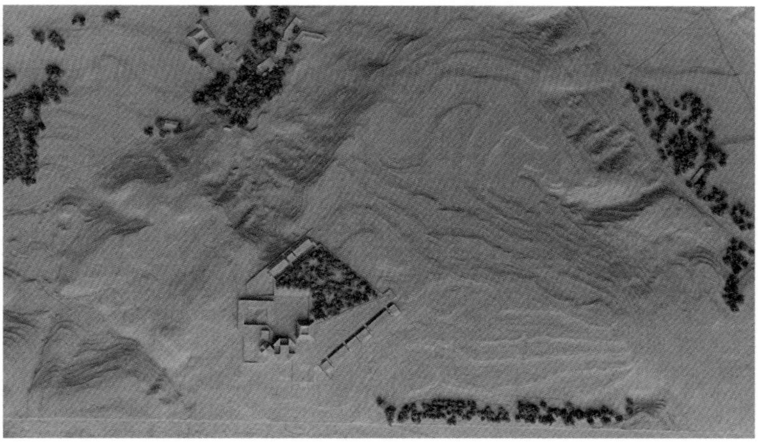

water flowing from the tower's reservoir follows gravity's pull through a series of long rivulets, irrigating the benevolent trees. A visitor following the water's flow would eventually be lead to the edge of the garden and to a tree-framed view over the desert. Forsaking a traditional cloister or the extensive galleries he first attempted at Media, Kahn offers in this desert a different kind of "space of appearance": the orchard as a sort of philosophers' grove or *sacro bosco.* Breezes, entering over the open border from the northeast, were to have mingled with shade and water to make this a place of meditative respite and to temper the microclimate of the monastery. Not only functionally and symbolically but also spatially, this grove is more than just some sort of pleasant landscape feature. Covering almost a third of the ensemble's total area, the shady roof of the trees, the dense space under the crowns, and the view out from under the leafy plane are all integral parts of the *architectural* composition, as necessary to its wholeness as any of the buildings.

As at Media, at Valyermo the monastery's relationship with the topography cannot be described in simple terms of contrast or harmony with the given condition. A series of different operations have been employed to establish the ensemble's complex relationship with the ground and the topography of the hill: here revealing, here exaggerating, and there contradicting. While the shaded terraces of the cells are cut as horizontal counterforms into the slope, the prismatic communal buildings celebrate the vertical, rising from a platform that has been established at entry-court level; the strong horizontals and verticals implying together a Euclidian frame of reference which serves as a foil to the landforms of the hills and the distant mountains. **Fig. 178** Drawing a diagonal in plan across the square of the base platform, we can see how the kitchen garden juts like a ship's prow into the landscape, while the opposite corner of the entry court wedges itself into the crest of the hill, the horizontal plane both anchoring the buildings and inflecting toward the landscape. **Fig. 184** By establishing this horizontal datum in the workshop court while letting the topography fall away within its interior, the artificial datum and the natural slope are juxtaposed to express the tension between the plan's ideal geometry and the circumstance of topography. **Fig. 181** An amphitheater-like outdoor chapel steps down the slope to the south, embracing the landscape with open arms.

The project offers a compelling paradox or inversion: although placed at the very center of the complex, the tower marks the entry and threshold between the monastery's "exterior" public realm and its interior spaces of retreat. A long diagonal drawn in plan through the tower and the chapel describes the demarcation between the public rooms outside of the threshold to the north (guest wing, entry court, workshop court) and the private rooms of the monks inside the threshold to the south (cells and living rooms, schoolrooms, private garden). Only by passing through the tower can the monks' cells be reached from the outside. **Fig. 185** With this floor-plan sleight of hand, using the tower as a kind of hub for the entire ensemble, Kahn has managed to solve the central functional conflict of the program without reverting to traditional models; that is, the one monastery, the two realms. It is a feat he found anything but simple to resolve at Media—as we have already observed at great length.

**Deep sources**

If our senses and psyche have grown up on the meanings of natural phenomena long before architecture existed, then nature, so the repeated and coherent argument goes, is architecture's strongest and most primary source of spatial and symbolic reference. The idea that architecture is at its deepest when it most closely resonates with its natural origins is integral to its history. This is not only manifest in theory's analogies such as the column-as-tree, the roof-as-firmament, the sacred mountain, natural proportion, and organic growth, etc., but in an ever-returning insight that an architecture whose authority has been sanctioned by that nature-in-us will have found a deep source of understanding and an originary source of expression.

After long looks at the Dominican Motherhouse and St. Andrew's Priory in their landscapes, something approaching recognition may begin to set in, and with that recognition a question arises. If in the meantime we've become accustomed to using Kahn's "Form" to talk about the revealing of deeper structures of use, of archetypes, might we not apply this thought to place? I conclude this chapter with an attempt—speculative, as Kahn never spoke of his monasteries in these terms—to describe the Dominican Motherhouse and St. Andrew's Priory in terms of the landscape archetypes they may be seen to reveal.

**Archetypes and counterforms: clearing and oasis**

Two landscape archetypes are the *clearing* and the *oasis*—both "strong" spaces, fairly laden with natural and cultural significance. So, the clearing: "In the dense, dark forest it was the glade or clearing that formed a natural inner world. Its meaning derives from its state of openness: the physical absence of the forest where that which was hidden is brought into view."[241] And the oasis: "The oasis is a microcosm, a complete world in itself. At its center is the source, the condition necessary for life on which the entire oasis depends."[242] In their history of the enclosed garden, Rob Aben and Saskia de Wit have reiterated the thesis that the gardens of Egypt, Persia, and

241 Aben and de Wit, *The Enclosed Garden*, pp. 22–33.

242 Ibid.

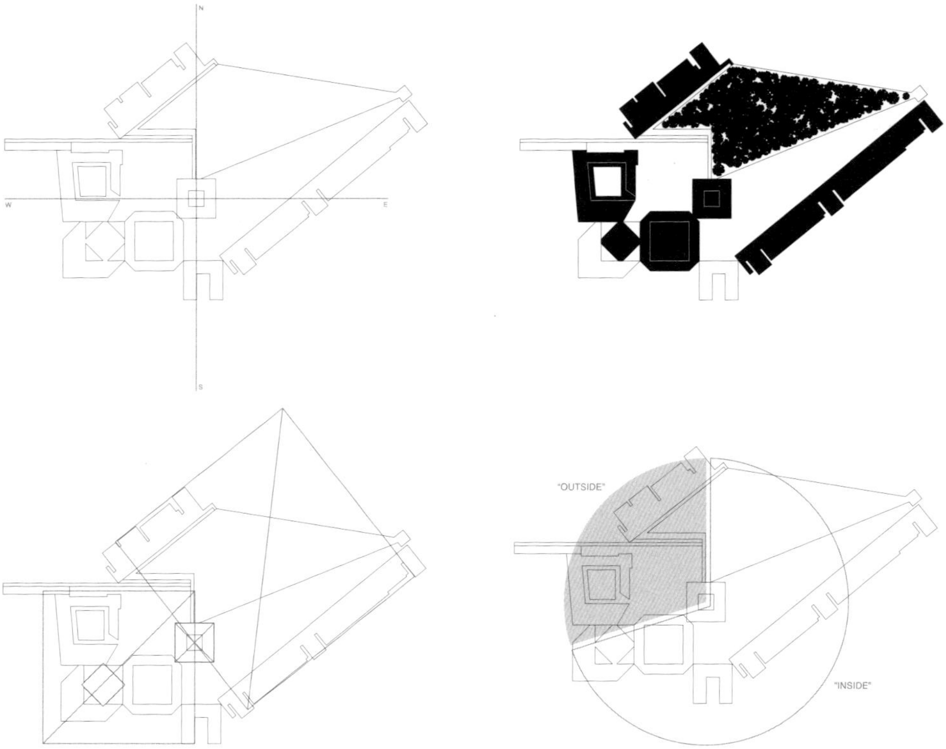


**182–85** St. Andrew's Priory, 1966–67: cardinal directions, figure-ground, geometry, tower as hub

**The Dominican Motherhouse: "Clearing"**

Mesopotamia were modeled on the natural archetype of the oasis, just as the medieval *hortus conclusus* was a natural product of the forested European landscape. Both oasis and clearing are counterforms to and offer respite from their respective landscapes; both establish central points in boundless space. As such, both archetypes have served as metaphors for the garden for the soul. The clearing has alternately meant salvation (the passage from darkness into light), insight (as in Heidegger's *Lichtung*), as well as the mythical space where human interaction and thus architecture began. (Vitruvius, in his *De Architectura Libri Decem,* places the locus of architecture's beginning in a forest clearing.) The oasis, on the other hand, has always served as the symbol for refuge and plenty—of paradise in the midst of paucity. Judeo-Christian literature—and architecture—is unthinkable without these two archetypes.[243]

Whether these are Kahn's conscious or unconscious evocations, I suggest that it requires only the slightest focusing of the eyes and imagination to see in his twin monasteries these counter-archetypes. As if in his mythical search for "volume zero" of the monastery he had excavated to their landscape sources.

243 Aben and de Wit, *The Enclosed Garden*, pp. 22–33.

**186** Dominican Motherhouse: site plan (final version), August 1968

With the Dominican Motherhouse, Kahn, seeking to engage the site's forest, transformed an edge condition through building and cutting into something approaching an artificial clearing. In the final scheme, a ring of horizontally oriented cells forms a border within which the communal world of vertically oriented spaces is assembled. Analogous to natural clearings, both courtyards and communal spaces receive their light and only visual respite from above. **Fig. 186** An axis linking earth and sky extends from the monastery's center, fixing a place in the natural continuum. The Dominican Motherhouse derives its expressive sway from multiple sources: from the tension of its skewed geometry; from its visualization/transformation of a type or "Form"; from its social function as a "people configuration"; from its tectonic articulation; and from its setting up of reciprocities between inside and outside, between architectural and arboreal mass. Is not an additional, intertwined source of expression the monastery's whispered evocation of a landscape archetype? In the foregoing text we have viewed the design of the Dominican Motherhouse as work-on-type (or "Form"), as work-on-configuration (or an "architecture of connections"), and as work-on-continuum (or "reciprocity"); an additional, equally valid way of viewing it is as work-on-place.

Once the Dominican Motherhouse is recognized in this way, it is no great leap to see in St. Andrew's Priory a manifestation of the oasis archetype—and of its more civilized forms, the sacred grove and the paradise garden.[244] As in Persian and Christian paradise gardens, the vertical axis of a well at the center (here, in the form of the water tower) is complemented by a protective horizontal wall (here, the blocks of cells). As in its antecedents, the monastery's irrigation channels flow from a central source and subdivide its garden. While architects of lesser import might have made of these ingredients something "merely" pleasant or beautiful, one great strength of Kahn's design is in its capacity for abstraction: the sense not of a monastery *with* paradise garden, but rather of a *monastery-as-paradise-garden.* (With the Dominican Motherhouse a *monastery-as-hortus conclusus.*)

Christian and Islamic traditions have derived layers of symbolic meaning from the natural, have seen in the enclosed garden as much a cosmogram as a garden for meditation or pleasure. The generic spatial diagram underlying both the *hortus conclusus* and the paradise garden may further tempt us to see in Kahn's monasteries something more fundamental than particular. At Valyermo, the water tower—the central vertical axis—may be seen as an *axis mundi,* fixing a horizontal cross that divides the monastery. **Fig. 183** This primal landscape-gathering diagram has been used to establish countless settlements in nature—bundling cardinal directions, a foil to the movement of the sun across the horizon. Like a Roman settlement's *cardo* and *decumanus,* a cross establishes an absolute reference and divides the monastery into four quadrants which correspond roughly to its areas of use: to the northwest, the "outside" of the entry court and guest quarters; to the southwest, the communal and sacred spaces; to the southeastern morning sun, the monks' quarters; to the northwest, the grove. The rotation of one half of the monastery around this axis to accommodate the topography serves to create tension without destroying this diagram. **Fig. 185** In St. Andrew's Priory, two elemental spatial voices speak in concert: the social-spatial significance established by the plan in regard to its use, and the natural/symbolic meaning latent in the plan and its interactions with both local and cosmic space.

The Dominican Motherhouse, the "clearing in the forest," invites a similar reading. Regarding built mass and forest mass as reciprocal, the (when seen without site plan, peripheral) entry tower becomes a central axis for the clearing/monastery and sets the conditions for its division. (Northwest: arrival, northeast: younger sisters/"secular" activities, southeast: older sisters/sacred activities, southwest: garden.)

244 Ibid.

What looking in this way reveals is how the two monasteries, at first glance so different in plan, do in fact share a common spatial scaffold.

Again, while it is not at all clear if Kahn was consciously thinking in these terms, I submit that this excursus has been more than merely seeing figures in clouds. With Kahn the paradigm of the beginning is always powerful and always close at hand. Of course, the danger in attempting to capture it in text and diagrams (as here) is to risk reducing something at once vague and potent into something academic and effete. The deep resonances of archetypes and of nature-in-us are not to be evoked by recipe or mere naming (as postmodernism's example taught), and Kahn, as always, was searching for strong, silent, and preverbal understanding. What may, perhaps, begin to emerge from between the text and diagrams here is how in both monasteries institution and site interact on multiple levels to transform and enrich each other. Kahn's tacit invitation to sense both institutional and landscape "beginnings" is an invitation to revisit both spaces and thus see them anew in light of each other.

### Architecture as Homecoming

This—by no means comprehensive—exploration of the emergence of *topos* or place in Kahn's mature work may begin to literally ground the previously discussed themes in the *conditio sine qua non* of architecture: the places of the earth. Beginning by showing the obvious—Kahn's turn away from modernism's lightfootedness toward an emphatically physical, space-fixing, grounding of his work—I've tried to intimate how his best architecture was often one of revealing and heightening the conditions of its context, be they physical, climatic, atmospheric, or cultural. The revealing could span from the scale of a sweeping landscape gesture down to that of a joint or the grain of a material. While sometimes direct, this revealing was often all the more uncanny and intense for its subliminal and indirect manner: Kahn's architecture often showing offhandedly or through contrast, by serving as a foil, a sounding board, or an amplifier. Beyond this focusing of the specific, the Dominican Motherhouse and St. Andrew's Priory suggest how Kahn's work could be about another kind of revealing: channeling those natural spatial archetypes which resonate deep in our consciousness. All these types of revealing, the physical, the tacit, and the mythic, begin to speak of an in-touchness with place, of getting close to sources of meaning, of architecture-as-homecoming. "Symbols are gentle reminders. They are stones left to find your path back to where you want to go back to."[245]

245 Kahn, quoted in Wurman, *What Will Be Has Always Been*, p. 219.

## EPILOGUE
## ON GOOD QUESTIONS

***For Pascal's message is that Man is great in that he searches for absolute values but small in that, without ever ceasing to search, he knows that he can never approach these values. The only form to express this content is, of course, one which does not prove the contrary: which doesn't show either a man who has abandoned the search or one who has approached the goal. The fragment is such a form.***

Lucien Goldmann, "Structure: Human Reality and Methodological Concept," 1972

***The only way to understand old art is to make it participate in our own artistic life.*** Lionello Venturi, 1925

A book's necessity for finding some kind of a conclusion in many ways contradicts the stubbornly "inconcludible" Dominican Motherhouse. As does the temptation to draw something like a capital-T Theory from either Kahn's design procedure or from his spatial paradigm run counter to his own skepticism toward normative theories of design. Kahn himself stated that "a good question is better than the most brilliant answer."[246] In this spirit, which seems so appropriate to the subject, this conclusion will take the form of a summary of what has been seen and a reflection on how this might be used to formulate additional "good questions."

The foregoing study has taken on a structure not unlike that of Kahn's monastery: quasi-independent parts (here, the chapters) inflecting toward a "difficult" whole. While posterity and the didactic potential of the material have called for a strong measure of exactitude and completeness, this obligation has been tempered by a wariness of closure's appeal. In the manner of a Kleistian "gradual formulation of thoughts while speaking,"[247]

246 Kahn, "New Frontiers in Architecture," p. 93.

247 Von Kleist, *Über die allmälige Verfassung*, pp. 23–34. In this text—a letter to a good friend—Kleist mused over a method in which clear thought might be teased out of darkness into light, not through meditation or brooding, but through unforced and ruminative speaking. He proposed an uncensored, successive thinking aloud—any listener will do—as a kind of self-generated act of Socratic thought-midwifery. In a parody of the French "l'appétit vient en mangeant," he suggested "l'idée vient en parlant." The sifting, evolutionary, self-feedback nature of designing on paper may be considered analogous to Kleist's method, with drawings, rather than words, being the means of inquiry.

the Motherhouse narrative has doubled as a form of inquiry, with the themes in the second half of this study first crystallizing through the questions raised by the drawings. This structure, for all its advantages, has demanded certain omissions of that which more conventionally academic texts would include. The question of internal coherence has, for example, been considered more important than have questions of influence, intellectual context, or how Kahn fits into the continuum of architectural history. And so, I have largely avoided those lines of questioning, although, for example, comparisons with historical relations and contemporary offspring of the Dominican Motherhouse would certainly be instructive.[248] It goes without saying that Kahn's development as an architect did not take place in isolation; yet important exchanges which may have effected the subjects of this book, also worthy of exploration, have been left largely unexamined here.[249] My drawing-board bias has been toward that synthetic, métier-specific means of designerly thinking, knowing, and doing Le Corbusier unapologetically dubbed "architecturing," with my own apologies for any resulting shortcomings and omissions.

## The Dominican Motherhouse: Looking, Showing, Situating

A first goal of this study has been to illuminate the (intended) realities of the Dominican Motherhouse. If this project has previously led an iconic yet enigmatic existence in Kahn literature—appearing more as a graphic plan-symbol than as a truly comprehensible "realm of spaces"—I've attempted to adequately fill this gap. I believe that it is evident that that which emerges from the drawings may indeed be counted among Kahn's most compelling space-creations: "a world within a world" and absolutely equal in its own rich and willful manner to many of its more famous siblings.[250] This extended revealing has, I hope, opened inroads to better demonstrate this project's place in Kahn's oeuvre. In contradiction to

248 Concerning the former: the Monastery of St. Catherine in Sinai or even certain Baroque monastic models loom vaguely, as do more recent additive/compositional models ranging from Beaux-Arts plans to Frank Lloyd Wright's oblique compositions for Florida Southern College or Taliesin West. Le Corbusier's recently completed ("deconstructed") Dominican monastery, La Tourette (actually discussed by Kahn and the sisters) must have been a yardstick for Kahn. Regarding possible offspring: Kahn's room-as-locale/plan-as-society-of-locales paradigm not only had direct contemporary parallels (Aalto, van Eyck, etc.) but has been both diffusely and directly influential in the last decades. It is tempting to speculate that the Dominican Motherhouse itself served as a direct model for James Stirling (Wissenschaftszentrum Berlin), Rafael Moneo (Kursaal, Chivite Winery), and even Zaha Hadid (Cardiff Bay Opera); while more recently, architects as diverse as David Chipperfield, SANAA, Sou Fujimoto, and Frank Gehry have regularly applied a related "difficult whole of specific locales" paradigm in their works.

249 For more here, I refer the reader to Williams Goldhagen's excellent *Louis Kahn's Situated Modernism.*

250 And if I have, dear colleague, largely relied upon the plan-partitas of Kahn and his associates in order to demonstrate these spaces—instead of making them more immediately accessible, e.g., via renderings—be assured that this is not for lack of opportunity. Rather, I did not wish to preempt your own pleasure of thinking yourself into those spaces; a process that, I believe, brings you that much closer to the architects who drew them.

**187** Louis Kahn in his office, ca. 1958–60

a relatively widespread opinion that the Dominican Motherhouse is an odd or isolated episode, it has, I believe, been demonstrated here that this project represents a logical and instructive manifestation of Kahn's continued research into a few fundamental architectural themes. One goal of exploring three of those themes in the second section has been to make explicit certain common internal threads that unite the Dominican Motherhouse with other, formally dissimilar works.

## Toward a Culture of Making

The dozens of drawings on the preceding pages (and their hundreds of companions in the Kahn Collection) were guided by Kahn's hard-won and cogent analysis of making: a broad evaluation which lead him to hypotheses on how works are conceived, how they are developed, how they are perceived, and how they find their place in common experience. Although largely removed from the world of academia today, Kahn's analysis is refreshingly provocative when seen in light of both modernist and popular contemporary paradigms of designing. Against modernist methodologies—which tended towards operational closure, tended to neglect or submerge the roles of intuition and human history in the process of making, tended to assume automatic links between analysis and synthesis where there were none[251]—Kahn described the act of designing as a self-reflective balance between knowing and not knowing, between an "arrogance of assumption" (the capacity of the individual to intuit and express cultural "Form") and modesty (the Socratic "I know that I do not know" which is made explicit in Kahn's asking what a thing "wants to be"). Kahn's reflexive *Denkraum* ("thinking space"), in this sense decidedly "un-modern," may be seen as a means of going beyond some of the unresolved conflicts of modernist thought.

On the other hand, against the current intellectual climate which gyrates wildly around the vortices of Big Theory, formalist solipsism, and an extreme relativity in which virtually anything may serve as the generator of a design (Michael Sorkin calls this the "empty authority of procedure"[252]), Kahn's thought is poignantly potent in its search for an *ethos* in the original sense of a common ground, in suggesting how "open" works might begin to emerge from the necessary search for commonality, how out of the status quo the new might arise. While his approach was grounded in a search for a reciprocal ethics and the origins of common understanding, Kahn realized that this agreement must be won anew with each project. In his work there is simultaneously a sense of authority grounded in the imperativeness of the search and the masterly demonstration of his craft, as well as a sense of the found coherence's fragility: a recognition that architecture is artifice grounded in reality and that each work is by necessity an approximation, a suggestion, an incomplete "offering to architecture."

Intertwined with this "what" of designing, the Motherhouse narrative has focused on the craftsman-like "how" of the development of architectural depth and of internal coherence in designing a work. In this case Kahn, that architects' architect, makes an ideal mentor: his exceptional collection of drawings allowing a glimpse of how this craft might look, a truncated snapshot of designerly intelligence at work. Beginning with the wagering of an architectural idea—here, an "educated guess" as to an institutional "Form"—moving over the testing of that hypothesis against the circumstances of reality, we have watched, while moving through the various scales of the project, the slow building of a linked chain of decisions. On one level, the goal of this linking has been the creation of internal coherence, of transparence (a linking which is both

251 And which, in one form or another, still linger among us, as evidenced by the recent forms of method-worship often involved in "datascapes" and "parametric designing."

252 Sorkin, "Family Values," p. 199.

conservative, in that we expect/depend on this coherence in our important artifacts, and progressive, in its invitation to take part as participants in an "open work"). On another level, Kahn's linking may be seen as an act of "drawing connections" between different (and sometimes apparently disparate) layers of reality: weaving the formal and social, the institutional and the natural, the tectonic and the topographical, the aesthetic and the ethical—a linking which thus shows architecture's great potential to be projective and experimental. And so, in practice, it is not surprising that something like a rhythm develops: as certain problems are solved, new ones are sought. This is not at all a linear "process"—doubling back, oscillating between scales, sometimes letting the part lead the whole, sometimes the whole lead the part, at once a collaborative effort and singularly in the hand of its author—as much about being receptive as being projective. We are reminded that an architectural idea is not simply "had," but must be constantly renegotiated, regained. Contingencies may sidetrack, even sink a project (as, alas, here), but in the end will also give it its realness and depth (as, indeed, here). Between the architects' knowledge of what and how (those rational, goal-directed elements which we may, in retrospect, "retrieve" from the procedure and, furthermore, teach) we gain glimpses of decisive and mysterious intangibles such as skill (yes, skill), courage, nerve, tacit knowledge, and embodied knowing—and, amid all that experience, something like innocence. Again, there's no normative theory to be won here, but perhaps a model: compellingly vital and instructive; a yardstick of mastery and conviction; a glimpse of a culture of making at once near and distant.[253]

## The Thoughtful Making of Spaces: Softening a Hard Spatial Paradigm

Growing out of the narrative, the three spatial themes explored in the second section of this study intimate where the thrust of this designing was aimed: "the thoughtful making of spaces." Viewed under the headings of "an architecture of connection," "reciprocity," and "place," the themes studied here might begin to supplement those of previous studies to provide a more comprehensive means for viewing Kahn's architecture. What they share is a notion of Kahn's space as both "charged" and relational—a space as much *revealed* as *made.* If Kahn's architecture has often been observed from the "outside" in—as exquisitely constructed objects, as Platonic bodies, or as built symbols—this is likely

253 Many colleagues would of course consider a strenuous, three-year-long, money-losing, unbuilt project a "failure" rather than a "model." I contend that if it was a failure, then a splendid one, and so, indeed, a model.

due to a deep-seated cultural tendency to see the object over the in-between, to see space as neutral and absolute rather than as relative and relational. And while Kahn's architecture is not alone in being seen in this manner, this view does in many ways explicitly contradict his own hard-won, mature thinking of space; this is revealed in the ripe works and, for those who take the trouble, may be gleaned from his many texts.

One may take, for example, an atomist view of the Dominican Motherhouse and see it as a collision of Platonic shapes in neutral space. Or one may take a complementary, Aristotelian view, and see it as a series of insides seeking resolved relationships among themselves and embeddedness within their specific place. The first view tends to see a hard conglomeration of colliding or assembled objects; the second, a soft sponge-like structure of self-linking spaces that extends beyond the plan to include the surrounding forest and hills. One may see the plan for its formal geometry, or may sense one's own movement—as a sentient body and social being—progressing through the multifarious and shifting spaces described by that geometry. It goes without saying that these ways of seeing apply to other of Kahn's mature works. While the former (masculine) ways of seeing Kahn's work have been the most common, the latter (feminine) are indeed the more timely due to their long-term neglect in our culture. As such I suggest that they are richer in their potential to reveal the contemporary relevance (and, yes, radicality) of Kahn's work, more fruitful and "progressive" in their capacity to inspire future thought. In the end, though, neither of these two views is the "correct" way of seeing Kahn's work; rather, a comprehensive understanding of the Dominican Motherhouse—and all of Kahn's mature work—must include both of these complements. Kahn's *coincidentia oppositorum* in thinking demands the same of those who wish to better understand how his work works. It is this complementary and intertwined nature of the work that at once gives it its richness and depth, and makes it so tantalizingly difficult to describe.

## Evoking Questions... and Responses

I've hoped to transport here at least a portion of the deep pleasure the hours spent with the drawings of Kahn and his associates have given me. One part of this pleasure has been the way in which those drawings have sparked this architect's curiosity and wonder; indeed, perhaps even more so than if the project had been built. Emerging from the drawings' story, two lines of inquiry have opened in *this* text: one regarding the

**"space" of designing, the other, the designing of spaces. Both of these merit deeper study and suggest, I hope, further exploration and shifted perspectives. Such explorations might take the form of musing, writing, drawing—or building. Kahn must have had this generative propensity of the unbuilt in mind when he suggested, "That which has not been built is not really lost. Once its value is established, its demand for presence is undeniable. It is merely waiting for the right circumstances."**[254]

254 Kahn, quoted in Lobell, *Between Silence and Light,* p. 84.

# APPENDIX

Evolution of the plan, 1966–1968

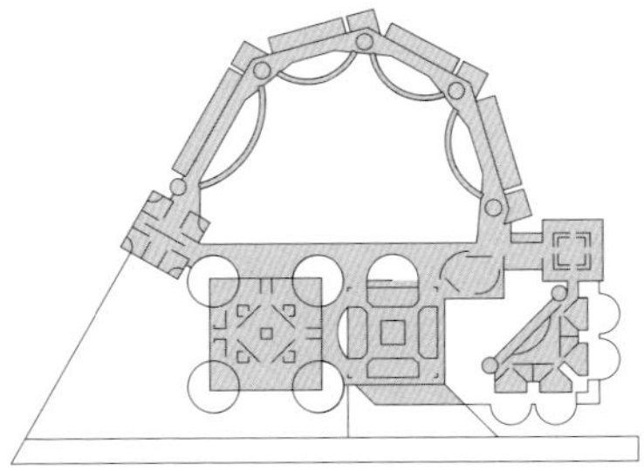

June 1966

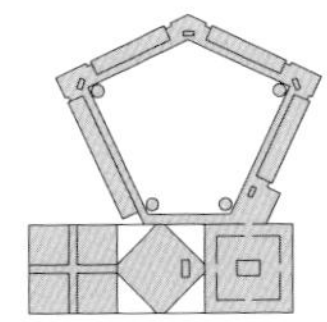

January–February 1967

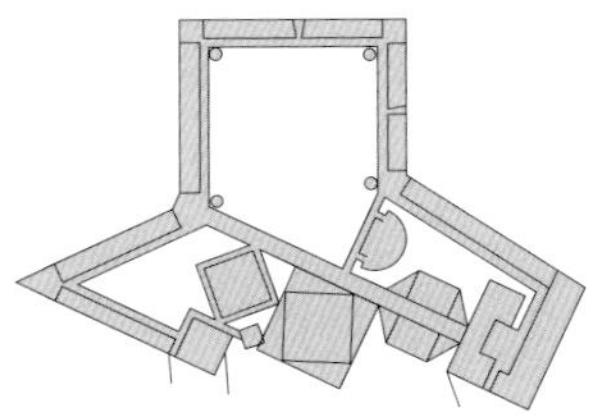

August–September 1966

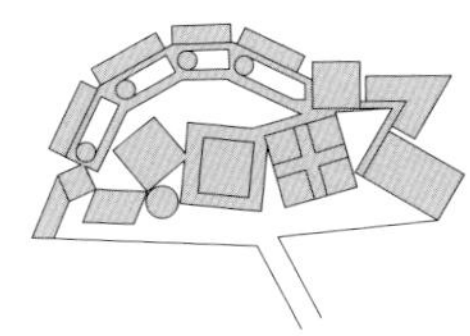

January–February 1967

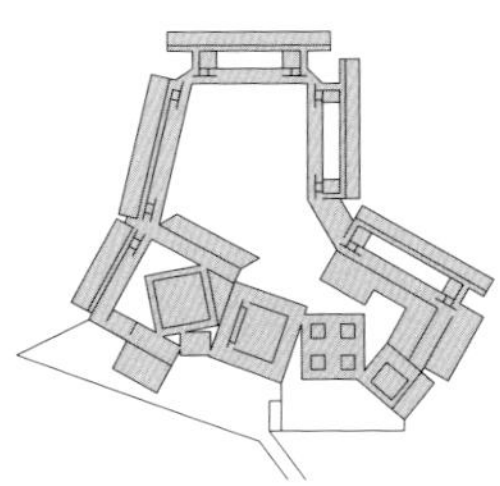

October–December 1966

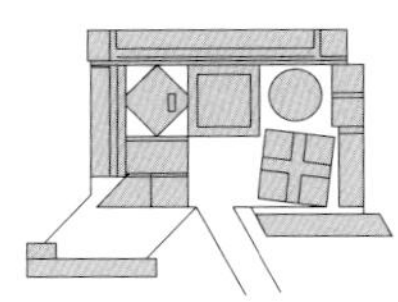

January–February 1967

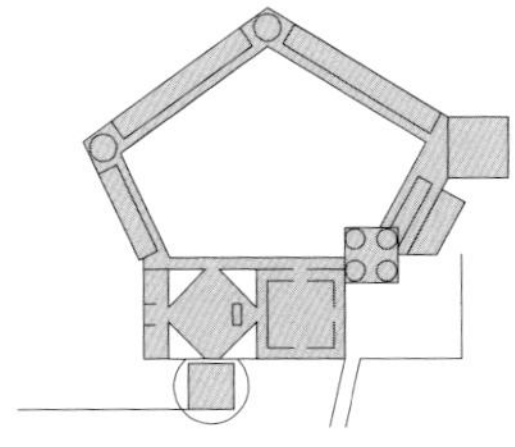

January–February 1967

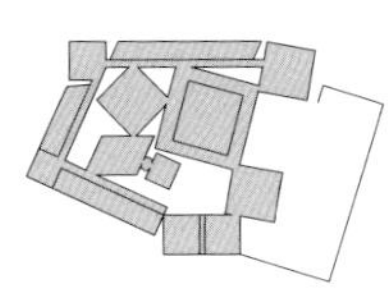

January–February 1967

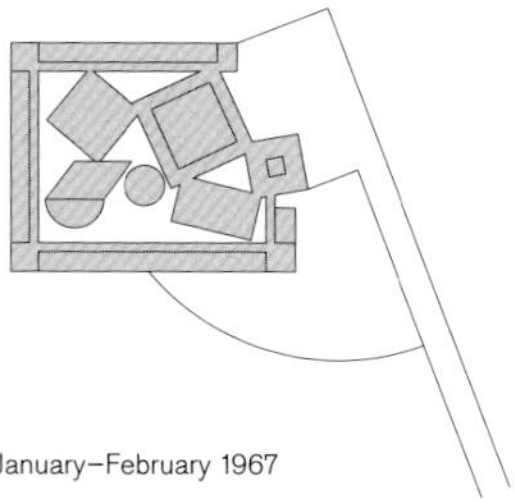

January–February 1967

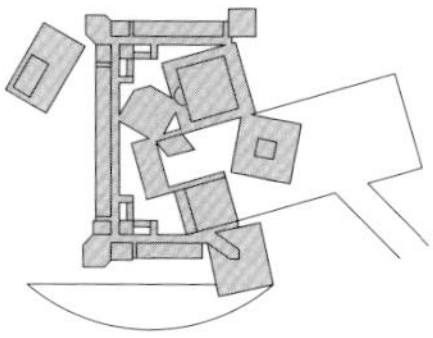

May 1967

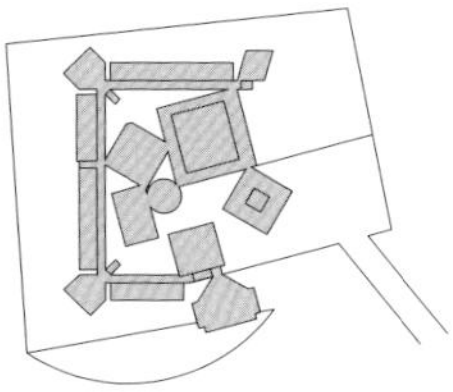

March–April 1967

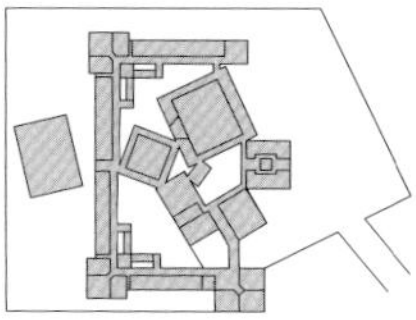

August 1967

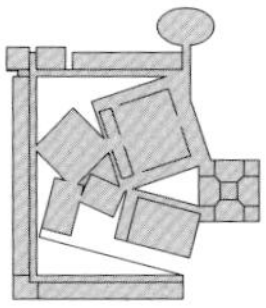

March–April 1967

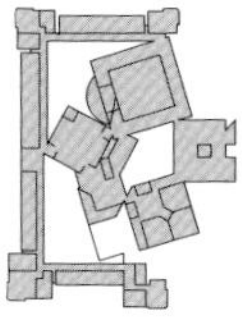

April 1968

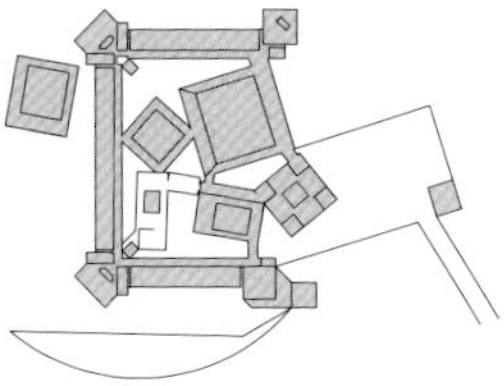

March–April 1967

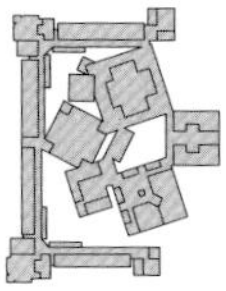

August 1968

Evolution of site plan, 1966–1968

June 1966

September 1966

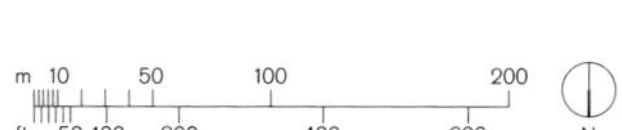

October 1966

August 1968

Floor plans of June, September, and October 1966

1 Tower/Entrance
2 Chapel
3 Refectory
4 Guest dining room
5 Auditorium
6 Library
7 School
8 Cells: postulants
9 Cells: novices
10 Cells: professed
11 Cells: older professed
12 Cells: guests
13 Living room
14 Kitchen
15 Service
16 Office
17 Cloister
18 Court
19 Entry court

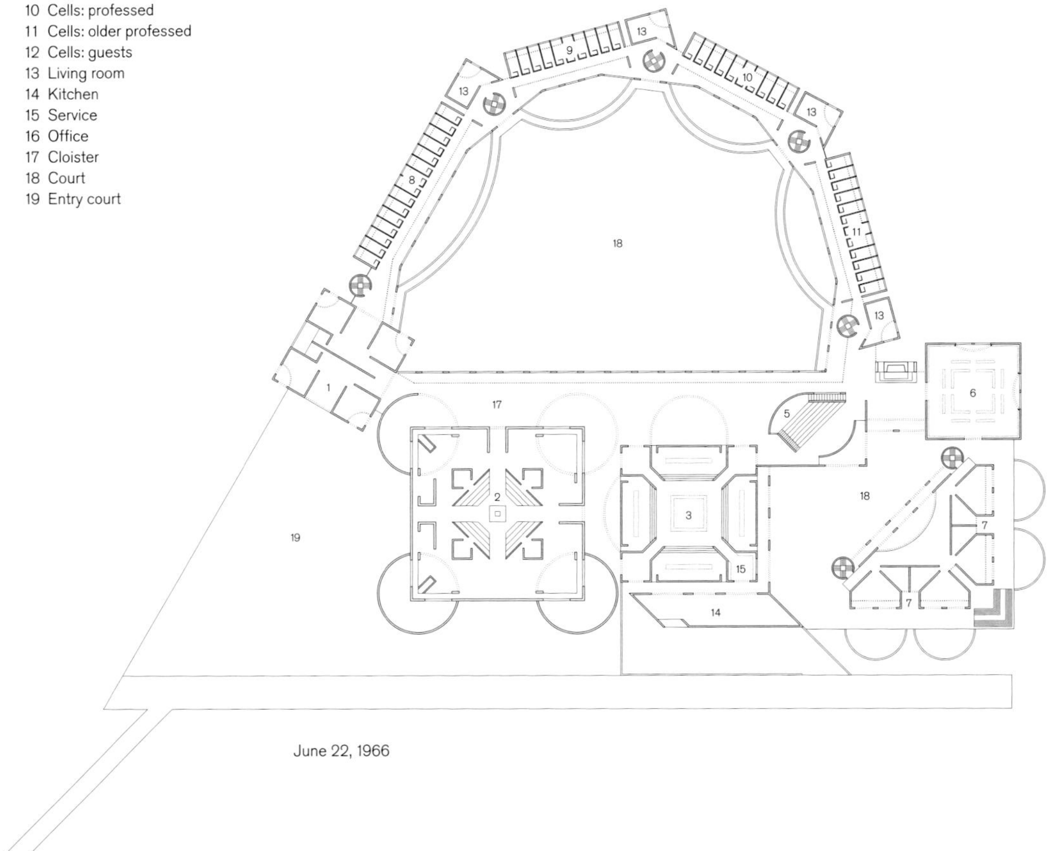

June 22, 1966

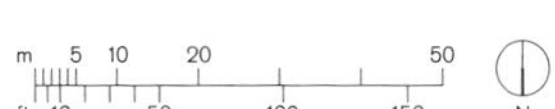

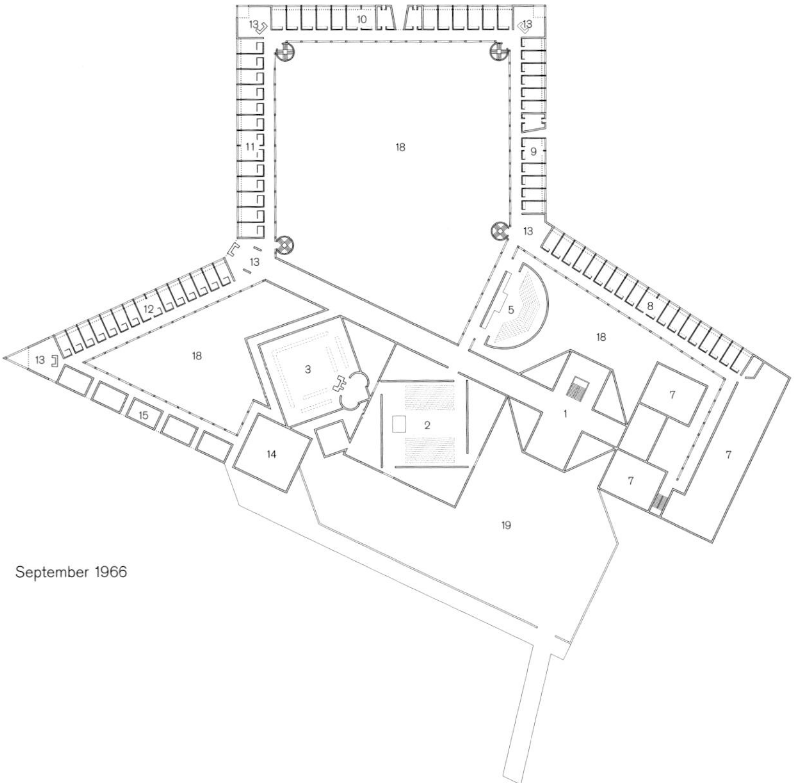


September 1966

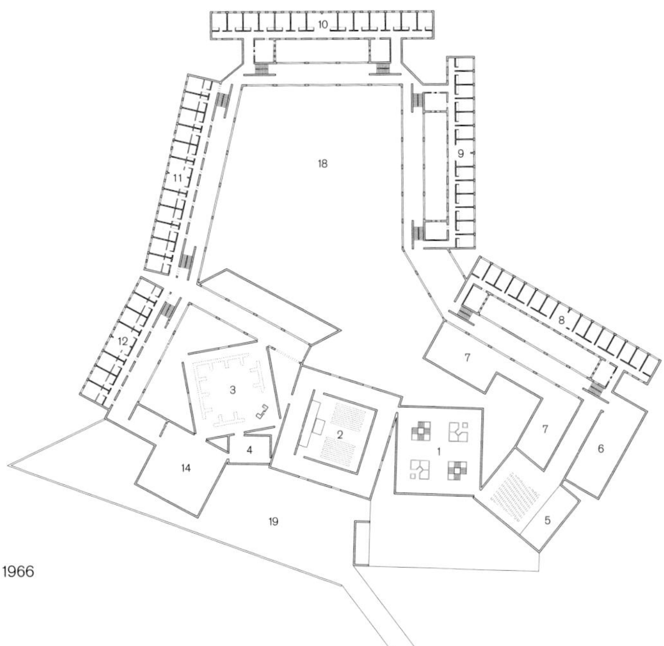


October 1966

Floor plan of August 5, 1968 (similar to other plans after February 1967)

1 Tower/Entrance
2 Chapel
3 Refectory
4 Guest dining room
5 Auditorium
6 Library
7 School
8 Cells: postulants
9 Cells: novices
10 Cells: professed
11 Cells: older professed
12 Cells: guests
13 Living room
14 Kitchen
15 Service
16 Office
17 Cloister
18 Court
19 Entry court

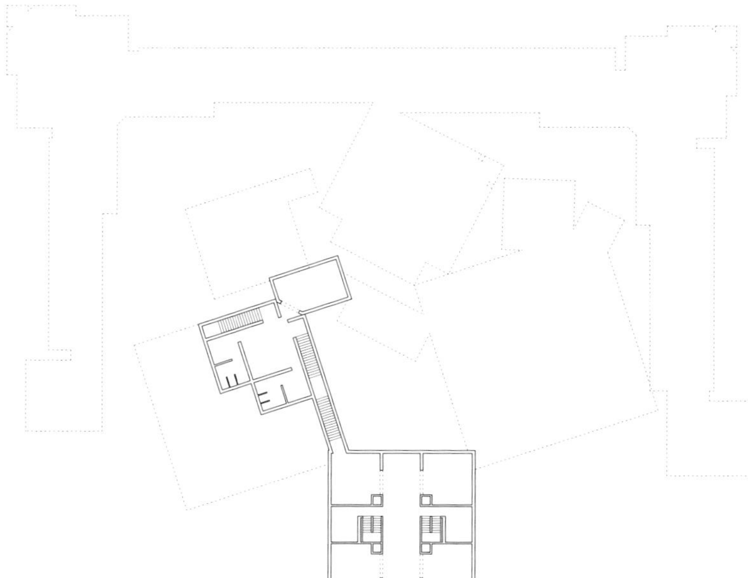

Basement

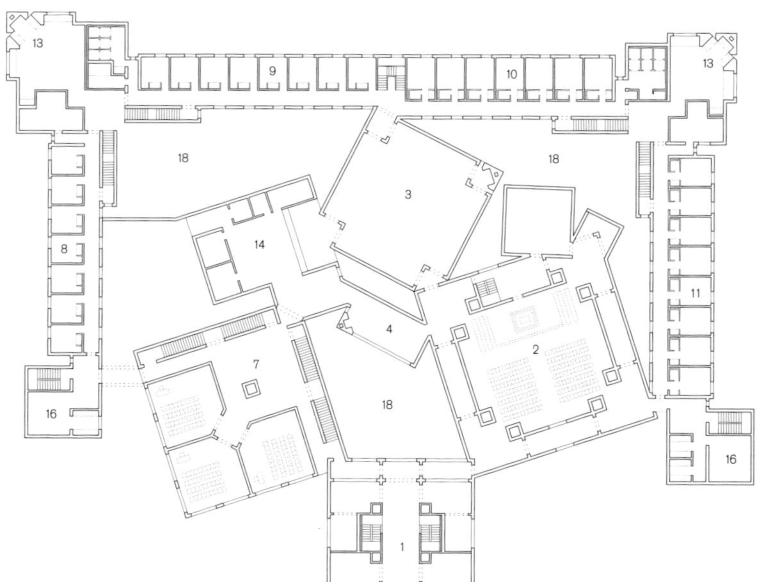


First floor

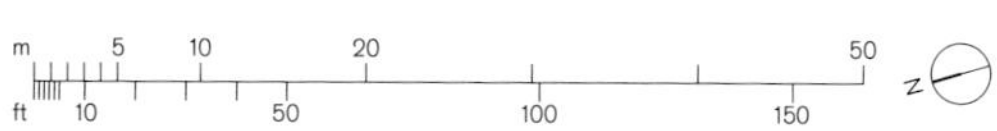

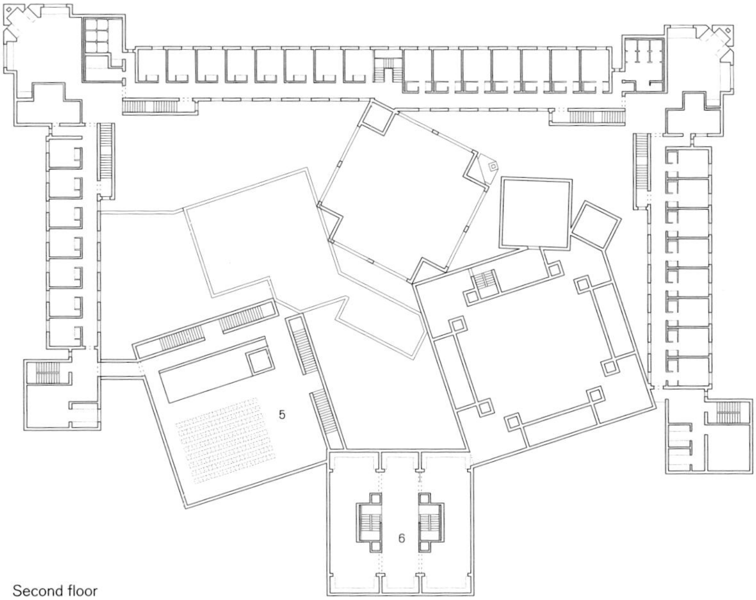


Second floor

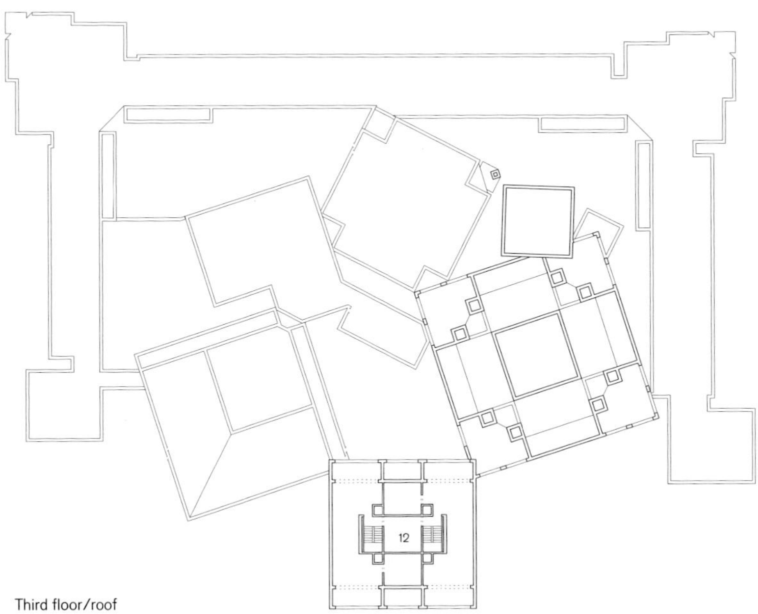


Third floor/roof

# INDEX

# LIST OF ILLUSTRATIONS

**The Louis I. Kahn Collection**
Unless otherwise noted, the drawings and documents reproduced in this book belong to the Louis I. Kahn Collection. Purchased by the Commonwealth of Pennsylvania from the Kahn estate and located in the Architectural Archives of the University of Pennsylvania, the Collection was placed on permanent loan to the University by the Pennsylvania Historical and Museum Commission in 1978. The richness of the Collection is almost overwhelming: encompassing over 200 of Kahn's projects, with over 6,300 drawings by Kahn, 40,000 developmental and working drawings from his office, 100 models, photographs, slides, and 150 linear feet of personal and office files and correspondence. The Collection also contains Kahn's personal library, awards, taped interviews, videos, and other memorabilia. In addition to the Kahn Collection, the Architectural Archives houses the works of more than 400 designers from the eighteenth century to the present, opening its doors to international visitors and scholars and serving as the basis for innumerous publications and exhibitions.

**Front cover** Collaged plan, October 9, 1966, Louis Kahn, see fig. 31
**1** Louis Kahn in his office, 1960, photo: George Pohl, Kahn Collection
**2** Dominican Motherhouse, 1965–69, in Romaldo Giurgola and Jaimini Mehta, *Louis I. Kahn,* Zurich, 1975. pp. 48–49
**3** St. Andrew's Priory, 1966–67, in Romaldo Giurgola and Jaimini Mehta, *Louis I. Kahn,* Zurich, 1975, pp. 50–51
**4** Letter from Mother Mary Emmanuel to Louis Kahn, March 26, 1965, Box LIK 10
**5** Auction poster (verso), Windy Hill, 1964, offset print, 18 × 10 in. (46 × 25 cm), Archive DMH
**6** Auction poster, Windy Hill, 1964, offset print, 18 × 10 in. (46 × 25 cm), Archive DMH
**7** Surveyor's plan, April 16, 1966, diazo print, 31 × 23 ¾ in. (79 × 60.5 cm), 1 in. = 100 ft., 030.I.C.700.010
**8** Louis Kahn and Mother Mary Emmanuel, *Signature Against the Sky,* documentary, WCAU-TV, Philadelphia, 1967
**9** Sister Eileen Patricia Primrose, *Signature Against the Sky,* documentary, WCAU-TV, Philadelphia, 1967
**10** Louis Kahn and David Polk, *Signature Against the Sky,* documentary, WCAU-TV, Philadelphia, 1967
**11** Louis Kahn at work, *Signature Against the Sky,* documentary, WCAU-TV, Philadelphia, 1967
**12** Elements of the plan, Spring 1966, Louis Kahn, charcoal on sketch paper, 22 ½ × 12 in. (57 × 30.5 cm), 1/16 in. = 1 ft., 030.I.A.700.1
**13** Plan, Spring 1966, Louis Kahn, charcoal on sketch paper, 22 ½ × 12 in. (57 × 30.5 cm), 030.I.A.700.1
**14** Plan, Spring 1966, Louis Kahn, graphite pencil on paper, 8 × 5 in. (20.5 × 13 cm), 030.I.A.700.1
**15** Chapel, Spring 1966, Louis Kahn, graphite pencil on paper, 8 × 5 in. (20.5 × 13 cm), 030.I.A.700.1
**16** First Unitarian Church, 1959–1963*: "Form diagram," Louis Kahn, Kahn Collection
**17** Letter, March 28, 1966, Louis Kahn, handwritten, 030.I.A.700.1
**18** Letter with plan sketch (verso), March 28, 1966, Louis Kahn, ink on paper, 8 ½ × 11 in. (21.5 × 28 cm), 030.I.A.700.1
**19** Elements of the plan, May/June 1966, David Polk, graphite pencil on sketch paper, 22 ½ × 12 in. (57 × 30.5 cm), 1/16 in. = 1 ft., 030.I.C.700.009
**20** Elements of the plan, May/June 1966, David Polk, graphite pencil on sketch paper, 20 ¾ × 12 in. (52.5 × 30.5 cm), 1/16 in. = 1 ft., 030.I.C.700.007
**21** Site plan, June 22, 1966, David Polk (attributed), sepia diazo print, 48 × 36 in. (122 × 91 cm), 1 in. = 50 ft., 030.I.C.700.012
**22** Plan: first floor, June 22, 1966, David Polk (attributed), graphite pencil on sketch paper, 21 ½ × 18 in. (54.5 × 45.5 cm), 1 in. = 50 ft., 030.I.C.700.010
**23** North elevation, June 1966, Louis Kahn, charcoal on sketch paper, 32 × 12 ½ in. (81.5 × 32 cm), 1 in. = 50 ft., 030.I.C.700.010
**24** North elevation, June 1966, Louis Kahn, graphite pencil on sketch paper, 30 × 11 ¾ in. (76 × 30 cm), 1 in. = 50 ft., 030.I.A.700.4
**25** North elevation, June 1966, Louis Kahn, graphite pencil on sketch paper, 29 ½ × 11 ¾ in. (75 × 30 cm), 1 in. = 50 ft., 030.I.A.700.4
**26** Plan variation, June 1966, Louis Kahn (attributed), charcoal on sketch paper, 20 × 12 ½ in. (51 × 32 cm), 030.I.C.700.010
**27** Plan variation, June 1966, graphite pencil on sketch paper, 26 ¾ × 21 in. (68 × 53.5 cm), 1 in. = 50 ft., 030.I.C.700.010
**28** Plan variation, June 1966, graphite and color pencil on sketch paper, 24 ½ × 18 in. (62 × 45.5 cm), 1 in. = 50 ft., 030.I.C.700.010
**29** Plan with notes, September 1966, Louis Kahn, graphite pencil on sketch paper, 30 ½ × 18 in. (77 × 45.5 cm), 1 in. = 50 ft., 030.I.C.700.010
**30** Plan, September 1966, Louis Kahn, charcoal on sketch paper, 22 × 11 ¾ in. (56 × 30 cm), 1 in. = 50 ft., 030.I.C.700.010

**31** Collaged plan, October 9, 1966, Louis Kahn, graphite pencil/diazo print, 19 ½ × 19 in. (49.5 × 48.5 cm), 1 in.=50 ft., 030.I.C.700.006

**32** Plan: first floor, October 1966, graphite pencil on vellum, 30 ½ × 23 ¼ in. (77 × 59 cm), 1 in.=50 ft., 030.I.C.700.008

**33** Model, October 1966, photo: Kahn Collection, B.700.1.1

**34** Chapel, tower, school, October 1966, Louis Kahn, charcoal on sketch paper, 23 ½ × 17 ¾ in. (60 × 45 cm), 030.I.A.700.4

**35** Tower, chapel, refectory, October 1966, Louis Kahn, charcoal on sketch paper, 6 ½ × 15 ½ in. (16 × 39.5 cm), 030.I.A.700.4

**36** North elevation, October 1966, Louis Kahn, charcoal on sketch paper, 15 ½ × 11 ¾ in. (39.5 × 30 cm), 030.I.A.700.4

**37** North elevation, October 1966, Louis Kahn, charcoal on sketch paper, 25 × 11 ¾ in. (63.5 × 30 cm), 1⁄16 in.= 1 ft., 030.I.A.700.3

**38** Section looking east, October 1966, Louis Kahn, charcoal on sketch paper, 25 × 11 ¾ in. (63.5 × 30 cm), 1⁄16 in.= 1 ft., 030.I.A.700.4

**39** Section: cell and cloister, October 1966, graphite pencil on sketch paper, 20 ½ × 11 ¾ in. (52 × 30 cm), ⅛ in.= 1 ft., 030.I.C.700.009

**40** Cell: plan, October 1966, Louis Kahn, graphite pencil on sketch paper, 9 ¾ × 11 ¾ in. (25 × 30 cm), ⅛ in.= 1 ft., 030.I.A.700.3

**41** Cell: interior, October 1966, Louis Kahn, charcoal on sketch paper, 29 × 11 ¾ in. (74 × 30 cm), ½ in.= 1 ft., 030.I.A.700.4

**42** Cell (professed): plan, October 1966, Louis Kahn, charcoal on sketch paper, 21 ½ × 11 ¾ in. (54 × 30 cm), ½ in.= 1 ft., 030.I.A.700.3

**43** Cell (young professed): plan, October 1966, Louis Kahn, charcoal on sketch paper, 22 × 11 ¾ in. (56 × 30 cm), ½ in.= 1 ft., 030.I.A.700.3

**44** Plan, January/February 1967, Louis Kahn (attributed), charcoal on sketch paper, 21 × 11 ¾ in. (53.5 × 30 cm), 030.I.C.700.010

**45** Plan, January/February 1967, David Polk (attributed), charcoal on sketch paper, 18 ½ × 11 ¾ in. (47 × 30 cm), 030.I.C.700.007

**46** Plan, January/February 1967, Louis Kahn (attributed), charcoal on sketch paper, 17 × 11 ¾ in. (43 × 30 cm), 030.I.C.700.010

**47** Plan, January/February 1967, Louis Kahn, charcoal on sketch paper, 20 × 11 ¾ in. (51 × 30 cm), 030.I.C.700.010

**48** Plan, January/February 1967, Louis Kahn, charcoal on sketch paper, 19 ½ × 11 ¾ in. (49 × 30 cm), 030.I.C.700.010

**49** Plan, January/February 1967, Louis Kahn, charcoal on sketch paper, 20 × 11 ¾ in. (51 × 30 cm), 030.I.C.700.010

**50** Plan, January/February 1967, Louis Kahn, charcoal on sketch paper, 18 ½ × 11 ¾ in. (47 × 30 cm), 030.I.C.700.010

**51** Plan with site, January/February 1967, Louis Kahn, charcoal on sketch paper, 23 ½ × 18 in. (60 × 45.5 cm), 1 in.=50 ft., 030.I.C.700.010

**52** Plan with site, February 1967, negro pencil on sketch paper, 28 ½ × 18 in. (72.5 × 45.5 cm), 1 in.= 50 ft., 030.I.C.700.001

**53** Core: plan, for June 28, 1967, Louis Kahn, charcoal on sketch paper, 27 ½ × 24 in. (70 × 61 cm), 1⁄16 in.= 1 ft., 030.I.A.700.1

**54** Core: plan, Spring 1967, Louis Kahn, charcoal on sketch paper, 19 ¾ × 11 ¾ in. (50 × 30 cm), ⅛ in.= 1 ft., 030.I.A.700.1

**55** Core: plan, for June 28, 1967, Louis Kahn, charcoal on sketch paper, 33 × 24 in. (84 × 61 cm), 1⁄16 in.= 1 ft., 030.I.A.700.1

**56** Core: plan, Spring 1967, graphite pencil on sketch paper, 16 × 11 ¾ in. (41 × 30 cm), ⅛ in.= 1 ft., 030.I.C.700.009

**57** Plan with site, May 19, 1967, Louis Kahn, charcoal on sketch paper, 28 ½ × 24 in. (72.5 × 61 cm), 1⁄16 in.= 1 ft., 030.I.A.700.1

**58** Plan fragment, for June 28, 1967, Louis Kahn (attributed), negro pencil on sketch paper, 23 ¼ × 18 in. (59 × 45.5 cm), 1⁄16 in.= 1 ft., 030.I.C.700.010

**59** Plan: first floor, June 28, 1967, graphite pencil on sketch paper, 36 × 28 in. (91.5 × 71 cm), 1⁄16 in.= 1 ft., 030.I.C.700.001

**60** Plan with site, August 1967, graphite pencil on vellum, 44 × 32 in. (112 × 81 cm), 1⁄16 in.= 1 ft., 030.I.C.700.008

**61** South elevation, August 7, 1967, Louis Kahn, Louis Kahn, diazo print, 30 ½ × 10 ½ in. (77.5 × 27 cm), ⅛ in.= 1 ft., 030.I.C.700.006

**62** East elevation, August 7, 1967, Louis Kahn, charcoal on sketch paper, 44 ½ × 18 in. (113 × 45.5 cm), ⅛ in.= 1 ft., 030.I.A.700.4

**63** East elevation, August 7, 1967, graphite pencil on vellum, 33 ½ × 11 ¾ in. (85 × 30 cm), 1⁄16 in.= 1 ft., 030.I.C.700.001

**64** North elevation, August 7, 1967, graphite pencil on vellum, 36 ¼ × 11 ¾ in. (92 × 30 cm), 1⁄16 in.= 1 ft., 030.I.C.700.001

**65** Chapel: plan, September/October 1967, Louis Kahn, charcoal on sketch paper, 19 ½ × 11 ¾ in. (49.5 × 30 cm), ⅛ in.= 1 ft., 030.I.C.700.010

**66** Chapel: plan, September/October 1967, Louis Kahn, charcoal on sketch paper, 22 × 18 in. (56 × 45.5 cm), ⅛ in.= 1 ft., 030.I.A.700.2

**67** Chapel: plan, September/October 1967, Louis Kahn, charcoal on sketch paper, 18 ¼ × 18 in. (46.5 × 45.5 cm), ⅛ in.= 1 ft., 030.I.C.700.010

**68** Chapel: plan, October 12, 1967, graphite pencil on sketch paper, 28 × 18 in. (71 × 45.5 cm), ⅛ in.= 1 ft., 030.I.C.700.001

**69** Entry tower: plan, October 12, 1967, graphite pencil on sketch paper, 21 × 18 in. (53.5 × 45.5 cm), ⅛ in.= 1 ft., 030.I.C.700.001

**70** Entry tower: plan, October 12, 1967, graphite pencil on sketch paper, 24 ½ × 18 in. (62 × 45.5 cm), ⅛ in.= 1 ft., 030.I.C.700.001

**71** Refectory: plan, October 12, 1967, graphite pencil on sketch paper, 23 × 18 in. (58.5 × 45.5 cm), ⅛ in.= 1 ft., 030.I.C.700.001

**72** Classrooms: plan, October 12, 1967, graphite pencil on sketch paper, 25 × 18 in. (63.5 × 45.5 cm), ⅛ in.= 1 ft., 030.I.C.700.001

**73** Parti sketch, March 7, 1968, Louis Kahn, charcoal on sketch paper, 22 × 18 in. (56 × 45.5 cm), 030.I.A.700.2

**74** Plan: first floor, February/March 1968, Louis Kahn, charcoal on sketch paper, 41 ½ × 33 ½ in. (105 × 85 cm), ⅛ in.= 1 ft., 030.I.A.700.1

**75** Plan: first floor, April 22, 1968, graphite pencil on sketch paper, 45 ¾ × 35 ¼ in. (116 × 89.5 cm), ⅛ in.= 1 ft., 030.I.C.700.010

**76** West elevation, April 22, 1968, graphite pencil on sketch paper, 32 ½ × 23 ½ in. (82.5 × 60 cm), 1⁄16 in.= 1 ft., 030.I.C.700.010

**77** East elevation, April 22, 1968, graphite pencil on sketch paper, 30 × 23 ¾ in. (79 × 60.5 cm), 1⁄16 in.= 1 ft., 030.I.C.700.010

**78** Section looking west, April 22, 1968, graphite pencil on sketch paper, 30 ½ × 18 in. (77.5 × 45.5 cm), 1/16 in. = 1 ft., 030.I.C.700.010
**79** Section looking south, April 22, 1968, graphite pencil on sketch paper, 37 × 24 in. (94 × 61 cm), 1/16 in. = 1 ft., 030.I.C.700.010
**80** Plan with site, April 17, 1968, sepia diazo print, 13 × 11 in. (33 × 28 cm), 030.I.C.700.12
**81** Plan: first floor, Spring 1968, graphite pencil on sketch paper, 35 ½ × 23 ½ in. (90 × 59.5 cm), 1/16 in. = 1 ft., 030.I.C.700.001
**82** Plan with overlay, May 20, 1968, diazo print/sepia diazo print, 21 × 15 in. (53 × 38 cm), 1/16 in. = 1 ft., 030.I.C.700.002
**83** Plan: first floor, May 20, 1968, graphite pencil on sketch paper, 31 × 23 ½ in. (79 × 59.5 cm), 1/16 in. = 1 ft., 030.I.C.700.010
**84** Plan: second floor, May 20, 1968, graphite pencil on sketch paper, 32 ¾ × 23 ½ in. (83 × 59.5 cm), 1/16 in. = 1 ft., 030.I.C.700.010
**85** Plan: third floor, May 20, 1968, graphite pencil on sketch paper, 34 × 23 ½ in. (86 × 59.5 cm), 1/16 in. = 1 ft., 030.I.C.700.010
**86** Plan: roof, May 20, 1968, graphite pencil on sketch paper, 34 × 23 ½ in. (86 × 59.5 cm), 1/16 in. = 1 ft., 030.I.C.700.010
**87** Site plan, Spring 1968, graphite pencil on sketch paper, 31 × 23 ¾ in. (79 × 60.5 cm), 1 in. = 50 ft., 030.I.C.700.010
**88** Plan: first floor, July 10, 1968, graphite pencil on sketch paper, 29 ½ × 24 in. (75 × 61 cm), 1/16 in. = 1 ft., 030.I.C.700.001
**89** Plan: second floor, July 10, 1968, graphite pencil on sketch paper, 31 × 18 in. (79 × 45.5 cm), 1/16 in. = 1 ft., 030.I.C.700.001
**90** Plan: first floor, August 5, 1968, graphite pencil on sketch paper, 26 ¾ × 18 in. (68 × 45.5 cm), 1/16 in. = 1 ft., 030.I.C.700.001
**91** Plan: second floor, August 5, 1968, graphite pencil on sketch paper, 27 × 18 in. (68.5 × 45.5 cm), 1/16 in. = 1 ft., 030.I.C.700.001
**92** Plan: third floor, August 5, 1968, graphite pencil on sketch paper, 27 × 18 in. (68.5 × 45.5 cm), 1/16 in. = 1 ft., 030.I.C.700.001
**93** Plan: basement, August 5, 1968, graphite pencil on sketch paper, 28 × 24 in. (71 × 61 cm), 1/16 in. = 1 ft., 030.I.C.700.001
**94** South elevation, August 5, 1968, graphite pencil on sketch paper, 27 ½ × 11 ¾ in. (70 × 30 cm), 1/16 in. = 1 ft., 030.I.C.700.001
**95** West elevation, August 5, 1968, graphite pencil on sketch paper, 21 ¾ × 11 ¾ in. (53.5 × 30 cm), 1/16 in. = 1 ft., 030.I.C.700.001
**96** Core: section, August 5, 1968, graphite pencil on sketch paper, 20 × 18 in. (51 × 45.59 cm), 1/16 in. = 1 ft., 030.I.C.700.001
**97** Core: section, August 5, 1968, graphite pencil on sketch paper, 21 ¼ × 13 ½ in. (54 × 34.5 cm), 1/16 in. = 1 ft., 030.I.C.700.001
**98** Entry tower: section, Summer 1968, graphite pencil on sketch paper, 18 × 8 in. (44.5 × 20.5 cm), 1/16 in. = 1 ft., 030.I.C.700.010
**99** Entry tower: section, Summer 1968, graphite pencil on sketch paper, 21 × 11 ¾ in. (53.5 × 30 cm), 1/16 in. = 1 ft., 030.I.C.700.010
**100** East elevation, August 5, 1968, graphite pencil on sketch paper, 27 ½ × 11 ¾ in. (70 × 30 cm), 1/16 in. = 1 ft., 030.I.C.700.001
**101** Small cell: plan, October 23, 1968, graphite pencil on sketch paper, 27 ½ × 11 ¾ in. 70 × 30, ½ in. = 1 ft., 030.I.C.700.001
**102** Large cell: plan, October 23, 1968, graphite pencil on sketch paper, 20 ¼ × 18 ½ in. (51.5 × 46.5 cm), ½ in. = 1 ft., 030.I.C.700.001
**103** Small cell: section, October 23, 1968, graphite pencil on sketch paper, 24 × 18 ½ in. (61 × 46.5 cm), ½ in. = 1 ft., 030.I.C.700.001
**104** Large cell: section, October 23, 1968, graphite pencil on sketch paper, 24 × 18 ½ in. (61 × 46.5 cm), ½ in. = 1 ft., 030.I.C.700.001
**105** Cells: partial elevation, Summer 1968, graphite pencil on sketch paper, 24 ½ × 11 ¾ in. (62 × 30 cm), ¼ in. = 1 ft., 030.I.C.700.007
**106** Core buildings: wall details, Summer/Fall 1968, graphite pencil on sketch paper, 30 × 11 ¾ in. (76 × 30 cm), ¼ in. = 1 ft., 030.I.C.700.007
**107** Cells: horizontal sections, Summer/Fall 1968, graphite pencil on sketch paper, 18 × 11 ¾ in. (45.5 × 30 cm), ¼ in. = 1 ft., 030.I.C.700.007
**108** Core buildings: wall details, Summer/Fall 1968, graphite pencil on sketch paper, 26 ¾ × 24 in. (68 × 61 cm), various scales, 030.I.C.700.007
**109** Wall sections, Summer/Fall 1968, graphite and color pencil on sketch paper, 26 × 17 ¼ in. (66 × 44 cm), ½ in. = 1 ft., 030.I.C.700.007
**110** School/auditorium: section, Summer/Fall 1968, sepia diazo print, 22 ½ × 18 ½ in. (57 × 46.5 cm), ¼ in. = 1 ft., 030.I.C.700.005
**111** Core buildings: wall details, Summer/Fall 1968, graphite pencil on sketch paper, 28 ¼ × 11 ¾ in. (72 × 30 cm), various scales, 030.I.C.700.007
**112** Chapel: section, Summer/Fall 1968, graphite pencil on sketch paper, 25 ½ × 18 ½ in. (65 × 46.5 cm), ⅛ in. = 1 ft., 030.I.C.700.007
**113** Drawing from the series "Silence and Light," 1970, Louis Kahn, Kahn Collection
**114** National Assembly Building, Dhaka, 1962–84: ambulatory, photo: Naquib Hossain
**115** Philadelphia Psychiatric Hospital, 1948–53, Kahn Collection
**116** Trenton Jewish Community Center, 1954–59, Kahn Collection
**117** Richards Medical Research Laboratories, 1957–64, Kahn Collection
**118** Weiss House, 1947–50, Kahn Collection
**119** Goldenberg House, 1959, Kahn Collection
**120** Philadelphia Traffic Study, 1953, Kahn Collection
**121** Philadelphia Bicentennial Plan, 1971, photo: Kahn Collection
**122–24** Salk Institute for Biological Studies, 1959–65: site plan, floor plan, section, photo: Kahn Collection, drawings: M. Merrill
**125** Salk Institute Meeting House, 1959–65: floor plan, drawing: M. Merrill
**126** Salk Institute, 1959–65: view across the plaza with studies and loggias, photo: Naquib Hossain
**127** Erdman Hall, Bryn Mawr College, 1960–65: intermediate scheme, Kahn Collection
**128** Erdman Hall, Bryn Mawr College, 1960–65: floor plan, Kahn Collection
**129** Erdman Hall, Bryn Mawr College, 1960–65: "architecture of connection," drawings: M. Merrill
**130** Dominican Motherhouse, 1966–68: "architecture of connection" (draft), drawings: M. Merrill
**131** Dominican Motherhouse, 1966–68: "architecture of connection" (final), drawings: M. Merrill
**132** Kimbell Art Museum, 1966–70: entry loggia, photo: Eduardo Ponce
**133** Suhrawardthy National Hospital, 1962–74: loggia, photo: Naquib Hossain

**134** Plan of Rome, 1748, Giambattista Nolli
**135** Rubin Vase, from Colin Rowe and Fred Koetter, *Collage City,* Basel et al., 1984, p. 88
**136** Design for a library, Ecole des Beaux-Arts, F. Boulanger (student), from *The Architecture of the Ecole des Beaux-Arts,* ed. Arthur Drexler, London, 1977
**137** Design for a hospice, Ecole des Beaux-Arts, Julian Guadet (student), from *The Architecture of the Ecole des Beaux-Arts,* ed. Arthur Drexler, London, 1977
**138** Adler House, 1954–55, diagrams: M. Merrill
**139** Fleisher House, 1959, diagrams: M. Merrill
**140–41** Research Institute for Advanced Studies, 1956–58, graphite pencil on vellum, 030.I.A.445.1
**142** Trenton Jewish Community Center, 1954–59: scheme 2, drawing: M. Merrill
**143** Trenton Jewish Community Center, 1954–59: scheme 3, drawing: M. Merrill
**144** Trenton Bath House, 1957: floor plan, drawing from Thomas Leslie, *Louis I. Kahn: Building Art, Building Science,* New York, 2005
**145–47** Fort Wayne Fine Arts Center, 1961–73: sketches, site plan, morphological plan, diagrams: M. Merrill
**148** De Menil Foundation, 1972: site plan, drawing: M. Merrill
**149–50** Dominican Motherhouse: figure-ground, June 1966; built and grown, August 1968, drawings: M. Merrill
**151–52** Salk Institute Meeting House, 1959–65: from membrane to border-space, Kahn Collection
**153–55** Dom Hans van der Laan, "threefold demarcation of space," from *De architectonische ruimte,* Leiden, 1977
**156–59** Kahn's threefold space: Salk Meeting House, Dominican Motherhouse, St. Andrew's Priory, Fort Wayne Fine Arts Center, diagrams: M. Merrill
**160** National Assembly Building, Dhaka, 1962–84, diagram, Louis Kahn
**161** Franklin D. Roosevelt Memorial, 1973–74, photo: Kahn Collection
**162–64** Kimbell Art Museum, 1966–72: porch, section, site plan, photo: Jeff Stvan, drawings: M. Merrill
**165** Library, Phillips Exeter Academy, 1965–72, photo: Ed Brodzinsky
**166** Salk Institute for Biological Studies, 1959–65, photo: Naquib Hossain
**167** Temple of Ammon at Karnak, Louis Kahn, 1951, charcoal on paper, 11 1/3 × 14 3/5 in. (29.2 × 37.5 cm), collection of Sue Ann Kahn
**168** President's Estate, Islamabad, 1963–66, Louis Kahn, charcoal on sketch paper, 9 1/2 × 19 in. (24 × 48.5 cm), 675.2
**169** Hurva Synagogue, Jerusalem, 1967–74, Louis Kahn, colored pencil on vellum, 9 3/4 × 41 3/4 in. (15 × 106 cm), 755.12
**170** U.S. Consulate, Luanda, 1959–62: section, Kahn Collection
**171** U.S. Consulate, Luanda, 1959–62: axonometric, Kahn Collection
**172** U.S. Consulate, Luanda, 1959–62: perspective, Kahn Collection
**173** Salk Institute for Biological Studies, 1959–65, Louis Kahn, charcoal on sketch paper, 11 3/4 × 19 1/2 in. (30 × 49 cm), 540.19
**174** Library, Phillips Exeter Academy, 1965–72, photo: Roberto Schezen, in Joseph Rykwert and Roberto Schezen, *Louis Kahn,* New York, 2001
**175** Academy Building, Phillips Exeter Academy, 1914–15, photo: Glenn Wiggins, in Glenn Wiggins, *The Library at Phillips Exeter Academy,* New York, 1997
**176** Kimbell Art Museum, 1966–72, photo: Jeff Stvan
**177** St. Andrew's Priory: section, Summer 1966, Louis Kahn, charcoal on sketch paper, 25 1/2 × 12 in. (65 × 30.5 cm), 030.I.A.715.1
**178** St. Andrew's Priory, 1966–67: elevation, Summer 1966, Louis Kahn, charcoal on sketch paper, 36 × 11 3/4 in. (91.5 × 30 cm), 030.I.A.715.1
**179** St. Andrew's Priory, 1966–67: plan, Kahn Collection
**180** St. Andrew's Priory, 1966–67, model photo, B.715.1.4
**181** St. Andrew's Priory, 1966–67, model photo, B.715.1.8
**182** St. Andrew's Priory, 1966–67: figure-ground, diagram: M. Merrill
**183** St. Andrew's Priory, 1966–67: plan and cardinal directions, diagram: M. Merrill
**184** St. Andrew's Priory, 1966–67: inside-outside/tower-as-hub, diagram: M. Merrill
**185** St. Andrew's Priory, 1966–67: geometry, diagram: M. Merrill
**186** Dominican Motherhouse: site plan (final version), August 1968, drawing: M. Merrill
**187** Louis Kahn in his office, ca. 1958–60, photo: unknown, Kahn Collection
**Back cover** Louis Kahn in his office, 1960, photo: George Pohl, Kahn Collection

The Mary, Queen of All Saints Motherhouse of St. Catherine de Ricci
North Providence Road, Media, PA
Earliest date: March 26, 1965
Date of contract: August 7, 1967
Last drawing date: December 15, 1969
Termination of contract: March 18, 1969
Mechanical/Electrical engineer: Vinokur-Pace Engineering Services

Project Material in the Louis I. Kahn Collection:
Portfolios 030.I.A.700.1–4: with original drawings by Louis Kahn
Portfolios 030.I.C.700.001–012: with original drawings by Kahn and his associates, prints
Project Files: Box LIK 10
Total of 956 drawings and prints, 1 model

## BIBLIOGRAPHY


Aben, Rob and Saskia de Wit. *The Enclosed Garden: History and Development of the Hortus Conclusus.* Rotterdam, 1999.

"A Discussion in Louis I. Kahn's Office." *Perspecta* 7 (1961), pp. 9–18.

Alexander, Christopher. "A City is Not a Tree." In *Architecture Culture: 1943–1968.* Ed. Joan Ockman. New York, 1993, pp. 379–88. Originally published in *Architectural Forum,* April 1965 (part 1) and May 1965 (part 2).

———. *Notes on the Synthesis of Form.* Cambridge, Mass., 1964.

Arendt, Hannah. *The Human Condition.* Chicago, 1958.

Ashraf, Kazi K. "Taking Place: Landscape in the Architecture of Louis Kahn." *Journal of Architectural Education* 61, no. 2 (October 2007), pp. 48–58.

Ashraf, Kazi K., and Yukio Futagawa, eds. *Louis I. Kahn: National Capital Complex of Bangladesh.* Tokyo, 1994.

Benedikt, Michael. *Deconstructing the Kimbell.* New York, 1991.

———. *For an Architecture of Reality.* New York, 1987.

———. "God, Creativity, and Evolution: The Argument from Designers." In *Center,* vol. 15: *Divinity, Creativity, Complexity.* Austin, 2006.

———. "On Adding to the Salk." *Progressive Architecture* (October 1993).

Barbaro, Daniele. *La Practica della Perpettia* [1568]. Facsimile ed. Bologna, 1977.

Berrizbeitia, Anita, and Linda Pollak. *Inside Outside: Between Architecture and Landscape.* Gloucester, Mass., 1999.

Bottero, Maria. "Organic and Rational Morphology in the Work of Louis Kahn." *Zodiac* 17 (1967).

Brady, Susan. "The Architectural Metaphysics of Louis Kahn." *New York Times Magazine,* November 15, 1970, p. 58.

Braunfels, Wolfgang. *Monasteries of Western Europe: The Architecture of the Orders.* London, 1972.

Broadbent, Geoffrey. *Design Methods in Architecture.* London, 1969.

Brownlee, David B. "The Houses of the Inspirations." In *Louis I. Kahn: In the Realm of Architecture.* Ed. Brownlee and De Long. New York, 1991.

———. "Turning a Corner with Louis I. Kahn." In *Das Bauwerk und die Stadt: Aufsätze für Eduard Sekler.* Ed. W. Boehm. Vienna et al., 1994, pp. 48–58.

Brownlee, David B., and David G. De Long, eds. *Louis I. Kahn: In the Realm of Architecture.* New York, 1991.

Canizaro, Vincent, ed. *Architectural Regionalism: Collected Writings on Place, Identity, Modernity, and Tradition.* New York, 2007.

Caragonne, Alexander. *The Texas Rangers.* Cambridge, Mass., 1995.

Colquhoun, Alan. "The Beaux-Arts Plan." *Architectural Design Profiles* 17, vol. 48, nos. 11–12 (1978), pp. 50–65.

———. "Typology and Design Method." In *Essays in Architectural Criticism.* Cambridge Mass. and London, 1981, pp. 43–50. Originally published in *Arena: Journal of the Architectural Association* 83 (June 1967).

Costa, Xavier, ed. *Kahn: Bibliotecas.* Barcelona, 1988.

Curtis, William J. R. "Cosmos and State: The National Assembly in Dhaka." *Monografías de Arquitectura y Vivienda* (February 2001).

De Quincy, Quatremère. *Dictionnaire Historique de l'Architecture.* Paris, 1832, pp. 629–30. Reproduced in *Oppositions,* no. 8 (Spring 1977).

Devillers, Christian. "Louis Kahn's Indian Institute of Management, 1962–1974." *Casabella* 54 (September 1990), pp. 36–63.

Evans, Robin. "Figures, Doors and Corridors." In *Translations from Drawing to Building and Other Essays.* London, 1997.

Flasch, Kurt. "Nikolaus von Kues: Die Idee der Koinzidenz." In *Grundprobleme der Großen Philosophen.* Ed. J. Speck. Göttingen, 1992, pp. 221–61.

Ford, Edward. *The Details of Modern Architecture.* Vol. 2. Cambridge, Mass. and London, 1996, ch. 9, pp. 305–35.

Forty, Adrian. "Language and Drawing." In *Words and Buildings: A Vocabulary of Modern Architecture.* London, 2000, pp. 28–41.

———. "Spatial Mechanics—Scientific Metaphors." In *Words and Buildings: A Vocabulary of Modern Architecture.* London, 2000, pp. 86–102.

———. *Words and Buildings.* New York, 2000.

Frampton, Kenneth. "Louis Kahn and the French Connection." *Oppositions,* no. 22 (1980), pp. 20–53.

———. *Studies in Tectonic Culture: The Poetics of Construction in 19th and 20th Century Architecture.* Cambridge, Mass. and London, 1995.

Friedman, Daniel S. "Salk Institute for Biological Studies" in *Louis I. Kahn: In the Realm of Architecture.* New York, 1991.

Giurgola, Romaldo, and Jaimini Mehta. *Louis I. Kahn.* Boulder, 1975.

Grassi, Giorgio. "Questions of Design" and "Choosing One's Masters: K.F. Schinkel." In *Giorgio Grassi: Obras y Proyectos, 1962–1993.* Valencia, 1994.

Graves, Michael. "The Necessity for Drawing: Tangible Speculation." In *Images of a Grand Tour.* By Brian M. Ambroziak and idem. New York, 2005, pp. 235–45. Originally published in 1997.

Gregotti, Vittorio. "Louis Kahn: Modern Connection." *Rassegna* 21 (1985).

———, ed. *Rassegna* 21 ("Louis I. Kahn 1901–1974"), special issue (March 1985).

Harries, Karsten. *The Ethical Function of Architecture.* Cambridge, Mass., 1997.

Heidegger, Martin. "Building Dwelling Thinking." In *Poetry, Language, Thought.* Trans. Albert Hofstadter. New York, 1971, pp. 145–61. Originally published in German as "Bauen, Wohnen, Denken" in 1951.

Hillier, Bill. *Space is the Machine.* Cambridge, UK, 1 996.

Hillier, Bill, and Julienne Hanson. *The Social Logic of Space.* Cambridge, UK, 1974.

Hinnebusch, William A., O.P. *Dominican Spirituality: Principles and Practice.* Washington, D.C., 1965.

———. *The History of the Dominican Order.* New York, 1966 (vol. 1) and 1973 (vol. 2).

Hochstim, Jan. *The Paintings and Drawings of Louis I. Kahn.* New York, 1991.

Jacobs, Jane. *The Death and Life of the Great American Cities.* New York, 1961.

*Jean-Michel Basquiat.* Exh. cat. Whitney Museum. New York, 1992.

Johnson, Eugene, and Michael J. Lewis. *Drawn From the Source: The Travel Sketches of Louis I. Kahn.* Cambridge, Mass. and London, 1996.

Johnson, Nell E., ed. *Light is the Theme: Louis I. Kahn and the Kimbell Art Museum.* Fort Worth, 1975.

Jordy, William. "The Span of Kahn." *Architectural Review* 155 (June 1974).

Judd, Donald. "Lecture at Yale, September 1983." In *Donald Judd: Architecture.* Ostfildern, 1992.

Kahn, Louis I. "The Architect Speaks" [1953]. Interviewed by Henry F. S. Cooper. *Yale Daily News,* special supplement: The New Art Gallery and Design Center Dedication Issue, November 6, 1953.

———. "Architecture is the Thoughtful Making of Spaces" [1957]. In *Architecture Culture: 1943–1968.* Ed. Joan Ockman. New York, 1993.

———. *Conversations with Students.* Ed. Dung Ngo. Architecture at Rice 26, 2nd ed. Houston, 1998. First published in 1969.

———. "Form and Design" [1961]. In *Louis I. Kahn: Writings, Lectures, Interviews.* Ed. Alessandra Latour. New York, 1991. Radio lecture for "Voice of America," November 1960. Published first as "A Statement from Louis I. Kahn," *Arts and Architecture* (February 1961), and later as "Form and Design," *Architectural Design* 31 (April 1961).

———. "I Love Beginnings." Lecture at "The Invisible City" International Design Conference, Aspen, CO, June 19, 1972. In *What Will Be Has Always Been: The Words of Louis I. Kahn.* Ed. Richard Saul Wurman. New York, 1986.

———. "The Institutions of Man." Lecture at Princeton University, March 13, 1968. In *What Will Be Has Always Been: The Words of Louis I. Kahn.* Ed. Richard Saul Wurman. New York, 1986.

———. "Louis I. Kahn: A Discussion." *Perspecta* 7 (1961). Reprinted in *Louis I. Kahn, Writings, Lectures, Interviews.* Ed. Alessandra Latour. New York, 1991

———. "Monumentality" [1944]. In *Louis I. Kahn: Writings, Lectures, Interviews.* Ed. Alessandra Latour. New York, 1991.

———. "New Frontiers in Architecture." Lecture at the 1959 CIAM Conference in Otterlo. In *Louis I. Kahn, Writings, Lectures, Interviews.* Ed. Alessandra Latour, New York, 1991.

———. "Not For the Faint-Hearted" [1971]. In *What Will Be Has Always Been: The Words of Louis I. Kahn.* Ed. Richard Saul Wurman. New York, 1986. Originally published in the *AIA Journal* (June 1971).

———. "Order Is" [1960]. In *Louis I. Kahn: Writings, Lectures, Interviews.* Ed. Alessandra Latour. New York, 1991.

———. "The Room, the Street and Human Agreement" [AIA Gold Medal Acceptance Speech, 1971]. In *Louis I. Kahn: Writings, Lectures, Interviews.* Ed. Alessandra Latour. New York, 1991. First published in the *AIA Journal* 56 (1971).

———. "Silence and Light." Lecture at ETH Zürich, February 12, 1969. In *Louis I. Kahn: Complete Work.* Ed. H. Ronner and M. Jhaveri.

———. "Talk at the Conclusion of the Otterlo Congress" [1959]. In *Louis I. Kahn: Essential Texts.* Ed. Robert Twombly. New York, 2003.

———. "Two Houses." *Perspecta: The Yale Architectural Journal,* no. 3 (1955), pp. 60–61.

———. "The Value and Aim of Sketching." In *Louis I. Kahn: Writings, Lectures, Interviews.* Ed. Alexandra Latour. New York, 1991. Originally published in *T-Square Club Journal* 1 (May 1931), pp. 19–21.

Kohane, Peter. "Library and Dining Hall, Phillips Exeter Academy." In *Louis I. Kahn: In the Realm of Architecture,* ed. Brownlee and De Long.

———. "Louis I. Kahn's Search for Form." In *Kahn Libraries/Bibliotecas.* Barcelona, 1989.

———. "Louis I. Kahn and the Library: Genesis and Expression of 'Form'." In *VIA* 10: *Ethics in Architecture.* New York, 1990.

Latour, Alessandra, ed. *Louis I. Kahn: L'uomo, il maestro.* Rome, 1986.

———, ed. *Louis I. Kahn: Writings, Lectures, Interviews.* New York, 1991.

Le Corbusier. "In Defense of Architecture" [1929]. *Oppositions Reader: Selected Readings from a Journal for Ideas and Criticism in Architecture.* Ed. K. Michael Hays. New York, 1998, pp. 611–12. First published in French as "Défense de l'Architecture" in *L'Architecture d'Aujourd'hui* 4, no. 10 (1933).

Leslie, Thomas. *Louis I. Kahn: Building Art, Building Science.* New York, 2005.

Lewis, Michael J. "The Dominican Motherhouse." In *Louis I. Kahn: In the Realm of Architecture.* New York, 1991.

Ligtelijn, Vincent. *Aldo van Eyck: Werke.* Basel et al., 1999.

Lobell, John. *Between Silence and Light: Spirit in the Architecture of Louis I. Kahn.* Boston, 1979.

Loud, Patricia Cummings. *The Art Museums of Louis I. Kahn.* Durham, NC, 1989.

"Louis I. Kahn." *Architecture + Urbanism,* special Issue (1975).

*The Louis I. Kahn Archive: Personal Drawings.* 7 vols. New York, 1987. Garland Archives, series editor: Alexander Tzonis.

"Louis I. Kahn: Oeuvres 1963–1969." *L'Architecture d'aujourd'hui* 40, no. 142, special issue (February/ March 1969).

Lynch, Kevin. *The Image of the City.* Cambridge, Mass., 1960.

Lynch, Kevin, et al. *The View from the Road.* Cambridge, Mass., 1964.

Mallgrave, Henry, and Eleftherios Ikonomou. Introduction. *Empathy, Form and Space: Problems in German Aesthetics, 1873–1893.* Santa Monica, 1994.
McCarter, Robert. *Louis I. Kahn.* London, 2005.
Meier, Raymond. *Louis Kahn Dhaka.* Zurich, 2004.
Merrill, Michael. "Louis Kahn and the Dominican Motherhouse: Problems of Space." PhD Diss., Universität Karlsruhe, 2008.
———. *Louis Kahn: Drawing to Find Out.* Baden, 2010.
Metzler, Wolfgang. *Gesetze des Sehens.* Frankfurt, 1936.
Meyers, Marshall. "Kahn and the Act of Drawing: Some Recollections." In *Sketches for the Kimbell Art Museum.* Fort Worth, 1975.
Moneo, Rafael. "End of the Century Paradigms." *El Croquis* 98 (1999).
———. "On Typology." *Oppositions,* no. 13 (Summer 1978), pp. 23–45.
*Monografías de Arquitectura & Vivienda,* ed. Jorge Sainz, "Louis I. Kahn" special issue (February 2001).
Moore, Charles. "Hadrian's Villa." *Perspecta* 6 (1960), pp. 16–27.
Nakamura, Toshio, ed. "Louis I. Kahn: Conception and Meaning." *Architecture + Urbanism,* special issue (November 1983).
Norberg-Schulz, Christian. *Architecture: Presence, Language, Space.* Milan, 2000.
———. *Genius Loci: Towards a Phenomenology of Architecture.* New York, 1980.
———. *Roots of Modern Architecture.* Tokyo, 1988.
Ockman, Joan, ed. *Architecture Culture: 1943–1968.* New York, 1993.
Padovan, Richard. *Dom Hans van der Laan: Modern Primitive.* Amsterdam, 1994.
Pena, William. *Problem Seeking: An Architectural Programming Primer.* Boston, 1977.
Polk, David. Interviewed by Kazumi Kawasaki. *Architecture + Urbanism,* special issue (November 1983).
Popper, Karl Raimund. *Conjecture and Refutations.* London, 1963.
Prown, Jules David. *The Architecture of the Yale Center for British Art.* 2nd ed. New Haven, 1982.
Riley, Terence. "The Landscapes of Frank Lloyd Wright: A Pattern of Work." In *Frank Lloyd Wright: Architect.* New York, 1994, pp. 96–107.
Ronner, Heinz, and Sharad Jhaveri. *Louis I. Kahn: Complete Work, 1935–1974.* 2nd ed. Basel and Boston, 1987.
Rowe, Colin. "Character and Composition." In *The Mathematics of the Ideal Villa and Other Essays.* Cambridge, Mass. and London, 1976.
———. "Neoclassicism and Modern Architecture II." In *The Mathematics of the Ideal Villa and Other Essays.* Cambridge, Mass. and London, 1976.
Rowe, Colin, and Fred Koetter. *Collage City.* Cambridge, Mass. and London, 1978.
Sabini, Maurizio. "Between Order and Form: Fragments and the Idea of Architecture." *Rassegna* 21 (1985).
Scully, Vincent. *Architecture: The Natural and the Manmade.* London, 1991.
———. "Introduction." In *Kahn Libraries/Bibliotecas.* Barcelona, 1989, pp. 16–44.
———. *Louis I. Kahn.* New York, 1962.
———. "Works of Louis I. Kahn and His Method." *Architecture + Urbanism,* special Issue (1975), pp. 286–99.
Smithson, Alison and Peter. "Louis I. Kahn." *Architect's Yearbook* 9 (1960).
———. *The Charged Void: Architecture.* New York, 2001.
Sorkin, Michael. "Family Values." In *Some Assembly Required.* Minneapolis and London, 2001.
Speck, Lawrence W. "Regionalism and Invention" [1987]. In *Architectural Regionalism: Collected Writings on Place, Identity, Modernity, and Tradition.* Ed. Vincent Canizaro, New York, 2007, pp. 70–79.
Steinmann, Martin. "Techne: zur Arbeit von Peter Zumthor." In *Partituren und Bilder.* Lucerne, 1989.
Till, Jeremy. *Architecture Depends.* Cambridge, Mass., 2009.
Twombly, Robert, ed. *Louis Kahn: Essential Texts.* New York, 2003.
Tyng, Alexandra. *Beginnings: Louis I. Kahn's Philosophy of Architecture.* New York, 1984.
Tyng, Anne. *Louis I. Kahn to Anne Tyng: The Rome Letters 1953–54.* New York, 1997.
Ungers, Oswald Mathias. *Architettura come tema/ Architecture as Theme.* Milan and New York, 1982.
———. "Designing and Thinking in Images, Metaphors and Analogies." In *Morphologie—City Metaphors.* Cologne, 1982. Originally published in *Man Transforms.* Exh. cat. Cooper-Hewitt Museum, New York, 1976.
Van de Ven, Cornelius. *Space in Architecture.* 3rd ed. Assen and Maastricht, 1987.
Van der Laan, Dom Hans. *Architectonic Space.* Leiden, 1987.
Van der Rohe, Mies. "Was wäre Beton, was Stahl ohne Spiegelglas?" [1933]. In *Das Kunstlose Wort.* Ed. Fritz Neumeyer. Berlin, 1986.
Van Eyck, Aldo. "Steps Towards a Configurative Discipline." In *Architecture Culture: 1943–1968.* Ed. Joan Ockman. New York, 1993. Originally published in *Forum,* no. 3 (August 1962), pp. 81–94.
———. "The Medicine of Reciprocity Tentatively Illustrated." *Architects Year Book,* no. 10 (1962), pp. 173–78.
Van Zanten, David. "Architectural Composition at the Ecole des Beaux-Arts." In *The Architecture of the Ecole des Beaux-Arts.* London, 1977, pp. 111–324.
———. "Louis I. Kahn and Composition." Unpublished manuscript of a lecture given at the Kahn Symposium, Yale University, January 23, 2004.
Venturi, Robert. "A Protest Concerning the Extension of the Salk Center." In *Iconography and Electronics Upon a Generic Architecture: A View from the Drafting Room.* Cambridge, Mass., 1996.
———. "Genius Betrayed." *Architecture* (July 1993).
———. "Ideas of Reconciliation in Architectural Composition." Proposal sent to John Entenza of the Graham Foundation, February 15, 1962. Unpublished. Architectural Archives of the University of Pennsylvania.
———. "The Obligation Toward the Difficult Whole." In *Complexity and Contradiction in Architecture.* New York, 1966, pp. 88–105.
Venturi, Robert, and Denise Scott Brown. "Genius Betrayed." *Architecture* (July 1993).
Vidler, Anthony. "The Idea of the Type: The Transformation of the Academic Ideal, 1750–1830." *Oppositions,* no. 8 (Spring 1977).
Von Kleist, Heinrich. "Über die almählige Verfertigung der Gedanken beim Reden." In *Heinrich von Kleist Sämtliche Werke und Briefe.* Vol. 3. Frankfurt am Main, 1990. Originally published in 1805–6.
Williams Goldhagen, Sarah. *Louis Kahn's Situated Modernism.* New Haven, 2001.
Wright, Frank Lloyd. "Concept and Plan." *The Architectural Record* (January/February 1928).
Wurman, Richard Saul. *What Will Be Has Always Been: The Words of Louis I. Kahn.* New York, 1986.

## QUOTES

Page 6:
Louis Kahn, in *The Notebooks and Drawings of Louis I. Kahn,* 1973, Wurman, *What Will Be Has Always Been,* p. 256.

Page 7:
"Die Gestalt ist ein Bewegliches, ein Werdendes, ein Vergehendes. Gestaltenlehre ist Verwandlungslehre." Johann Wolfgang von Goethe, Diary [1796], quoted in Oswald Spengler, *The Decline of the West,* vol. 1, trans. Charles Francis Atkinson, London, 1926, p. 97.
Louis Kahn, 1965, quoted in Wurman, *What Will Be Has Always Been,* p. 223.
Louis Kahn, quoted in John Lobell, *Between Silence and Light,* p. 80.

Page 15:
Louis Kahn, "The Institutions of Man," p. 22.
Louis Kahn, "White Light, Black Shadow," lecture, in *Conversations with Students,* p. 28.

Page 25:
Le Corbusier, "In Defense of Architecture," pp. 611–12.
Gerhard Richter, *Text: Writings, Interviews and Letters, 1961–2007,* ed. Dietmar Elger, Hans-Ulrich Obrist, London, 2009.
Joseph Brodsky, "Less Than One," in *Less Than One: Selected Essays,* New York, 1986.

Page 115:
Karsten Harries, *The Ethical Function of Architecture,* p. 180.
Louis Kahn, "The Room, the Street, and Human Agreement," p. 33.

Page 123:
Bill Hillier, *Space is the Machine,* p. 30.
Adrian Forty, "Spatial Mechanics—Scientific Metaphors," p. 94.

Page 145:
Louis Kahn, letter to landscape architect, Karl Linn, May 1965, Box LIK 58, Kahn Collection.
Aldo van Eyck, "Steps Towards a Configurative Discipline," p. 348.
Miles Davis [1959], quoted in Ian Carr, *Miles Davis: The Definitive Biography,* New York, 1999.

Page 163:
José Ortega y Gasset, *The Revolt of the Masses,* New York, 1993, pp. 151–52. Originally published in Spanish as *La Rebelión de las Masas* in 1930.

Page 165:
Louis Kahn, transcript of a talk to the Board of Standards and Planning for the Living Theater, Box LIK 57, Kahn Collection quoted in Brownlee and De Long, *Louis I. Kahn,* p. 71.

Page 179:
Louis Kahn, transcribed notes of a discussion in his Master's Studio, University of Pennsylvania, September 29, 1969, quoted in Wurman, *What Will Be Has Always Been,* p. 78.
Louis Kahn, "Monumentality," p. 25.

Page 205:
Lucien Goldmann, "Structure: Human Reality and Methodological Concept," in *The Structuralist Controversy: The Languages of Criticism and the Sciences of Man,* ed. R. Macksey and E. Donato, Baltimore, 1972, p. 107.
Lionello Venturi, from 1925 essay on Caravaggio, quoted in *New York Times,* March 9, 2010.

Cover:
Louis Kahn, "I Love Beginnings," p. 291.

## THE DOMINICAN MOTHERHOUSE IN THE LOUIS I. KAHN COLLECTION

| Portfolio Call Number | Description | Quantity |
|---|---|---|
| LIK 700.01–700.39 | DMH. design drawings from Louis Kahn, 39 originals, dated/undated | 39 drawings |
| LIK 700.40–700.84 | DMH. design drawings from Louis Kahn, 44 originals, dated/undated | 44 drawings |
| 030.I.C.700.001 | DMH. design drawings on yellow and white trace, 59 originals, dated 16.04.66–17.01.69 | 59 drawings |
| 030.I.C.700.002 | DMH. design drawings, 74 prints, dated 02.05.67–15.12.68 | 74 prints |
| 030.I.C.700.003 | DMH. design drawings, 50 prints, undated | 50 prints |
| 030.I.C.700.004 | DMH. design and presentation drawings, 32 prints, dated 12.03.67–23.10.68 | 32 prints |
| 030.I.C.700.005 | DMH. design and presentation drawings, 20 prints, dated 09.10.66–28.06.67 | 20 prints |
| 030.I.C.700.006 | DMH. design drawings, 25 prints, dated 16.04.66–15.12.68 | 25 prints |
| 030.I.C.700.007 | DMH. design drawings on yellow trace, 208 originals, undated | 208 drawings |
| 030.I.C.700.008 | DMH. design drawings on white trace, vellum, 31 originals, undated | 31 drawings |
| 030.I.C.700.009 | DMH. design drawings on yellow trace, 139 originals, undated | 139 drawings |
| 030.I.C.700.010 | DMH. design drawings on yellow trace, 142 originals, undated | 142 drawings |
| 030.I.C.700.011 | DMH. design drawings, 32 prints, undated | 32 prints |
| 030.I.C.700.012 | DMH. design drawings, 61 prints, undated | 61 prints |
| | | 956 total<br>662 drawings<br>294 prints |

## COLLABORATORS ON THE DOMINICAN MOTHERHOUSE, 1966–1969

Source: Kahn Collection, Boxes 71 (F2), 75 (F6), 77 (F8): Payroll

1966:
David Polk (Project Architect)
David Slovik
Cengiz Yetkin
Vincent Rivera
Gabor Szalontay
W. Neuman
Steve Hill
Kazi Abdul-Razzah
Anant Raje
Galen Schlosser
Frank Kawasaki
David Wisdom
Henry Wilcots
Peter Kaack

1967:
David Polk (Project Architect)
Anant Raje
Leslie Vallhonrat
David Slovik
Al Baxter
John M. Lucas
Galen Schlosser
W. Neil Thompson
David Wisdom
Hugh Zimmers
M. Garfield

1968–69:
David Polk (Project Architect)
Anant Raje (Project Architect)
Frank Kawasaki
David Wisdom
Vincent Rivera
Martin Verman
Anthony Pellecchia
Heina Patel

# BIOGRAPHIES

Michael Merrill studied at the Art Center College of Design in Los Angeles and graduated with his professional degree in architecture from California Polytechnic State University and a doctorate in architecture from the University of Karlsruhe in Germany. He is a registered architect in California and in Germany, where he has practiced both collaboratively and independently. He is currently Assistant Professor for Architectural Design at the Karlsruhe Institute of Technology.

Louis Kahn (1901–1974), B. Arch, University of Pennsylvania (1924); Danish Architectural Association's F.A.I.A. Medal of Honor (1965); American Institute of Architect's Gold Medal (1971); Royal Institute of British Architect's Gold Medal for Architecture (1972); Paul Philippe Cret Professor of Architecture, University of Pennsylvania (1957–74). As a builder, teacher, and participant in international discourse, Kahn acted to challenge many fundamental premises of mainstream modernism in the decades following World War II, becoming one of the most influential architects of the twentieth century. Defying simple categorization, works such as the Salk Institute for Biological Studies (1959–65), the Kimbell Art Museum (1966–72), the Library of the Phillips Exeter Academy (1965–72), the Indian Institute of Management (1962–74) and Sher-e-Bangla Nagar, the capital of Bangladesh (1962–83) have remained lasting touchstones for generations of architects.

## ACKNOWLEDGMENTS

Lou Kahn knew that "Nobody ever paid for the price of a book. They paid for the printing." This book was paid for with many forms of help given by many others. Not all of them can be listed here, nor are those mentioned responsible for any errors, omissions, or exaggerations, for which I alone am responsible. My warmest thanks go to:

In Philadelphia and the U.S.:
Bill Whitaker, Collections Manger of the University of Pennsylvania's Architectural Archives, for his generous support, good advice, and for being such an excellent and good humored source on all things Kahn;
Nancy Thorne, for her great patience and beyond-the-call-of-duty help with my research;
Julia Moore Converse, former Director of Penn's Architectural Archives, for organizing such a wonderful place of research;
Harriet Pattison, for a long and memorable discussion on Kahn and landscape;
Amy Brown Polk for her kind hospitality during my meeting with her late husband David Polk;
Sister Mary Irene Lolli, O.P., and Sister Eileen Patricia Primrose, O.P., of the Dominican Motherhouse of St. Catherine De Ricci for opening their archive and sharing their experiences of working together with Louis Kahn;
Michael J. Lewis for his repeated support and his kind appraisal of the rough text;
David van Zanten for his friendly help and for sharing an excellent lecture on Kahn and Composition;
Contributing photographers Naquib Hossain, Eduardo Ponce, Ed Brodzinsky, and Jeff Stvan;
The many others who took their time to discuss this project with me, among them David G. De Long, David B. Brownlee, Duncan Buell, and Jim Kise;

Carolyn Kelly of the Graham Foundation for helping me to get the most out of a generous grant;
Those who have backed up their enthusiasm for Louis Kahn's work and for this project with other forms of generous support: Nathaniel Kahn, Larry Korman, Moshe Safdie, and Steven Holl.

In Karlsruhe:
Walter Nägeli, chairman of the Institute for Architectural Design, where I have taught for the past years, for his support and for the culture of critical inquiry and exploration within which this book—and the dissertation that preceded it—grew;
Dr. Hans J. Böker, for his expertise and advice on that dissertation;
All of my colleagues at our institute, for sharing in the adventure of this project, contributing to the discourse around it, and for taking up the slack created by my own involvement;
Especially to Gudrun Wiedemer, who in spite of her own workload, always took time for serious evaluation and encouragement;
Susanne Elisabeth Berger and Karin Bierlich for their skill and assistance with drawings and diagrams;
Werner Sewing, for helping out in a pinch;
Steffie Gawlik, for her generous support when it was needed;
Walter Kohne, for being a long-term sounding board on this subject and others around it;
The many students of my seminars who, with their own explorations helped sharpen my eyes and deepen my understanding of Kahn's work.

In Switzerland and Barcelona:
Lars Müller, for his enthusiasm, skill and commitment. With his eye for both the small detail and the big picture, I cannot imagine a better partner for this project;
Ellen Mey, for guiding this project surely forward from first contact to bound book;
Martina Mullis, for her skill and patience in laying out this book and its partner publication;
Jonathan Fox, for his sure hand and unerring eye in editing the text.

At Home:
Most of all, my thanks go to my partner Helena Hörig, for all of the patient and loving support which made this project possible.

This reprint was made possible with the generous support of:

Karlsruhe Institute of Technology, Institute for Building Typology

Stuart Weitzman School of Design, University of Pennsylvania

Alphawood Foundation, Chicago

Michael Merrill
LOUIS KAHN
ON THE THOUGHTFUL MAKING OF SPACES
The Dominican Motherhouse and a Modern Culture of Space

Design: Integral Lars Müller/Lars Müller and Martina Mullis
Copyediting: Jonathan Fox
Lithography: connova GmbH, Appenweier, Germany
Paper: Hello Fat Matt, 135 g/m²
Printing and binding: Eberl & Kœsel, Altusried-Krugzell, Germany



Lars Müller Publishers
Zürich, Switzerland
www.lars-mueller-publishers.com

ISBN 978-3-03778-220-0

Distributed in North America by ARTBOOK | D.A.P.
www.artbook.com

Printed in Germany